C000130001

A THOUSAND YEARS OF A LONDON STREET:
DENMARK STREET

MIKE READ

CRANTHORPE
—MILLNER—

Copyright © Mike Read (2019)

The right of Mike Read to be identified as author of this work has been asserted by him in accordance with section 77 and 78 of the Copyright, Designs and Patents Act 1988.

All rights reserved. No part of this publication may be reproduced, stored in a retrieval system, or transmitted in any form or by any means, electronic, mechanical, photocopying, recording, or otherwise, without the prior permission of the publishers.

Any person who commits any unauthorised act in relation to this publication may be liable to criminal prosecution and civil claims for damages.

A CIP catalogue record for this title is available from the British Library.

ISBN 978-1-912964-20-8 (Paperback)

www.cranthorpemillner.com

First Published (2019)

Cranthorpe Millner Publishers
18 Soho Square
London
W1D 3QL

About the Author

Mike Read was created a Knight of Malta in 2011 and is Chairman of the British Plaque Trust. During 2018 he expanded the Blue Plaque scheme into the Commonwealth. Mike is also an Ambassador for the Prince's Trust and founder of the Rupert Brooke Museum & Society. Mike has won ten National Broadcaster of the Year Awards, an International Music award and has been awarded the Gold Badge of Merit by the British Academy for his special contribution to Britain's music industry. He has been a household name in Britain for over 35 years having fronted three top-rated long-running TV series, *Top of the Pops, Pop Quiz & Saturday Superstore* and three national radio breakfast shows, including Radio One, Classic FM and currently United DJs Radio. 2016 saw him still presenting front line programmes for the BBC as well as producing and presenting a new TV series, Tin Pan Alley, which ran for 8 weeks on Sky. During 2016 and 2017 he was writing, shooting, producing and presenting a six-part series, *Jamaicaphiles.* A best-selling author, he has had some forty books published. Mike has written several film scripts, had eight musicals staged and penned songs for over forty major artists as well as having several chart hits, twice topping the Independent Singles Chart and recently writing a No.1 in the North American Chart. 2019 sees his musical *Great Expectations* undertaking another national tour. He has played himself in such perennial TV favourites as *Only Fools and Horses* and *Midsomer Murders* and has interviewed 100s of major artists on his live TV show and on stage. Mike has also presented for and worked with most of the Royal Family. He regularly travels to different parts of the world broadcasting or giving talks.

Acknowledgements

I'd like to thank:

All the songwriters and publishers who gave Denmark Street a global identity as Tin Pan Alley.

Laurence Kirschal & Richard Metcalfe at Consolidated Development.

Cover Designer Martin Madigan.

Kirsty-Ellen Smillie and David Hahn at Cranthorpe Millner Publishers

Regent Sounds of Denmark Street

Other titles by the Author

Guinness Book of Hit Singles 1-5
Guinness Book of Hit Albums 1-2
Guinness Book of the 1970s
The Guinness Hits Challenge
Guinness Book of 500 No.1s
Mike Read's Pop Quiz Book
The Cliff Richard File 1 & 2
The Story of the Shadows
The Aldermoor Poems
Elizabethan Dragonflies
Cliff Richard: The Complete Chronicle
Major to Minor
One Hundred Favourite Poems (20 years of reprints)
One Hundred Favourite Humorous Poems (20 years of reprints)
Forever England: The Life of Rupert Brooke
A Room with Books
Rupert Brooke: His Life & Poetry (Audio Book)
Labatt's 500
Inspirations
Read's Musical Reciter
The South Coast Beat Scene of the 1960s
New Poems for Old Paintings
Dead Finger Pointing
The Little Book of Cliff Richard
Seize the Day
Forever England (Re-published with new material)
Caversham Park and its People: BC to BBC
The Writing on the Wall

Introduction

Denmark Street, and the site on which it was built, has witnessed a millennium of mass murderers, rock stars, inventors, serial killers, queens, rebels, rogues, lepers, poets, explorers, arsonists, swordsmen, activists, criminals, anarchists, racing drivers, reformers, schemers, dreamers, pirates, plague victims, great lovers, pioneers, regicides and…songwriters.

The Beatles, Queen Matilda, Jimi Hendrix, The Kray Twins, David Bowie, Karl Marx, General Tom Thumb, Elton John, Tom Jones, Casanova, Claud Duval, The Rolling Stones, Denis Nilson, The Sex Pistols, Paul Simon, Charlie Chaplin, Johan Zoffany and hundreds of other familiar names, all walked, worked, or wrote in this site. The New Musical Express and the Melody Maker were born here, and it was, for a century, the home of our great songwriters and the British music publishing industry. Of course not every publisher and songwriter that ever worked in Denmark Street is mentioned in these pages, but a representative cross-section gives an idea of the atmosphere of the era.

In 1670 women were fainting, screaming and weeping at the end of Denmark Street as the 'dandy highwayman' Claude Duval, stopped to drink from the St. Giles Bowl on his way to the Tyburn gallows. Almost three hundred years later, the Rolling Stones would have the same effect after they recorded their first album on the same site. The lyrics to Denmark Street's first big hit were written here in the 1680s, the song helping to bring down James II and put William III on the throne. A hymn written in the street in the 1840s would become a No.1 in the late 1960s, well over a hundred years before the likes of David Bowie and Elton John started their careers here. Denis Nilson, who admitted to murdering over twelve young men between 1978 and 1983 worked in the street during his killing spree. On the verge of dying here was the sister, and victim, of serial poisoner Graham Young. Karl Marx and Frederick Engels came here to listen to talks by the Chartists and O'Brienites in the mid-1800s, while at the same time the street played host to the country's first dog show. William Paterson, the man responsible for the creation of the Bank of England, lived here. Paterson also attempted to make Scotland a world power by establishing the new colony of Caledonia in Panama, and becoming pivotal to world trade. He failed and crippled Scotland financially, which led to them reluctantly accepting the Acts of Union. Three of Byron and Shelley's children were christened here in 1818, following in the footsteps of John Milton who had his daughter christened here in 1647. Another great poet, Andrew Marvell, is buried in the churchyard. The street's first writer and publisher, Lawrence Wright, settled here a century later, creating what would become Tin Pan Alley, the centre of the UK's songwriters and publishers for almost a century. The street is not without a plethora of royal connections. Henry I's Queen, Matilda, founded a leper hospital here in 1101 and the architect of the street's current church, built in the 1720s, also designed for the family home of the Duchess of Cambridge. General Tom Thumb's carriage was made here while he was in London performing for Queen Victoria and young Paul Lemaitre was arrested at no.13 on a charge of attempting to kill George III. In the Victorian period, several Denmark Street residents were hanged or transported, for crimes ranging from stealing a handkerchief to cold-blooded murder. There are also unsolvable crimes of passion, with bullet-ridden bodies and questionable alibis. In the mid-Victorian era one eleven-year-old boy from the street was in court having stolen the equivalent of £10,000 in today's money in just one week from people's pockets. In the 1980s, Denmark Street was the scene of the most horrific fire, in terms of loss of life, since the Blitz in WWII, with thirty-seven people being burned alive. The arsonist got life and died in prison on the 28th anniversary of the fire.

The only woman to turn down Casanova lived in Denmark Street - the 17-year-old prostitute who allowed him to visit and to give her money and jewellery, but denied him anything else. Who would have guessed that the hard men of the gangster world, the Kray Twins, would have come here for secret dancing lessons, or that the seeds of Indian independence were sown here in the 1920s. Both Charlie Chaplin and the Sex Pistols wrote here, in the same street where the destitute Johan Zoffany worked decorating clocks, little knowing that 250 years later, his paintings would sell for multi-millions. The street has been full of inventors, with futuristic ideas for steam-powered cars, water-powered railways and underground travel all being explored in the here in the 1820s, as well as other inventions such as the ice-making machine, diving helmet and paper-making machine. One of the street's residents helped Brunel to build the first tunnel under the Thames, known as 'The Eighth Wonder of the World'. The sword for Admiral Collingwood for his part in the Battle of Trafalgar was made in the street as were many other ceremonial swords. Jimi Hendrix was ejected from Regent Sound studio as his guitar was too loud and annoyed the neighbours, but Black Sabbath's volume, it seemed, was quite acceptable. Thousands of our great songs have emanated from this street, where our two great music magazines, *New Musical Express* and *Melody Maker* were both born and where the first hit parade was devised. The only song that the Beatles recorded for EMI outside Abbey Road was recorded in Regent Sounds studio: 'Fixing a Hole' for the Sgt Pepper album ... oh, and Jesus Christ was present at the session. Well, if you're going to name-drop...

.

Reelin' In The Years

Denmark Street may only have been in existence as an official thoroughfare for something short of 350 years, but many have passed this way over the millennium; heading for sanctuary, to be laid to rest at St Giles-in-the-Fields churchyard, to murder, to take arms, to pursue criminal activities, to plot, to pause on their way to the gallows at Tyburn, or even to write hit songs over two hundred years before the creation of Tin Pan Alley.

Occupying a few hundred feet at the far western point of the Parish of St. Giles, Denmark Street lies north of Covent Garden and the Parish of St. Martin's and to the east of Soho in the Parish of St. Ann's. During the 20th century it would become known as both Tin Pan Alley and Little Tokyo. The street was built in the 1680s, joining St Giles High Street with what is now Charing Cross Road but was then Hog Lane, and before that Elde Strate, whose narrow way led down through uninterrupted fields to Westminster. The road would be given many names over the years, including The Waye to Uxbridge, The King's Highway, the Road to Oxford, the Road to Acton, and The Tyburn Way. Eight of the original buildings still stand in Denmark Street, the site having had a rich and chequered history both before and since the 17th century.

To put Denmark Street and the surrounding area of St. Giles into its historical setting - Palaeolithic hand axes and other flint artefacts were found close by, but that doesn't necessarily indicate a settlement as settlers at this time were usually on the move. The Roman Road, Watling Street, almost certainly followed the line of today's Oxford Street which ran just a few yards north of Denmark Street and was part of the roman route connecting Hampshire with the Suffolk Coast. Four Roman burials were discovered in the area and it's thought that the Roman thoroughfare was on the site of an earlier Iron-age trackway. By the late 5th century though, the Romano-British settlement of Londinium had been abandoned and by the early 7th century an Anglo-Saxon settlement had been established called Lundenwic (London trading town), about a mile to the west of Londinium. The Saxon road followed the old Roman road, probably looping down through what is now St. Giles. The village of St Giles had Saxon origins, with a chapel almost certainly being on the site of what is now St. Giles in the Fields. The original dwelling place, the Westminster Berewic may well be the one referred to as being granted to Westminster Abbey by Ethelred in 1002. A copper alloy long-cross brooch, the earliest Saxon find from the area is now in the British Museum. The whole area around what would become St Giles (including what is now Denmark Street) was essentially a medieval rural landscape. This landscape was characterised by small settlements and agricultural activity between the abandonment of Lundenwic in the 9th century and the urban development of the area in the late 16th or early 17th centuries.

After some to-ing and fro-ing between Mercia, Wessex and the arrival of the Vikings, Alfred the Great re-established control of London by the 880s. With the Roman walls repaired and new ditches and fortifications in place, it now became known as Lundenburh. This was the beginning of the City of London, which by 1016 was, with the rest of England, under the control of King Cnut. The abandoned Lundenwic became known as Ealdwic, which survives today as Aldwych. Cnut's step-son, Edward the Confessor, built Westminster Abbey, but it was Edward's death that led to a succession crisis which brought about the Norman Conquest. Duke William of Normandy claimed the throne, but Edward's brother-in-law Harold Godwinson was elected and crowned, at Westminster Abbey. William was so incensed that he famously invaded England in 1066. His success saw more than 90% of the English landowners lose their titles and land, which were given to Normans who'd supported his cause. In the 1980s and again in the 2000s an extensive Anglo-Saxon settlement was uncovered, just to the south of what is now Denmark Street and environs.

In 1101, on the site of what is now St Giles-in-the-Fields, at the end of Denmark Street, a chapel was founded by Henry I's wife Matilda as a house of prayer for the leper hospital which she also created here. Built on the site of a small Saxon chapel, which served the isolated village of Alde Wyche, she named it St Giles, after the adopted patron saint of beggars, cripples and lepers. The innovative Matilda was also the first Queen to create a musical court. Among her musicians were William LeHarpur, who had four and a half bovates (land that could be worked by one eighth of a plough) given to him by Henry I, William Rufus's one-time minstrel, Rahere and Adelard of Bath who may well have played his guitar-like cithara for the Queen. If these musicians also performed at the chapel of her leper hospital, Tin Pan Alley effectively came about 800 years earlier than we thought. *The Song of Roland*, dating from the early 1100s is the earliest known

work performed at court, the epic being based on the hero of the Battle of Roncevaux in 778 when Charlemagne fought the Saracens in Spain. Maybe this area echoed the lengthy work in the early 1100s.

Matilda

Born in Scotland, Matilda had been christened Edith, and was educated in the South of England. After the suspicious death of William II, his brother Henry I ascended to the English throne, taking Edith, the great-granddaughter of King Edmund Ironside, for his Queen, who then became Matilda, a name favoured by the Normans. She was passionately interested in architecture and music, commissioning many Norman-style buildings including Bow Bridge which spanned the River Lea and connected Essex to Middlesex. Matilda, Queen Elizabeth's 21st great-grandmother died in 1118 at Westminster Palace and is buried at Westminster Abbey.

In the early 1100s the church and the hospital stood among corn fields and water mills, well outside the City walls, being recorded in 1120 as *Hospitali Sancti Egidii extra Londonium*. It was the custom to retain fourteen lepers, a clerk, a messenger, matrons, the master and other members of the establishment, but much of the time there were no more than a handful of lepers benefitting from Matilda's philanthropy.

Like all disease, leprosy had no respect for class or position and during the medieval period was widespread across England, having arrived in the country in the 4th century. By the time Matilda set up the hospital at St. Giles it was commonplace, with lepers at risk of losing fingers and toes, losing their sight and suffering from gangrene, ulcerations and lesions. Many believed that these people who were suffering on earth would go directly to heaven and therefore were closer to God. Matilda's hospital was one of over 300 leper, or lazar, houses and hospitals established across the country between 1000 and 1350. 'Leprous brothers and sisters' were often accepted into the religious order of the house that had taken them in. The outlook in the treatment of the lepers is startlingly modern in concept. Cleanliness was of paramount importance, clothes were washed regularly and diet was as healthy as possible, with food often being home grown. Fresh air and exercise were also on the agenda, with many of the sick tending the gardens and growing flowers, vegetables and healing herbs. Those being cared for at St. Giles, weren't locked away or kept within the walls, they could visit their home if it was geographically possible and their family and friends were welcome to visit. Maybe the Black Death created some form of immunity in those that survived, but whatever the reason, leprosy was on the wane and would eventually die out. It would pass a torch though to future generations and lay down a structure for how we would deal with care for people with disability and deformity in the coming centuries.

With an endowment of £3 per annum it was necessary for the lepers to go out on market days to beg for money. The practice soon stopped as their unfortunate appearance deterred people from being charitable. There was division within the church as well, with the lepers praying on the south side and the local parishioners on the north side.

The altar at the east side of the church was dedicated to St Giles, next to which burned a great taper called the St Giles Light. In 1200, one William Christmas bequeathed the sum of 12 pence towards it. Mr. Parton, the vestry clerk in the early 1800s, drew a map of how the hospital and surrounding area looked circa 1200. Many of the buildings created as leper hospitals would disappear in the mid-1500s with the dissolution of the monasteries.

The church, hospital, gatehouse, gardens and orchard are all visible. The area at the time was in the Ossulvestane or Ossulton Hundred with Pituance Croft Ditch to the north of the church, with the Great Marshland Ditch, which later became known as the Cock and Pye Ditch, to the south. Listed in the St Giles hospital records is linen draper Gervasele Lyngedrap and in the late 1270s, during the reign of Edward I, the hospital cook, Herbert de Redemere, is documented as owning a local hostelry called 'The Croche House' (the Crossed Stockings).

The present site of the Phoenix Garden shown within a plan of St. Giles Leper Hospital and precincts

Parton's map of 1200

The 1200 map, drawn by Mr. Parton, the vestry clerk to St Giles-in-the-Fields in the early 1800s, shows the exact position of Pool Close, probably the water supply for the hospital, now the site of the Odeon cinema in Shaftesbury Avenue. The cottages to the east of the hospital are on the site of what has been The Angel public house for centuries, and Le Lane, running SW to NE across the middle of the map, was to become Monmouth Street. St Giles High Street, then *strata Sancti Egidij,* has retained the same curvature as it had eight hundred years ago. The eastern end of what is now Oxford Street is visible as *via ad Tiborne.*

For two hundred years St. Giles Hospital was administered by the City and supported by the Crown, but in 1299 Edward I ordered that St Giles was to be administered by the Order of St Lazarus, one of the chivalric orders dating from the Crusades. This became a cell to the Hospital of Burton Lazars in Leicestershire, who were often accused by the authorities of putting monastic affairs before caring for the sick. On several occasions Edward III would intervene and replace the head of the hospital; the monarchy still retaining an influence and interest in St. Giles over two hundred years after its conception. In

1391 St Giles hospital was sold by Richard II, Edward's grandson and successor, to the Cistercian Abbey of St Mary de Graces (close to the Tower of London), an action which riled the Lazars. They withheld rent money in protest and even used force to express their dissatisfaction with the King's ruling. The property at the time included 8 acres of farmland, eight horses, twelve oxen, two cows, one-hundred and fifty-six pigs, sixty geese and one-hundred and eighty-six domestic fowl. Just eight years later in 1399, Richard abdicated, or rather was coerced into abdicating, and Henry IV manoeuvred his way on to the throne. This was good news for the Lazars as St. Giles was returned to them, at least until the dissolution in 1539, by which time leprosy had died out in England, the hospital serving as a refuge for people with general infirmities. Even later it became abused and used by the 'decayed domestics' of the court.

The precinct of the hospital occupied the area that is now Shaftesbury Avenue, St Giles High Street and Charing Cross Road, with what is now Denmark Street at its north end. The other buildings included the Master's House, later the Mansion House, to the west of the church, the Gatehouse, to the north-west of the church and the Spittle Houses, which probably stood to the south east of the church. In the 1300s and 1400s St Giles village was a cluster of houses that lay on the route between Holborn and Tyburn, whose gardens stretched behind them to St Blemund's Dyke, bordering the mansion and lands of William Blemund, after whom Bloomsbury would take its name. The many local ditches and dykes can be traced to the area's modern-day sewers. The land was distinctly marshy, with 'Marlyn's-pond' 'Capper's-pond' and 'Smith's-pond' often being referred to. The building of the hospital and chapel started the commencement of the draining of the St. Giles area. At the turn of the century, during the reign of Henry IV, there were around two hundred house-holders in the vicinity who could never have imagined that their pastoral landscape and pace of life would turn into a glass city where images and messages could be flashed instantaneously around the world, and their descendants could travel at high speed under the ground or fly eight miles above it *en route* to as yet undiscovered places. The pace may well have been leisurely but there was still plenty of action.

Out in the Fields

Henry V ascended the throne in 1413, and he wasn't well-received by all his subjects. On the night of 9th January 1414 there was an uprising against the Roman Catholic Church and Henry V in the fields by St Giles Hospital by the Lollards, led by Sir John Oldcastle, whose beliefs were heavily influenced by Lollard cleric William Swynderby. Lollardy was a politic-religious movement that was opposed to capital punishment, rejected religious celibacy and believed that the clergy should be accountable to civil laws. Oldcastle headed up what had become a full-scale conspiracy, which included a plan to seize the king, establish a commonwealth of which Oldcastle was to be Regent and dissolve the abbeys and share out their wealth. Forewarned by one of his spies, Henry V and his forces were ready for Oldcastle and his Lollards when they assembled in St Giles Fields and dispersed them easily. Oldcastle was taken to the Tower of London and, following his denouncement of the Pope as the Antichrist, was condemned to be executed, despite Henry V's attempt to show

leniency to his old friend. He managed to escape to Herefordshire, where he evaded capture for three years, before being caught in Wales and brought back to the scene of the 1414 uprising, where, on December 14th 1417 he was dragged through the streets to St Giles-in-the-Fields tied to a hurdle.

Sir John Oldcastle

sentenced to be hanged, drawn and quartered. His offer of £1,000 to Elizabeth to buy his pardon, cut no ice. He and his fellow conspirators

were strapped to sledges and dragged through the London streets to St Giles Field, where they were executed and parts of their bodies distributed to prominent locations around the City, as a warning to any contemplating treason. The Pound was finally removed in 1765.

(Left) An old marker in Highgate for St. Giles Pound. Irrelevant now for 250 years!

In 1606 an Act of Parliament condemned the area, that was pockmarked with open ditches, conduits and marsh, as '*deepe foul and dangerous to all who pass those ways.*' A man born into that St Giles in the Fields landscape, albeit into a prominent family, was John Okey, who was also baptised in the church. Before the start of the English Civil War, he enlisted in the Parliamentary army, soon rising to become a colonel in Cromwell's New Model Army of 1645. He and his regiment achieved lasting fame for their actions at the Battle of Naseby as well as engaging successfully in several other battles during the ongoing conflict. In 1648, with Charles I having been denounced as a traitor, Okey was appointed as commissioner to the High Court of Justice and was active during most of the king's trial. He was also one of the fifty-nine regicides who signed the king's death warrant and had a close friendship with the Earl of Leven, whose Scottish army assisted Cromwell against the king. At the Restoration, despite political compromise allowing many who sided with Cromwell to go free, Charles II declared that most of the regicides would stand trial. Okey, by now an MP and major landowner, fled to Germany and was declared an outlaw. He was eventually caught in the Netherlands, brought to trial and executed for high treason by being hanged, drawn and quartered in April 1662. By confessing his own culpability, the man from St Giles in the Fields hoped to have his body returned to his wife for burial, but fearing a demonstration from those opposed to the Restoration, Okey was buried in the precincts of the Tower of London. His son fled to Connecticut USA, the Christian name Leven remaining prevalent through the generations.

In 1631 Lady Dudley also purchased The White House, which stood roughly where Denmark Place is today, occupying a triangle of land between the existing Hog Lane and what would later become Denmark Street and Denmark Place. Described as 'all that one messuage or tenement, with appurtenances, commonly known by the name of the White House, and one yeard, one garden and one long walke, and one stable with a hay lofte over the same.' Three years later she transferred the property to trustees to be used for the purposes of a parsonage. Also known as 'Duchess Dudley' Alice was the second wife of the explorer Sir Robert Dudley, the son of Queen Elizabeth's favourite, the Earl of Leicester. Alice gave birth to seven daughters and Dudley abandoned her in 1605, fleeing to France to marry his first cousin. The philanthropic Alice also paid the major portion of the money needed to rebuild the church between 1623 and 1630. The new buildings became Dudley Court, later renamed Denmark Place.

In 1633 a number of people from the St Giles area embarked on the four-month voyage to America on the *Dove* and the *Ark* to form a colony in Maryland, one of the original thirteen colonies of British North America. A year before their epic voyage came the very first reference to the area that begins just a few yards away from Denmark Street, Soho. It was first written as 'So Ho' in a rate book dating from 1632, the word being a hunting cry, much like 'Tally Ho.' The journey of the *Dove* and the *Ark* from the Isle of Wight to Barbados took the *Ark* forty-two days and the smaller *Dove,* a further two weeks. They eventually landed on the Potomac River in March 1634, the entire trip having taken just over three months. A large cross was planted, the land claimed in the name of Charles I and March 25th would be celebrated annually as 'Maryland Day.' Notable for having been established with religious freedom for Catholics, this almost certainly came about as George Calvert, 1st Baron Baltimore, who had originally applied for a charter for the Maryland Colony, had been stripped of his title of Secretary of State by Charles I for announcing his Roman Catholicism. Maryland's economy was based on tobacco and relied on slave labour. His son, Cecil (or Cecilius) Calvert 2nd, Lord Baltimore, had taken up the Charter for the Maryland Colony given to his father and fitted out the ships that would administer the Colony from London. Cecilius' younger brother, Leonard, who had undertaken the voyage, became the first Governor of Maryland. Cecilius Calvert is buried in St Giles-in-the-Fields church, as are his son and daughters-in-law. A memorial was unveiled in May 1996 by the Governor of Maryland, Parris N. Glendening. They may have just been here long enough to hear the neighbouring area referred to by its new name.

(right) Cecil Calvert, Lord Baltimore

In 1644 Charles I made Alice Dudley a duchess in her own right: 'And whereas, our father not knowing the truth of the lawful birth of the said Sir

Robert (as we piously believe) granted away the titles of the said earldom to others…and holding ourselves in honour and conscience obliged to make reparation; and also the said great estate which the Lady Alice had in Kenilworth, and sold at our desire to us at a very great undervalue…we do…and give and grant unto the said Lady Alice Dudley the title of Duchess of Dudley for life.'

Lady Dudley was finally widowed in 1649 when Sir Robert died in Florence, after forty years in exile, but she was generous with her money, being recorded as a major benefactor to the parish of St Giles-in-the-Fields, Middlesex, a few yards from her property.

That same year, Sir John Wolstenholme 3rd, the son of Sir Thomas Wolstenholme, was born in Denmark Street and baptised at St Giles in the Fields. Thomas's great-grandfather had farmed the customs for Charles I and his grandfather became collector for the Port of London, for which service he was given a baronetcy. John Wolstenholme attended Trinity College in Cambridge and in 1675 married Mary Raynton, the daughter and heiress of Nicholas Raynton of Forty Hall, Enfield. Eighteen years later at the age of forty-nine, Wolstenholme was put up for election, being described as 'A very honest man.' With the support of luminaries such as Charles Montagu, 1st Earl of Halifax, he won and became a staunch supporter of the court at Westminster. Two years later he inherited Forty Hall Estate, which came to him on the death of his father-in-law and held on to his seat at the Middlesex election. He appears to have introduced a bill to improve river and harbour navigation, but he failed to get re-elected in 1701 despite being touted as a member who had 'honourably and faithfully served his country and the government.' In December 1701 his son Nicholas was put forward as a Whig candidate but narrowly failed to be returned. Nicholas stood again at the first election of Queen Anne's reign, but disrespectful words uttered about the monarch appear to have skewered his chances. Having taken time out to try and reclaim family monies owed, John Wolstenholme ran again in the next election, helping the Middlesex Whigs achieve a clear victory over the Tories. Just seven days after the Lords ruled in his favour on a debt owed to his great-grandfather, John Wolstenholme, the man born in Denmark Street, was dead, and was said to have been suffering from 'A lingering disposition.' By 1762 the baronetcy had become extinct. The fortunes of the Royalist Wolstenholme's had dipped during the time of the Commonwealth but risen again with the Restoration. The pattern of everyday life was also temporarily changed by the Civil War of 1642-51, which not only had a political impact on London but temporarily changed the landscape of some of its outlying areas such as St. Giles. London was surrounded by a defensive bank and ditch with forts and batteries set into them. Part of the east-west section of the ditch almost certainly passed across the top of St. Giles with two forts flanking Tottenham Court Road, the eastern fort not being too far away from where Denmark Street would be built just three decades later.

The size of Lady Dudley's property on the site, and the buildings around her can be roughly ascertained by the Hearth Tax of 1662-63. With the restoration of the Stuart dynasty in 1660, Charles II found himself desperately short of funds with the result that a bill was passed granting the king the proceeds of a tax on all hearths in the Kingdom, which came into force on 25th March (then New Year's Day) 1662. The tax, also referred to as 'Chimney Money', consisted of an annual charge of two shillings on every fire hearth. In the vicinity of St. Giles' Churchyard, Lady Dudley was taxed on twenty hearths, Lord Wharton on eighteen, Susan Bethell on fifteen and Alice Haywood on eleven. In some areas of the country the tax led to violence, riots and bloodshed, but there is no record of that in the area around St. Giles in the Fields and those also paying to the 'chimney men', were Will Turppin, Edward Harris, John Miller, Roger Stephens, John Gabe,

Rich Welles, John Colleman, John Twele, Margrey Sargent and Henery Welch.

Lady Alice Dudley died in her house in January 1669, at the age of ninety, having outlived all but one of her seven daughters. Her White House property, which had a lease on it '*for three lives*', was also held by Edward Smith and this was not determined until 1681 when the house had become '*very ruinous and scarcely habitable.*' The rector entered into an agreement with John Boswell of St. Dunstan's West for rebuilding, and it was arranged that houses erected on the site should be built '*with all materials and scantlings conformable to the third rate buildings prescribed by the Act of Parliament for rebuilding the City of London.*' Her other house would soon be pulled down to make way for the regeneration of the area and the building of Denmark Street. In her will Lady Dudley left '*The sum of one hundred

pounds for ever, for the redemption of poor English captives taken by the Turks.*'

(Left) Lady Alice Dudley

The church organ was destroyed during the English Civil War, George Dallam building a replacement in 1678. It was rebuilt again in 1699 by Christian Smith, nephew of the great organ builder 'Father' Smith, and rebuilt yet again in 1734 by Gerard Smith the Younger. A final rebuilding was undertaken by London organ builders, Gray and Davison in 1856 and was extensively restored in 2006 by William Drake. The Regency font dates from 1810 and bears a relief of St. Giles.

St Giles-in-the-Fields.

The Great Plague of 1665 started in St Giles, leading many to blame the area for the outbreak and naively imagining it to be contained entirely within the vicinity of the outbreak. The first victims were buried in the St Giles churchyard and the increasingly familiar red crosses began appearing on many local doors; the sign that the plaque was within. The plague killed well over 3,000 victims in a parish which had fewer than 2,000 households and led to more than a thousand people being buried in the plague pits of St Giles graveyard.

The plague pits.

Stand and Deliver

In 1670, Claude Duval, the notorious French-born highwayman, famed for his alleged gentlemanly behaviour, courtesy to the ladies, good looks, lack of violence and fine clothes, was finally relieved of his duties on Hounslow Heath after being captured in the Hole-in-the-Wall tavern in Covent Garden. An abundance of inconsolable and weeping ladies visited him in Newgate, with many more accompanying him to the gallows at Tyburn, where he was executed. The scene was more like the mass-mobbing of a film star than the execution of a tyrant, the crowds following his body to the Tangier Tavern in St. Giles. It was there that a paper was discovered in his pocket, which began, 'I should be very ungrateful to you fair, English ladies, should I not acknowledge the obligations you have laid me under. I could not have hoped that a person of my birth, nation,

education and condition could have had charms enough to captivate you all...I am confident that many among you would be glad to receive me to your arms, even from the gallows.' A real dandy highwayman, who, even in death, was writing his own self-promoting PR.

Claude Duval at work in Windsor Forest.

Some claim the urbane Duval is buried at St Giles, but St Paul's Covent Garden is said to be his actual resting place. Word of mouth places his remains under the centre aisle, but the current incumbent feels that it would have been highly irregular for a criminal to be buried in consecrated ground. That was true of murderers, but he wasn't tried or executed for murder, and who can tell at this distance whether, with a wink and a nod, money changed hands and the deed was done, either at St Giles or St Pauls. Nine years later, eleven Roman Catholics who were said to be plotting to kill Charles II, *were* buried at St Giles. The false claims of the so-called 'Popish Plot' were made by Titus Oates, the son of an Anabaptist chaplain. The King's reluctance to order the execution of men he knew to be innocent was outweighed by public pressure and they were duly executed at Tyburn. They were all interred at St Giles between January and July 1679. Three-hundred and fifty years later, in 1929, the eleven men were beatified with another ninety-seven martyrs by Pope Pius XI. Two years later, the final victim of the 'Popish Plot', Oliver Plunkett, the Roman Catholic Archbishop of Armagh and primate of All Ireland, was buried here having been hanged, drawn and quartered. Plunkett was executed for an alleged plot for a French invasion of Ireland, but beatified in 1920 and canonised in 1975, becoming the first new Irish saint for almost seven hundred years.

After the Great Fire and subsequent expansion, St Giles began to grow into a cosmopolitan area, with many Irish settling in the area as well as Armenians, Greeks and a sizeable number of French Huguenots. To the south of what would become Denmark Street lay the wasteland of the future Shaftesbury Avenue and the Cock and Pye fields which would be developed as Seven Dials in the late 1690s. The village of St Giles was on the route to Tyburn, so many criminals would be given as a final drink, the 'St Giles Bowl' at the hospital before their hanging. There was even an inn called The Bowl just north of the Denmark Street area, where St. Giles High Street met with Hog Lane.

In November 1724, at the Crown Inn, just off Denmark Street, the celebrated pickpocket and jail-breaker, Jack Sheppard was offered the 'St Giles Bowl' filled with strong ale, and to the cheers of the crowd, he downed it one draught. Just twenty-three years old and something of a pin-up, young women fought and scrambled to throw posies of flowers at him, as they had at highwayman Claude Duval here fifty years earlier. Soldiers brandishing javelins kept the crowd at bay, fearing a last-minute rescue attempt. Sheppard was *en route* from Newgate to Tyburn, sitting in his own coffin, where some 100,000 people turned up for a day of revelry and to watch him die on the 18ft high gallows.

Among the crowd at both St Giles and Tyburn would have been 'rampsmen' (muggers) 'toolers' (pickpockets) speelers (conmen who fleeced people at card and dice, dragsmen (carriage robbers) 'prigs' (thieves) 'swells' (pickpockets dressed a aristocrats) and gonolphs (child pickpockets). But there were more heinous crimes afoot, with the *Weekly Journal* reporting that a man called White, the Innkeeper of the King's Head ale-house in Hog Lane was committed to Newgate in 1726 by Justice Ellis in Denmark Street (being charged upon oath) for raping his own child, a girl of about 11 or 12 years of age.

Sir Edward Cope's mansion on the site of what would become Denmark Street and its environs was now occupied by Philip, 4th Lord Wharton circa 1677. 'The garden of Lord Wharton' is mentioned in 1687 as being the southern boundary of a premises in Denmark Street. The house was demolished soon after the building of Denmark Street, with the garden not being built on until much later. Philip, 4th Baron Wharton was a soldier, politician, diplomat and puritan who'd fought with Cromwell during the Civil War. Following the Restoration, he was imprisoned in the Tower in 1676 and later, in 1685, fled the country when James II came to the throne. He was back in the country and back in favour when William of Orange became King. His Trust still delivers bibles to under eighteen-year-olds. The property passed to his son, Thomas, 5th Lord Wharton. He had immense charm and was a gifted politician, but if Thomas had any of his father's puritanical blood in him it certainly wasn't apparent, as he was described as a man 'devoid of moral or religious principles.' Queen Anne disliked him, but under King George I, he returned to favour and just months before his death in April 1715, the King created him Marquess of Catherlough, Earl of Rathfarnham, Baron Trim in the Peerage of Ireland and Marquess of Wharton and Marquess of Malmesbury in the Peerage of England. Wharton wrote the stirring words to *Lilliburlero* in 1686, the song said to have 'sung James II out of three Kingdoms.' How delightful that the lyrics to what was the 17th century's most successful song were written by the owner of the house that was on the site where the NME would publish the UK's first top twelve, 266 years later. The South side of Denmark Street bordered Wharton's land and some may have even gone to build the thoroughfare. The melody of *Lilliburlero* first appeared in print in a collection of songs entitled *An Antidote Against Melancholy* in 1661, but its popularity soared due to Wharton's new lyrics and played a major part in the Glorious Revolution when the Catholic King, James II was deposed by the choice of the English Protestants, William of Orange and his wife, Mary. The anti-Catholic ballad really touched a nerve, the words depicting two Irish Catholics discussing what would happen if a Catholic Monarch were allowed to remain on the English

throne. The title took its name from the Papist watchword of the Irish rebellion massacre of 1641, which kicked off the Irish Confederate wars, and it's thought that Wharton wrote the words as revenge for James II having made Richard Talbot (Tyr Connell), a fierce Papist, Viceroy of Ireland.

Lord Wharton: Lilliburlero lyricist.

'Lilliburlero, bullen-a-la.
Lero, lero, lilli burlero, lero lero, bullen-a-la,
Lero, lero, lilli burlero, lero lero, bullen-a-la.'

Lord Wharton was very aware that Englishmen prized their political liberty, so wrote of what might happen if William failed to take England and the country were to fall back into Popish tyranny. The song was so popular that many believed that it seriously contributed to the downfall of James II. It may be far-fetched to think that an English king could be brought down by a song from Denmark Street, but there was no denying that it played a vital role. One contemporary observer, Bishop Burnett commented that it, 'made an impression on the [king's] army that cannot be imagined by those that saw it not. The whole army, and at last the people, in both city and country, were singing it perpetually. And perhaps never had so slight a thing had so great an effect.'

The melody is the theme tune for the BBC World Service, having first been used by the corporation during World War II. On the death of Wharton's son, Philip 1st Duke of Wharton, all his titles, except the baronetcy, became extinct. In Stow's map of 1720, the triangular gardens, enclosed by Loyde Court, Denmark Street and Hog Lane, are still shown as 'Whartons.'

On the Street Where You Live

Denmark Street, just 354 feet in length, was begun c. 1685, cutting between the church and Hog Lane (later Charing Cross Road). It was laid out by developers Samuel Fortrey and Jacques Wiseman, who also petitioned to build a sewer from their new houses to Hog Lane. Samuel Fortrey died in 1689, the year the buildings were completed, their construction having taken place during the entire four-year reign of James II. Lessons had been learned from the Great Fire of London in 1666 and the London Building Act of 1667 encouraged the building of terrace house in brick rather than timber. More measures would be taken in 1707 with the Fire Prevention Act. Most of the original buildings in Denmark Street would have been panelled, but apart from No. 26, most of this has long vanished. The best-preserved properties are probably Nos. 6 and 7. Six of the surviving Grade II listed buildings are Nos. 5, 6, 7, 9, 10 and 20, constructed between 1686 and 1689, no. 27 was constructed late 17th century, while No. 26, the oldest building in the street, dates from 1635. Presiding over them at their eastern end is St Giles-in-the-Fields. Two years after Fortrey's death, his widow Elizabeth leased a piece of ground at the end of Denmark Street, in Hog Lane, to an Innkeeper, Leonard Cunditt, for 'the second ground plot or new house built or intended to be built,' and another for 'the fourth house'. Both leases were from 99 years at a rent of £3 a year. The street built by her husband was named after Prince George of Denmark, the husband of the future Queen Anne, daughter of the newly-crowned James II. Due to the street being virtually overtaken by our publishers and songwriters for almost a hundred years, part of his title will have been included in tens of thousands of conversations over the best part of a century, but who was he?

Prince George, the son of Frederick III of Denmark, was born in Copenhagen in 1653. As their youngest son, there was little chance he would inherit the Danish throne. He toured Europe, he was a devout Lutherian and was good at putting people at ease. He was proposed as a candidate for the Polish throne but refused to denounce his faith for Catholicism. He fought with distinction in the Scanian War between Denmark and Sweden, but across the sea Charles II's quest would change his life. He was looking for a husband for Princess Anne, the daughter of his brother, the Duke of York (later James II) and with anti-Catholicism riding high, the choice was, in reality, confined to a Protestant. Who was more ideal then, than Prince George? Against all odds, this suggestion was supported by the Catholic King of France, Louis XIV, as he had hopes of it bringing about an Anglo-Danish Alliance against the Dutch, and opposed by the Dutch Prince of Orange, a Protestant, who was married to Anne's sister. Anne's father was a staunch Catholic but approved of the marriage as it both pleased Louis XIV and angered his protestant son-in-Law, the Prince of Orange. In July 1683 Princess Anne and Prince George were married at St James's Palace. George wasn't too keen on the pace of London or the gossiping tittle-tattle of court life, he was all for a quiet life and domestic bliss. His idea of domestic bliss may not have been Anne's, but they were happy enough. Anne became pregnant on eighteen occasions, but only one child, William, survived infancy and even he died of smallpox in 1700 at the age of eleven.

On the death of Charles II, Anne's father James II became King. When William of Orange was preparing to invade England, George refused to accept any position from his father-in-law, declaring that he thought William would prove to be successful and take the English throne. He was right, and James II was shocked that George, the son-in-law he liked, declared for William, the son-in-law he disliked.

After the Glorious Revolution and William and Mary were ensconced on the English throne, George was made Duke of Cumberland. Despite support from George, William never trusted him with any seriously responsible positions and easy-going George was probably fine with that. Although it became synonymous with music, Denmark Street isn't the only musical connection to George as Jeremiah Clarke, then the organist in the newly-built St. Paul's Cathedral, composed *The Prince of Denmark's March* in 1700. It commonly became known as the Trumpet Voluntary, and hundreds of years later it became strongly associated with the opposition to the Nazi occupation of Denmark, having been played as support during WWII by the BBC. For many years the piece remained the European Service signature tune of the BBC World Service. It has also proved to be popular at weddings over a long period of time, even being played at Prince Charles and Lady Diana Spencer's wedding in 1981. Now who suggested prominently featuring a tune named after the husband of the Queen's second cousin eight times removed! Maybe the St Pauls

eight times removed organist.

(Left) Prince George of Denmark.

In 1702, when William died, Anne came to the throne as Queen of England, Scotland and Ireland, and appointed George to what were basically ceremonial positions: Commander of the Army and Lord High Admiral. A humble and trustworthy man, he demanded little and remained a devoted, supportive and loyal husband to his Queen, but was rather partial to a groaning table. The Acts of Union meant from 1707 Anne became the first monarch of Great Britain and Ireland.

For many years George suffered from asthma and dropsy, which got noticeably worse by 1706. He died two years later at Kensington Palace at the age of fifty-five but is commemorated by a street that had always been far more active than he ever was: Denmark Street.

Possibly one of the first people to move in to the new street was Scottish trader and financier, William Paterson, an entrepreneur who'd traded in Jamaica in the late 1670s and early 1680s, around the time of the buccaneer raids. Paterson took part in the development of property to the west of London but plumped for making his home in Denmark Street. He was, apparently, humourless and serious but very honest and was constantly promoting new commercial ideas. He propounded one of his major proposals to the Committee of the House of Commons: the creation of the Bank of England, which would give credit and take loans on government security. The bank was established on this basis in 1694, with business associates of Paterson's, the Houblon Family, being one source of the bank's financial backing. For the first time, England assumed a national debt

and issued promissory bank-notes to acknowledge its debts: the country's first paper currency. Paterson was one of the first directors of the Bank of England.

He had long championed the idea of establishing a colony called Caledonia (*pictured left*), on the Isthmus of Panama on the Gulf of Darien, in an attempt to establish the

- 45 -

Kingdom of Scotland as a world trading nation. The aim was that the colony would be a strategic overland route linking the Atlantic and Pacific Oceans. Paterson, his wife and 1,200 Scots attempted to set up a new colony in 1698, undertaking a three-month voyage in five ships, with many of the passengers not entirely sure where they were going. After a couple of years, poor planning, inadequate provisions, an English blockade, disease and a siege by the Spanish, forced them to abandon what could have been a serious economic success. Many of the colonists survived by eating lizards and roots, but approximately 2,000 died. The Scottish Darien Company was backed by 25-50% of all the money circulating in Scotland, some £300,000. Its failure ruined many parts of the country and weakening its resistance to the Act of Union in 1707. Paterson's idea was brilliant and could have made the Scots a major trading nation, but the flaws virtually cost the country its independence and Paterson his wealth and health.

William Paterson

Like Paterson, Haberdasher Richard Dickson who had a house close to St Giles church was also one of the first people to live on Denmark Street. A monument on the middle pillar on the North side of the church commemorates his wife Sarah Dickson who died in 1709 and his daughter Elizabeth Downing born in 1675 and died in 1713. Dickson, who caught the plague but survived, was described as a citizen of London, and an important member of the Haberdasher's Company. Family letters also reveal that Elizabeth's son, Dickson Downing, inherited a considerable fortune on his mother's death, when he was just twelve-years-old, but lent it out unwisely it seems and by the time of his death in 1745 he'd lost most of it. In 1720, he married 16-year-old Bridget Baldwin and in his will of 1742 wrote that he did, 'bequeath all the rest residue and remainder of my estate [presumably including the property in Denmark Street] whatsoever and wheresoever real and personal to my dear wife Bridget Downing her hears and assigns for ever not doubting of her maternal care of my two dear children George and Bridget Downing.' Three years later, in his mid-forties, Dickson Downing tripped over a carpet and died from

the effects of the fall. Being a resident of Demark Street he may well have named his son after Prince George of Denmark. He is buried in the churchyard of St Giles-in-the-Fields.

(Left) Dickson Downing

Not all the deaths in the street were accidental. Two men, known to the court as J. W. and J. P. were indicted for killing Peter Penrose, bell-man in the Parish of St Giles-in-the-Fields on 30th November 1686. The man referred to as J.W. was alleged to have murdered him by stabbing him with a rapier, delivering, 'one mortal Wound upon the Brest, near to the Right Pap, of the breadth of one Inch, and of the depth of six Inches, of which he instantly died.' It was said that as the deceased was ringing his bell and saying his verses on St Andrew's Day at one or two o'clock in the morning he encountered the two prisoners in the street who complained about the noise. An argument ensued between the two prisoners and two other bellmen from the Watch who'd come on to the scene, the miscreants having made towards them with their swords drawn. They argued, in their defence, that they were abused by the two men from the Watch, were highly provoked and that the bell-man had set his dog on them. They also complained that he'd knocked one of them down, which had made them seek refuge in an empty hansom cab. It was there that they were apprehended and committed to the St. Giles Gate-House. Also in their defence, they said that they had been set upon and mistaken for thieves. At the trial at the Old Bailey in January 1687, they called 'several persons of very great Quality to Evidence on their sides that they had never been wont to quarrel, nor to keep any unreasonable hours.' The pair were found Guilty of Manslaughter.

Avenues and Alleyways

One can get a good idea of the many alleyways, snickets and yards in the vicinity that could harbour criminals. There is an insight in curate John Strype's 1720 book, A Survey of the Cities of London and Westminster. 'This Place crosseth Stacies street; thence falleth into Kendrick Yard, and so into St. Giles by the Church. Out of Stedwael street is Vinegar Yard, which leadeth into Pheonix street, butting on Hog Lane, against the French Church, and runs down to the back side of St. Giles Churchyard, where there is a little passage into Leydes Court; and out of this place there is a Passage without a Name into Monmouth Street, about the Middle of which is a Passage into Stedwel street. All these Streets and Places are very meanly built, and as ordinarily inhabited, the greatest Part by French and the poorer sort. Denmark Street fronts St. Giles Church and falls into Hog Lane; a fair, broad street, with good Houses, well inhabited by Gentry. On the back side of this Street is Dudley Court, which falls into Hog Lane, and hath a passage into the said Street. Loyds Court, or rather Alley, paved with Freestone, is parted from Denmark Street by the Lord Wharton's House and Garden, which fronts St. Giles on the West side. From St. Giless by the Pound, I shall lead you down the South side unto great Turnstile, taking in all the Places of Note not yet named; and after that shall do the same on the North side within the limits of the Parish. And according to this Method, the first place that offers itself is the Church, called St. Giles-in-the-Fields, built in the Place with the antient Church stood; which was so decayed as not to be repaired. This good work of building the church anew was carried on and finished by charitable Contributions of the Inhabitants, and others: And afterwards the Churchyard was enclosed with the brick wall.'

London was growing and expanding into its surrounding countryside, marsh and farmland. By 1715, a year after George I came to the throne, there were over 21,000 living in some 3,000 dwellings in the vicinity at a time when London had a population of some three-quarters of a million. The folk from St. Giles and Denmark Street were living in a city divided by politics and religion, many remaining unconvinced about the legitimacy of the new Hanovarian regime. Religious bigotry raised its head; on many occasions erupting into violence. The need for a controlled force to deal with riots, criminality and unrest would lead to Henry and John Fielding forming the Bow Street Runners in 1749. London was a city of Jacobitism and anti-Catholicism, economic instability and unrest, alcoholism and inadequate living conditions. On the positive side, it was Britain's largest manufacturing centre and the centre of trade and finance, the number of hospitals increased, coffee houses sprang up and

newspapers flourished. In the 1730s a new church was built on the site of the existing St Giles Church, along with a vestry house. It would be the first English church built in the Palladian style. The architect was Henry Flitcroft (*pictured left*), the son of one of William III's gardeners at Hampton Court, Henry's birthplace. His talent at design was spotted while he was working for Lord Burlington, who subsequently employed him as his draughtsman and architectural assistant. Flitcroft swiftly worked his way up until he was Comptroller of the King's Works. He designed for several members of the Royal Family and created the famous lake at Virginia Water. His royal connections have reached into the 21st century, when it was discovered that the panelling and a mantelpiece in the study at Sutton

Hall, Yorkshire, the home of Samantha Cameron's family, had been designed by Flitcroft in the 1720s. It had been taken there from Potternewton Hall near Leeds, the ancestral estate of Olive Middleton, the Great-Grandmother of Catherine, Duchess of Cambridge. The Vestry House was also designed by Flitcroft and has a panelled vestry room with the names of the rectors from 1547 and churchwardens from 1730 painted on the panelling. The royal arms on the front of the gallery are those of George II, who was the King at the time of Flitcroft's rebuilding. The church also has a blue plaque commemorating George Odger, who moved here when 18, and helped to establish the Trade Unions. There is also a tablet commemorating Luke Hansard who initiated printing and publishing verbatim reports of proceedings in Parliament. Another tablet commemorates John Coleridge Patteson, the first Bishop of Melanesia, who was baptised in the church in 1827 and forty-four years later was murdered by the natives of Nukapu. The pulpit was given to the church by John Sharp, the Rector here in 1676 who became Archbishop of York. The wooden pulpit on the north side of the church is from the nearby West Street Chapel. Founders of the Methodist Church John and Charles Wesley both preached from it between 1741 and 1793. The gate at the west end of the churchyard was designed by Thomas Leverton in 1800 and originally stood at the main entrance. It was moved in 1865 when there were plans for a new road to be driven through the area, but Charing Cross Road was built slightly further west. The Church itself s built of Portland stone, with vaults beneath the building, the steeple rising to 160 feet, whilst above the clock is an octangular tower.

Stow's map of 1720 of St Giles (*Pictured below*) still shows what would become Oxford Street as Tiborn Road and Wharton's Gardens, unbuilt on and still running the length of the south side of Denmark

Street. There is still very little infilling between the St Giles thoroughfares.

Despite the crowded area around it, in 1720 Denmark Street was described as 'a fair, broad street, with good houses, well inhabited by gentry.' A hundred years later however, the local population would increase to 30,000 and the north of the area would become one of the most impoverished parts of London, known as St Giles Rookery. There would often be twenty people living in one room, with child prostitution, gin shops, criminal gangs, drunks, robbery and murder becoming commonplace. St Giles was on its way to becoming the worst of the London slums. The late 1720s seemed plagued by incessant rain and foul roads, house-breaking increased dramatically, criminals worked in gangs and footpads and street-robbers were becoming increasingly fearless. It was reported that, 'there was no stirring out after dark for fear of mischief. These ruffians knocked people down and wounded them before they demanded their money…half the Hackney coachmen were in league with the thieves…the mails coming and going into London were seized and rifled. Post-boys, stage-coaches, every-body and everything that travelled were attacked. People were robbed in Chelsea, in Cheapside, in White Conduit Fields, in Denmark Street, St. Giles.'

A painting by Hogarth (*pictured below*) from Hog Lane (now Charing Cross Road) in 1736, features the view over Denmark Street to St Giles Church and was one of a series of four that Jonathan Tyers

commissioned, to adorn the supper boxes at Vauxhall Gardens. The Duke of Ancaster bought the original painting of *Noon,* for £38-17s-0d (£5,800 today).

To protect our economy while we were at war with France, the government slapped a heavy duty on the import of spirits and lifted restrictions on domestic spirit production. This led to an increasing number of people distilling their own gin, known as 'Old Tom.' This generally meant that unless it was laced with copious amounts of sugar, it usually tasted pretty foul. Some even added turpentine or, bizarrely, sulphuric acid, but nevertheless it sparked a gin craze in London from around 1720. Not only adults averaged half a pint of gin a day, many children did too, so it's not surprising that some 10 million of gallons of it were being distilled in the capital each year. At one point, one in six houses in London sold gin and a quarter of all residences in St. Giles were gin shops. Gin was blamed for the rise in crime, prostitution, insanity, a higher mortality rate and lower birth rate. The Vice-Chamberlain, Lord Hervey, remarked that; 'Drunkenness of the common people was universal, the whole town of London swarmed with drunken people, morning till night.' The Gin act of 1736 played into the hands of the bootleggers by taxing the reputable sellers. Gins known as 'Cuckold's Comfort' and 'Ladies Delight' were readily and cheaply available, and there was still little or no quality control. It was another picture by William Hogarth, *Gin Lane*, set in St. Giles, which helped to push the government into passing more stringent laws and ensuring that premises were properly licensed. A new act was passed in 1751 which charged higher fees for licenses and that, together with a couple of bad harvests, which led to a ban on distilling grain, helped to reduce consumption. By 1760 the gin craze was more or less over, but crime was still rife in Denmark Street and the surrounding area and no-one at the lower levels of society was above the law...if they were caught. Soldiers Joseph Wolf and Robert Martin were charged with stealing two damask napkins, some aprons, stockings and table-cloths. After the robbery, the court was told that they, 'Lock'd the outside door...and went to the Two Brewers in St. Gyles's.' They also tried to sell the goods at the Brown Bear in St. Giles before admitting, 'We came back to a pawnbroker in Denmark-Street.' Mr. Harris, the Denmark Street pawnbroker gave evidence. Wolf was acquitted and Martin transported.

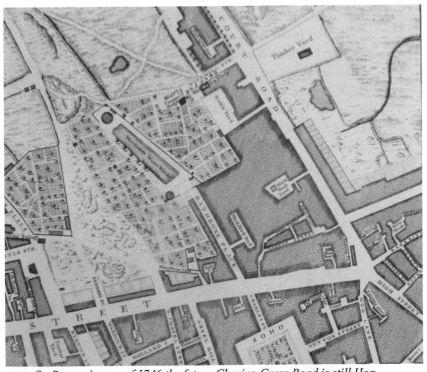

On Rocque's map of 1746 the future Charing Cross Road is still Hog
Lane and Denmark Place is marked as Farmer's Alley (bottom right).

Shop Around

There is little record of the wheelings and dealings of the street's pawnbrokers in the 1750s, one Mr. Fell and a Mr. Harrison, except that John Fell was called upon to give evidence in a case brought against two sisters. He claimed that on the 29th of October, one of the sisters, Ann Smith, and a man named James M'Daniel offered him child's cap, a child's apron and a child's shirt. He said he lent her 8 shillings on them.' Ann and Elizabeth Smith stole these various items from Joseph Wilkin to whom Elizabeth Smith was apprenticed, Wilkin having saved her from the workhouse.

Possibly the only existing image of a Denmark St Trader's advert

Joseph Wilkin told the court: 'I sell milk. I took Elizabeth Smith upon liking from out of St. Martin's workhouse, to be an apprentice in last October. Ann Smith came to my house, and wanted employment; we took her in. My wife and I went out with milk the 26th of October in the afternoon, and left the two prisoners in the house, we returned about six, and found the doors all open and the things and they gone; I found some of them at James M'Daniel's in St. Giles's on the 30th of October, and some I found at a pawnbroker's.'

The court decided that Elizabeth's older sister, Ann, was the guilty party and sentenced her to be transported, while the eleven-year-old Elizabeth was acquitted.

The October 9th 1755 edition of the *Whitehall Evening Post, or London Intelligencer* carried the news that one of Fell's neighbour's former linen-draper and later author of several religious tracts, James Buscarlet, was found dead in his bed in Denmark Street. His will is in the National Archives. Natural causes or foul play? And what of Sarah Dawkins, a widow who lived in the street and died in 1758 but whose estate was still unclaimed fifty years later? Nor will we probably ever know the real reasons why another neighbour, Anthony Gilbert, a merchant of Denmark Street went out of business five years later in 1760. None of them may have been particularly significant historically, but these and many other comings and goings of daily life created the Denmark Street footprint that included everyone from the British shopkeeper to master craftsmen, thieves and murderers. In 1761, bricklayer John Duke murdered his wife in Drury Lane and then cut his own throat, dying later in hospital. His body was buried close to the St Giles pound, a few yards to the north of Denmark Street. It wasn't unusual for a murderer to be refused a churchyard burial, but it was rare to be buried with a stake driven through your heart. That was the fate of John Duke. Suicide was considered to be such an offence against God that he was buried with a stake through his heart to stop him returning to plague the living. And just to make doubly sure, people who had committed suicide were often buried at a crossroads in order to confuse their ghost. If it escaped from beyond the pale of course. Maybe the new road layout and the regeneration of the area are simply a 21st century attempt to further confuse the wraith of John Duke. The document condemning Duke ends with the verdict *Felo de se,* Latin for 'felon of himself' an archaic way of saying 'suicide'. Baker Harris was a Harpsichord Maker in Denmark Street at the time and may well have witnessed, or at least been aware of, the gruesome acts against Duke's body after his death. Active for at least forty years, one of his spinets, dated 1740, was exhibited in London in 1904 and there is a Baker Harris spinet in the Victoria and Albert Museum dating from 1770, restored by Arnold Dolmetsch in 1966. The inscription reads: *Baker Harris London Fecit 1770.* (*pictured below*). Harris's latest surviving instrument is a double-manual harpsichord from 1780.

Many of the rock stars that would frequent Denmark Street in the mid-1900s where often portrayed as latter-day Casanovas, but in 1763, exactly two hundred years before the Beatles' publishing deal was signed in the street, Casanova himself was there. He'd arrived in the summer, to try to sell English officials the idea of a state lottery and also to visit his ten-year-old daughter Sophia, who was living with her mother, Teresa Imer at Carlisle House in Soho Square. Teresa may have been an old friend and the mother of his child, but by then she had a wealthy English lover and had established Carlisle House as London's most fashionable entertainment venue. Under the pseudonym Mrs Cornelys she had become the capital's leading music impresario with an annual income of some £24,000, making her the highest-earning businesswoman in the country. The ballroom in the house was 93 feet long, the supper room, 80 feet long and a Chinese bridge connected the main house to the new rooms. On the day he arrived, she was too busy to see Casanova, being otherwise engaged, but had organised somewhere for him stay. In high dudgeon at the low-class lodgings and her dismissive treatment of him, he found rooms in Pall Mall. His attention was soon focused elsewhere, as he became besotted with seventeen-year-old Marianne de Charpillon who lived with her Swiss mother, grandmother and aunts in Denmark Street, a stone's throw from Teresa's house. This group of women were incredibly adept at persuading wealthy men to part with their money. Casanova certainly spent a lot of money on her, but she teased him, tormented him and refused to have sex with a man very used to getting his own way with women. Even when he decided enough was enough, she'd reel him back in again with empty promises. His frustration was such that he became violent and so she had him arrested. He'd already spent some time in prison in France eight years earlier having been arrested for 'affront to religion and common decency.' His revenge on the unforthcoming Marianne was bizarre to say the least, as he bought a parrot and taught it to say 'Miss Charpillon is more of a whore than her mother' before putting the bird on sale at the Royal Exchange in the City. Casanova had never experienced treatment like that from a woman and it damaged his notorious self-confidence as a lover. In the Courtesan of Denmark Street the great Casanova had met his nemesis. He did, unsurprisingly, have other liaisons while he was here, even advertising in the paper for the 'right' woman. He came to sell us the idea of a national lottery and left with venereal disease.

By the 1770s it all started to go wrong for Mrs Cornelys and she was arrested and gaoled for staging unlicensed performances. The house was sold and by 1789 music publisher Thomas Jeffreys was operating from there, missing being the first music publisher in Denmark Street by a matter of yards and over one hundred years. Carlisle House, on the east side of Soho Square, the rear of which looked down Sutton Street, over Hog Lane to Denmark Street, was pulled down in 1791 and replaced three years later with two new houses, of which the southern one survives The other was demolished a century later for the building of St Patrick's Church.

(Left) The Courtesan of Denmark Street

There was some consummation taking place in Denmark Street as actor and dramatist, Joseph George Holman was born here in 1764. He attended Barwis's school across the road in Soho Square, an establishment known as the Soho Academy, where acting was very much in vogue. Reverend Cuthbert Barwis ran what was recognised as London's first academy, until 1751, when his nephew John Barwis took over on his uncle's death. It instilled a love of acting into the young Holman.

Despite going up to Oxford, he realised that the stage was his calling, first performing as Romeo at Covent Garden in 1784. He remained at Covent Garden until 1800, performing as Harry Thunder in *Wild Oats* in 1791, Harry Dornton in *Road to Ruin* in 1972, the title role of *Cyrus* in 1795, as Hippolitus in 1796 in *Phaedra and Hippolitus* and appearing in the 1798 production of *The Grecian Daughter*. Edinburgh and New York.

In 1798 Holman married Jane, youngest daughter of the Hon. and Rev. Frederick Hamilton, a direct descendant of the Duke of Hamilton. At the end of his third season (1799-1800) he left Covent Garden after a major row broke out between the actors and the proprietors. Although some actors bit the bullet and stayed, Holman couldn't agree on terms and was either dismissed or resigned. After spells at Edinburgh and various other towns and cities, he returned to Covent Garden. He also acted at The Haymarket, where he produced the comic opera *What a Blunder*, playing Count Alphonso d'Esparza. His wife died in 1810 and after that he spent some time in theatrical management in Dublin, where he also acted and dabbled in farming. In 1812 after an absence of many years, he reappeared at the Haymarket in *Venice Preserved*. The same year he went to the States with one of his daughters and played the Chestnut Street Theatre in Philadelphia. He undertook management of the theatre, but it failed as a business. He went on to manage a theatre in Charleston, Virginia

and on returning to England for actors, married a singer. One account has him dying in 1817 of apoplexy in Rockaway, Long Island, another has both he and his new wife expiring after contracting yellow fever.

Samuel de Wildes' 1795 painting of Joseph George Holman

Five years after Holman, the English Unitarian Divine and archaeologist, Charles Wellbeloved (*left*), was born in Denmark Street, where his father was a joiner. He arrived on 6th April 1769 and was baptised on 25th April at St Giles-in-the-Fields. He became an assistant at St Saviourgate Chapel, York in 1792 and was elevated to minister in 1801. He was asked to become divinity tutor of the Manchester Academy, if it were to be moved to York. Wellbeloved agreed and held the divine chair from1803-1840 when it was known as Manchester College, York, before becoming Harris Manchester College, Oxford. Wellbeloved was passionate about the archaeology of York and participated in several excavations as well as being one of the founders of the York Subscription Library, the Yorkshire Philosophical Society and the York Institute. His son, Robert married heiress Sarah Scott and became deputy lieutenant for Worcestershire and MP for Walsall. His youngest daughter married Sir James Carter, the Chief Justice of New Brunswick and a school chum of Benjamin Disraeli. Yet another fascinating and varied journey that began in Denmark Street. Some devoted their lives to the scriptures, others fell by the wayside.

The lawlessness of the St. Giles area meant that it was a pretty good place to try and seek refuge from justice and retribution. One footpad mistakenly imagined that Denmark Street would be an ideal place to hide. In 1772, Robert Astrop was accused of making an assault on John Stern, a servant of Colonel Woolaston in Wimpole Street, putting him in 'coporal fear and danger of his life.' He was also charged with stealing from him, 'a silver watch, value 40 shillings, a steel watch chain, value sixpence, a cornelian stone seal set in silver, value one shilling, a brass watch key, value one penny and eight pence in money.' The assault took place in Park Lane, but the culprit was taken at Denmark Street. Giving evidence, John Heley said that he, a Mr. Bond and a Mr. Taylor had gone to St. Giles to apprehend a man accused of footpad robbery: 'We had been searching there about half an hour, and as we were coming away, I saw the prisoner with another young fellow, I don't know his name. I said to Mr. Bond, there is Astrop; Mr. Bond said, 'You must take him, for last night he went to pawn a watch and got off.' As soon as he saw us come towards him, he run off; we pursued him, and took him in a court in Denmark-Street, St Giles; when we came up to him, I put my hand in his coat pocket and found a hammer. The hammer, with which he had knocked out John Stern was then produced in court. Astrop was found Guilty and sentenced to death.

Thomas Gaugain, engraver, print seller, painter and picture cleaner lived and worked in Denmark Street, from 1786 to 1789. Born in Abbeville, France, he moved to London with his family as a boy n 1756, and entered the Royal Academy Schools in 1771, initially working as an artist and exhibiting portraits at the Royal Academy between 1778 and 1782. His advertisement as a picture cleaner read, 'Pictures cleaned by Thomas Gaugain, who has a peculiar Method, by which the most delicate are in no Danger of being damaged.' On moving to Denmark Street, Gaugain took insured his stock for £400 and the following year he married Mariane Ame Le Cointe at St Anne, Soho. He also published engravings printed by his brother, Peter John, who married Jane, another member of the Le Cointe family. After three years in Denmark Street, he moved to Manor St, Chelsea. The lives of Thomas and his brother, were closely linked, having shared a business premises at 4, Little Compton Street. Gaugain died in 1810 and his brother Peter in 1813.

In 1784, Yorkshireman, Joseph Bramah *(left)* opened a factory in Denmark Street where he made substantial changes to the water closet, with flushing, a method of stopping the water from freezing and a hinged flap which sealed the bowl. He had obtained the patent for this early form of flush toilet in 1778, so from 1784, Denmark Street saw thousands of toilets, generally housed in fine mahogany, heading from the factory to such eminent households as that of Kew Palace and Queen Victoria's residence, Osborne House on the Isle of Wight. The young Henry Maudsley *(right)* came to work for Bramah at Denmark Street, having already been responsible for devising the maritime pulley block system, with Samuel Bentham and Marc Isambard Brunel. Maudsley married Bramah's housekeeper and had four children, although even after eight years' service, he still

remained on 30 shillings a week. Having cut his teeth in the street, Maudsley later went on to help Brunel create the Thames Tunnel between Wapping and Rotherhithe, that many called 'The Eighth Wonder of the World'. Maudsley, whose inventions and designs contributed greatly the Industrial Revolution, would be referred to as the 'Founding father of machine tool technology.' He would later invent a printing press for bank notes. Bramah also patented a brass and steel lock which gave a new level of security to boxes. It was described as 'A LOCK, constructed on a *new* and i*nfallible* Principle, which, possessing all the Properties essential to Security, will prevent the most ruinous Consequences of HOUSE ROBBERIES, and be a certain Protection against Thieves of all Descriptions.' He soon moved his showroom to Piccadilly, but retained his factory at Denmark Street. In 1790 Bramah's famous 'Challenge Lock' was displayed in their London shop linked to an inscription which read, 'The artist that can make an instrument that will pick or open this lock shall receive 200 guineas the moment it is produced.' The lock withstood attempts to open it for over sixty years. Joseph Bramah, the Denmark Street toilet and lock inventor, died in 1814. His son Timothy took over the business which is still active today as Bramah Security Equipment.

Police and Thieves

Of course, not every felon or criminal was a professional that needed to break a lock or enter a premises, there were also chancers and petty thieves. Just around the corner from Denmark Street, in Hog Lane, by then also referred to as Crown street, William Vandamme had his house broken into while he was abroad: 'I found some of the shirts myself at a pawnbrokers; he is here. The lock of the door was broke, and three of the locks of the bureau appeared to have been opened, with a pick-lock. I missed all the things mentioned in the indictment.' The case was heard against John Allies and John Mince at the Old Bailey in July 1774. Found Guilty of stealing a quantity of watches, silver, boxes, silver tea spoons, Dresden ruffles and linen shirts, they were both transported.

In 1786 Elizabeth Fitzgerald was sentenced to be transported for stealing a cotton gown worth seven shillings. In court, Henry Clark, the brother of shopkeeper Thomas Clark and a pawnbroker of No.4 St Giles High Street gave evidence that the prisoner had come in and asked for a handkerchief in the name of Moreing: 'There was another customer in the shop; the boy went up to look for it and he could not find it; there was a little girl playing with a child and the prisoner pretended to faint away. I sent the little girl for some cold water, in the meantime my brother went up to look for it (the handkerchief); I was in the shop all the time he was looking for it; she said it was not hers, she would go and ask the woman about it and she went out. Presently my brother came down and he missed the gown directly. It was a cotton gown and we suspected the prisoner as she was sitting close by; I found the gown in Denmark Street in a quarter of an hour after at a pawnbrokers and I desired them to stop the person if she came in again. The next morning she was stopped.' Maybe she was an habitual criminal, maybe she was penniless, hungry and desperate. Whatever the reason, she risked her life for a few shillings. In

December 1786 Elizabeth Fitzgerald was transported for seven years. Born in 1760, Elizabeth was twenty-six when she was put on the 338-ton transport ship *Lady Penrhyn*, and despatched to Australia. The vessel carried 101 female convicts, two male convicts and twelve children. She was part of a convoy of eleven ships, the so-called 'First Fleet', which brought over 1000 convicts, marines, and seamen to establish European settlement in Australia.

(Left) The Lady Penhryn

After two years at Port Jackson, Elizabeth was sent to Norfolk Island on the ill-fated Sirius. In 1791 she gave birth to twin girls by a man named William Mitchell. The couple returned to Port Jackson on *Kitty* in 1793, but by 1806, Mitchell having returned to England, she was living with a soldier from New South Wales and had three children with him. In 1809 she arrived at Norfolk Plains, Van Dieman's Land, on *Porpoise,* having used a variety of surnames during her time in Australia. In 1914 she married former convict Henry Wilkinson at Launceston and the couple had three children. A simple cotton gown, recovered from a pawnbrokers in Denmark Street in 1796, led to Elizabeth living with a fellow transport on a 50-acre farm on the other side of the world, at Norfolk Plains, having had many children and spending more time at sea than she could ever have imagined. Elizabeth died aged seventy-two on their farm, in 1832, twenty-four years before the country would be re-named Tasmania.

Hannah Rowney appeared to have been a serial bible-snatcher. Having been brought before the court once for pawning a stolen bible, her defence had been that her husband had given it to her to pawn and had then run away, never to be seen again. She was again indicted for 'feloniously stealing on the 1st day of August last, in the parish of St. Giles in the Fields, a folio-printed common prayer book, value 5 shillings'. There was also a second charge for stealing another book from the church. Elizabeth French was a witness: 'I am a pew-opener at St Giles; I was in church the 31st July, about twenty minutes before three; I staid rather better than half an hour; there was a poor woman to be churched; and I saw the clerk's book on his desk then; on Friday morning I went in about twenty minutes before eleven, and the clerk's book was missing; it was prayer day on Friday; I came out and said the book was gone; and a person went and found it at the pawnbrokers.' William Tomlinson also gave evidence: 'I am a pawn-broker in Denmark-street…I saw the prisoner take it in her hand….the boy took it in….she came in in the evening with another, I detained her, and sent for a constable.' Even a boy, David Lamb, gave evidence: 'I am servant to Mr. Tomlinson…she came in and offered me a book to pledge; which I lent her half a crown on….I am positive that she is the woman that pledged it.'

Rather bizarrely, Hannah Rowney made the same defence, that her husband had given her the books to pawn and then disappeared. The court decided that Hannah too would disappear. They sentenced her to be transported for seven years, away from the temptation of purloining religious tomes. She sailed in June 1789 with 150 other convicts on the Lady Juliana to New South Wales. She died in 1829 aged seventy-four. 216 years and eight generations later, her great-great-great-great-great-great grand-daughter, Louise, came to London and walked in her footsteps. The difference was that she was given a bible rather taking one.

It may seem that the judicial system was draconian by default, but not everyone was found Guilty. John Parsley, James Williams, John

Brown and John Barber were tried for grand larceny in January 1794. They were indicted for stealing two cloth great coats, value fifteen shillings, a pair of stays, value eight shillings, a muslin gown, value five shillings, a silk petticoat, value one shilling, a silk cloak, value two shillings, a cotton bed gown, value one shilling, a stuff gown, value one shilling and a silk handkerchief, value sixpence, from a man named William Smith. Smith gave evidence, saying that his wife had told him she had lost his great coats and some other items. The prisoners were apprehended by two officers from Bow Street (Croker and Hatch) and a man called Kane, who lived in Denmark Street. He was the first to see them, unluckily for them, on Friday 13th: 'I am bearer and grave-digger of the Parish of St Giles-in-the-Fields. On Friday 13th of December, I saw the four prisoners at the bar about two o'clock: Parsley, Williams, Barber and Brown. I saw them in Lloyd's Court leading to Denmark Street. I saw first in company together, Parsley and Williams separate from Barber and Brown. Parsley and Williams, which, I cannot swear to, having a bundle in possession, went into the shop of Mr. Burlance's. I saw as they were going along, a green silk petticoat hanging out of a bundle. I had a suspicion that they had been stolen from the fire, there had been a fire that morning. I went to the adjoining public house and communicated my suspicion; the landlord did not seem very anxious towards helping me take him.' The landlord, Mr. Goby, who kept the Eight Bells at 5, Little Denmark Street, wasn't in the best of health. Things took a turn though when Kane bumped into Croker, who had apprehended Barber and Brown on suspicion. Kane said, 'I says to Croker I am glad I have seen you, as if anybody had given me five guineas there are two gone in a shop over the way with a swag. Croker and I immediately went into the shop...we found the prisoners, Parsley and Williams, standing on one side of the counter, the things were on the opposite side of the counter on a little shelf on the left hand, the things that were brought in...we took the prisoners into custody.' The defence for Parsley asked among other things, where Kane lived, to which he replied, 'Five, Denmark Street.' He was also asked where he had learned the word 'swag', to which he replied, 'When I was on patrol, in the Parish of St. Giles-in-the-Fields.' The gentlemen of the jury were duly instructed that 'swag' referred to the stolen goods'. The keeper of the clothes shop, William Burlance, also gave evidence, but was suitably vague about whether he recognised any of the prisoners. When pressed he was a little more forthcoming: 'I was in the back room and I saw through the window, between that and the shop, the shadow of a person and a knock on the counter, saying 'do you buy clothes?' There was one person only, I came out, and the bundle was on the counter, and I naturally went to look at the bundle...I was looking over the bundle, to ascertain the value, as I had just done that, there came in, I fancy, two police officers...' He was asked specifically several times if he was sure he didn't know the man who had brought in the bundle, even being threatened with Newgate Gaol if he was deemed to not be telling the truth. He remained evasive, but the court felt that his character had been impeached. Croker, the policeman based at Bow Street testified: 'I was going towards Tottenham Court Road, me and Mr. Hatch, a constable, belonging to Pancras near St. Giles church. I saw Barber and Brown, the two lads, standing near the church, near Denmark Street. I says to the officer that was with me, 'there is a couple of young prigs,' I immediately went with him towards them and desired that he would not let them run away as I meant to search them.' It was as Croker and Hatch were steering the lads towards a public house, that Kane approached them about the two men in the clothes shop. Croker left Barber and Brown in Hatch's care while he went to apprehend Williams and Parsley, the latter claiming he was only in there to buy a pair of boots. Croker said that he felt the old shopkeeper was terrified. Prisoner Williams told the Grand jury, 'I was coming down Denmark Street and I saw a clothes shop, Bulrance's shop, I went into it and asked him for a pair of boots.' He swore that he'd never taken clothes into the shop. Prisoner Brown said, 'I met this John Barber about six years ago, I went to school with him. I stopped him in St Giles church, I had not stopped with him there five minutes before a man they call Mr. Croker and Mr. Hatch came up and took me over to the public house, and when I was set down they came and brought the two men in, and those clothes. The men nor the property I never saw with my eyes before; but John Barber I know by going to school with him.' Brown concurred, stating: 'Mr. Croker and Hatch took us to a public house to search us, and they brought over two others, and laid a charge of robbery to us that I am innocent of.' Twenty-six-year-old John Parsley and nineteen-year-old James Williams were found Guilty and sentenced by Mr. Justice Grose to be transported for seven years. John Brown and John Barber were found Not Guilty and acquitted. Williams and Parsley were 'removed on board the Lion Hulk at Portsmouth Harbour, to the care of J Bradley Esq.'

There was a feeling that as well as a decline in formal apprenticeships, industrialisation was having a disruptive affect, leading to law-abiding citizens fearing the ever-increasing activities of criminal gangs of boys and girls in London. Lurid details of juvenile crime began to appear in newspapers, broadsides and pamphlets, with tales of men training young boys to steal and acting as a fence (the middle man between thieves and buyers) for the stolen goods they brought to them. One of the most famous was the St Giles 'thief-trainer' Thomas Duggin, who worked the area until he was caught in 1817. Jemima Matthews, a few streets away, had a team of eight children working the area on a daily basis. Isaac 'Ikey' Solomon was also a well-known receiver of stolen goods in the 1810s and 1820s, having been arrested several times and even escaping from custody.

A police drawing of Isaac 'Ikey' Solomon

Solomon's father was a 'fence' who introduced his son to a life of crime. Arrested in 1810, he was sentenced to transportation, but somehow slipped through the net, and spent four years on the prison hulk *Zetland* before escaping. Arrested again in 1818, he went to Newgate, came to trial and escaped on his return to the gaol, the hackney carriage he was being transported in being driven by Isaac's father-in-law. A great self-publicist, he published pamphlets grossly exaggerating his criminal activities. Solomon fled to Denmark and then New York, as his wife was sentenced to transportation. On hearing this he made his way to Hobart via Rio de Janeiro. He was later arrested in Hobart and returned to England to be sentenced to transportation to…Hobart. His trial at the Old Bailey in 1830 caused a sensation in the press, as he'd been on the run and half way round the world and is generally considered to have aroused Charles Dickens' interest to such an extent that he used Solomon as the model for Fagin in *Oliver Twist.*

On the more cultural side of life is Scots-born naval surgeon, William Balmain, who lies in peace at the foot of Denmark Street. Balmain was one of a group of officers who sailed with the First Fleet on the convict ship Alexander, to establish a new colony in New South

Wales. Eleven ships carried 772 convicts, officers, crew, wives and children more than 10,000 miles to an unknown shore. During the voyage Balmain delivered the Fleet's first child. By 1797 Balmain had become principal surgeon of the colony comprising 1,600 settlers and thousands of convicts. Away from his professional duties he formed a relationship with a young convict, Margaret Dawson, and the couple had a child. He was appointed a magistrate of New South Wales, and was given 1,500 acres of land, part of which would become a suburb of Sydney, which would take his name. William Balmain was buried in St Giles-in-the-Fields in 1803, where a memorial was placed on the north-west wall in the mid-1990s with the assistance of the Balmain Society of Sydney.

Poetry in Motion

The children of the Romantic Poets, Byron and Shelley, were baptised at the font in St Giles-in-the-Fields in 1818, and thus it became known as 'The Poets' Church'. This took place on the 9th March, a few weeks after the publication of Mary Shelly's *Frankenstein*, with Byron's daughter, Allegra and the young children of the Shelleys, William and Clara Everina being baptised. Allegra was the result of a liaison between Byron and Mark Shelley's step-sister, Claire Clairmont. The Shelleys had been looking after the one-year-old and probably organised the baptism, as the child was about to be delivered to the care of Byron in Italy, who therefore would not have been present. He had also dissociated himself from Claire Clairmont, but Percy and Mary Shelley and Clairmont would have been at the ceremony at St Giles-in-the-Fields. None of the three children baptised that day would live past the age of five. The church register contains the following entry for Allegra: 'Reputed daughter of Rt.Hon. George Gordon, Lord Byron, peer of no fixed address, travelling on the continent.' Allegra died in an Italian convent at the age of five and was buried at Harrow School. Clara Shelley also died in Italy at the age of one, with her brother William dying there at the age of three.

But the links to writers stretch back much farther than that. Mary Milton, the daughter of John Milton and his wife, also Mary, was baptised there in 1647. Mary lived to the age of fifty, passing away in Devon in 1697. There are memorials to both George Chapman, the translator of Homer, and poet Andrew Marvell (*right*), who is buried here under the pews in the south aisle next to the pulpit. Born in 1621 he became tutor to Oliver Cromwell's ward, William Dutton, before being given the role of Cromwell's unofficial laureate. He took over from Milton as Latin secretary to the council of state and in 1657 became MP for Hull. Andrew Marvell, satirist, wit and poet died in August 1678, while suffering from tertian ague, although it was rumoured that he'd been poisoned by Jesuits.

This is an extract from one of his most enduring poem, *To His Coy Mistress:*

> 'But at my back I always hear
> Time's winged chariot hurrying near;
> And yonder all before us lie
> Deserts of vast eternity.
> Thy beauty shall no more be found,
> Nor, in thy marble vault, shall sound
> My echoing song: then worms shall try
> That long preserved virginity
> And your quaint honour turns to dust,
> And into ashes all my lust.
> The grave's a fine and private place,
> But none, I think, do there embrace'

There is also memorial to Richard Penderall (or Pendrill) who accompanied Charles II as he fled the country following the Battle of Worcester. The wording on his tomb must surely outshine any future Tin Pan Alley spin!

> 'Hold, passenger, here's shrouded in his hearse,
> Unparallel'd Pendrill through the universe;
> Like whom the Eastern star from heaven gave light
> To three lost kings, so he in such dark night
> To Britain's Monarch, toss'd by adverse war,

On earth appear'd, a second Eastern star;
A pole, a stem in her rebellious main,
A pilot to her royal sovereign.
Now to triumph in heaven's eternal sphere
He's hence advanced for his just steerage here;
Whilst Albion's chronicles with matchless fame
Embalm the story of great Pendrill's name.'

There is a stone in the churchyard which commemorates a lady from he area who certainly lived the longest. Eleanor Stewart died in 1725 at the astounding age of 123 years and five months. Two years short of having existed in three different centuries and having lived in the reign of nine monarchs from Elizabeth I to George I. Her stone reads:

'Neare this place lyes the body of Eleanor Stewart
who died the first day of May 1725 aged 123 years
and above five months. She lived in the Parish near
sixty years and received £150 by a pension of 4s a
week in the last 15 years of her life.'

Among the other monuments is one to, 'Thomas Edwardes, gent. Who died January 21st 1793, and left £500, 4 per cent stock to provide forever for the poor of this parish to be distributed every Sabbath day; also £300 in the same stock, for the use of the charity school.' There is also a monument dating from 1611, that was put up by John Thornton to his wife who died in childbirth and this, the family tomb, is inscribed;

'Full south this stone four-foot doth lie,
His father John and grandsire Harvey
Thornton of Thornton in Yorkshire bred,
Where lives the fame of Thornton being dead.'

There are also memorials to another devout Royalist Lord Belasyse, Sir Roger L'Estrange, the last public censor, sculptor John Flaxman, Luke Hansard, printer to the House of Commons and Thomas Earnshaw, a noted watch and chronometer maker. Lord Herbert of Cherbury reposes in the churchyard, as do actor Michael Mohun, Oliver Plunkett, the Roman Catholic archbishop of Armagh, who, as we've heard, was executed at Tyburn on a charge of high treason in 1681. The remains of a relation of Belasyse, James Radclyffe, 3rd Earl of Derwentwater, English Jacobite and companion to the 'Old Pretender', is still marked in the churchyard by a well-worn stone. Having lain by what would become Tin Pan Alley, it's fitting that he is remembered in song. 'Lord Allenwater' was collected by Ralph Vaughan Williams in 1904 from the singing of Emily Stears. Robert Walpole was offered £60,000 (around £8 million now) to save Derwentwater, but Walpole was determined to make an example of him and he was beheaded on Tower Hill in February 1716. His remains were later removed from St. Giles churchyard to Northumberland.

Among the other memorials are former St. Giles choirmaster Francis Smith who died in 1964 and the painter Arthur William Devis (1762-1822) who painted the heroic picture *The Death of Nelson* and had sixty-five of his works exhibited at the Royal Academy There are also plaques to slave owner William Robinson of Trinidad, who died aged thirty-five and Luke Hansard, printer to the House of Commons, who came to London with just one guinea in his pocket and gave his name to Hansard, the record of Parliamentary debate. The memorials are a delightful mix. George Parsons, bell-ringer for forty-six years sits with Sir Roger L'Estrange, pamphleteer, devout Royalist, a champion of Charles I and Charles II, who was knighted by James II. Sir Roger died in 1704 having lived to the then ripe old age of eighty-seven.

John Coleridge Patteson (1827-1871) missionary and the first Bishop of Melanesia is commemorated here. An Old Etonian and fellow of Merton College Oxford, he played first class cricket, spoke twenty-three Melanasian languages and his mother was a niece of the poet Samuel Taylor Coleridge. He was murdered by natives on Nukapu in the Solomon islands. His body was found covered with palm fibre matting adrift on a canoe, with a palm branch in his hand.

To give you an idea of how rife the crime and punishment in and around Denmark Street was in the 1820s, this is simply a small sample of the hundreds and hundreds of cases that were laid before the justice system…

40-year-old Mary Kelly was in court for passing counterfeit coins. Matthew Langle, assistant overseer for the Parish of St Giles, spoke about her previous convictions and term in prison. Mary Kelly refuted his evidence, saying: 'Do not believe a word that he says…he would swear his life away for one shilling…that is the way in St. Giles.' Despite telling the court that she had six children and a sick husband, Mary Kelly was sentenced to death.

Michael Bagley, an 18-year-old orphan fending for himself, was transported for 14 years for stealing a handkerchief valued at 3 shillings. Bagley sailed with two hundred other convicts to New South Wales on the Surrey in 1831. 18-year-old John Dudley was also transported in 1831, on the Lord Lyndoch, for 14 years for stealing a handkerchief and three years later another 18-year-old Daniel Duggan was transported, on the Surrey, for 7 years for stealing a handkerchief, despite the fact that he'd never been in trouble before. 29-year-old Mary Aveleigh, who claimed 'distress and poverty drove me to it', was transported for seven years for stealing two table-spoons. Samuel Panton was sentenced to death for stealing a horse as was 20-year-old

George Smith. John Hayes, 35, was sentenced to death for stealing a watch to buy bread, as he told the court that he was starving, couldn't find a job and was distressed. 27-year-old Henry Bradfield, in court for stealing three loaves, asked for clemency as he too was starving: 'There was a large piece of ham and a piece of bacon there, but I always considered myself an honest man, and wished to keep myself honest. I was prompted by starvation to do it. I was in want of victuals and throw myself on your mercy, hoping you will pity a man who has been driven to this.' Henry Bradfield was found Guilty and sentenced to death. Almost two centuries on, one wants to turn back the clock, stop them taking the bread and buy Henry and John large baskets of food.

Money, Money, Money.

Some Denmark Street residents of the time, like goldsmiths G. Worgman and J. Golibert, made an honest living in the street, others donated money to the church, some had it picked from their pockets while others played it safe and put their savings in the bank. Well, in one case, not so safe.

A Denmark Street resident suffered badly in the crash of the private bank, Marsh, Sibbald and Co., in 1824. Seventeen years earlier, in 1807, after seven years as a clerk at Marsh, Sibbald & Co., of which his father was one of the founders, Henry Fauntleroy was taken into partnership, and effectively became responsible for the running of the firm. By 1824 Fauntleroy's criminal activities began to manifest themselves; the bank suspended payments and subsequently crashed. Fauntleroy was arrested on the charge of appropriating trust funds by forging the trustees' signatures and was committed for trial. It was alleged that he had appropriated £250,000, which he had squandered in debauchery.

William Marsh's handwritten notebook listed *'Frost, Jno. Denmark Street. St. Giles's £62,16,11d'* as one of the bank's creditors. But it's unlikely that he ever saw his money. It had been spent, along with everybody else's by Henry Fauntleroy, who was charged with some thirty counts of counterfeiting and forgery at the Old Bailey. The prosecution was conducted by Mr. Attorney General, Mr. Sergeant Bosanquet and Messrs. Bolland and Law, before Mr. Justice Park. In court, Fauntleroy admitted his guilt, but insisted that he'd only misappropriated funds to pay the firm's debts. Despite some seventeen eminent merchants and bankers speaking up for his integrity, the prisoner was found Guilty and sentenced to be hanged at Newgate. An Italian named Angelini even offered, heaven knows why, to take Fauntleroy's place on the scaffold and a rumour went around that the condemned man escaped by inserting a silver tube in his throat, thus escaping strangulation. It was also erroneously put about that he was living a life of ease on the continent. Fauntleroy was one of the last to be hanged for forgery, before it ceased to be a capital crime in 1832. The £62,16,11d never found its way back to Mr. Frost in Denmark Street.

That particular crime had long been a problem. From the time that Denmark Street had been built until decimal currency was introduced, the currency was pounds, shillings and pence, written as £.s.d., the pound sign standing for Libra, Latin for a pound weight, the 's' being an abbreviation for 'shilling' and the 'd' for 'denarious', a Roman coin. There were twenty shillings to the pound and twenty-shillings to the guinea, for which we can thank Sir Isaac Newton, Master of the Mint from 1699-1727, and man of gravity. There were twelve pence to the shilling and other coins were crowns, worth five shillings, half-crowns, worth two shillings and sixpence, Florins, worth two shillings, sixpence, threepence, two pence, halfpennies and farthings, worth a quarter of a penny. The Bank of England also introduced £10 and £15 notes from 1759 and notes of higher and lower denominations later in the century. Counterfeiting had been a popular crime throughout the 1600s, as was 'clipping', where bits of silver were taken from the edges of coins, leaving them underweight. By 1696 forged coins represented some 10% of the nation's currency and coins were also being melted down and shipped abroad, as the value of silver bullion in Paris and Amsterdam was greater than the face value of the coins in London. Recoinage was tried in an attempt to thwart the criminal fraternity, but it didn't really work and the counterfeiters of the St. Giles area continued with their activities. The death penalty for forging bank notes was changed from death to transportation for life in 1832 and later still, life imprisonment, despite which, by 1850, trials for forgery and fraud comprised 20%

of all trials. This reached a high point in the 1860s when over 2,300 cases of forgery and passing off, often referred to as 'uttering', were heard at the Old Bailey alone. Newton himself cross-questioned many counterfeiters, sending some, including William Challoner, to Tyburn, to be hanged, drawn and quartered, via the top of Denmark Street and with a final drink from the St. Giles bowl. As well as being Master of the Mint Newton was the President of the Royal Society and became close friends with society member Prince George of Denmark, after whom the street is named. Through his friendship, he was knighted by George's wife, Queen Anne in 1705.

During the 1700s, annual wage in the area could be as low as £2 to £3 a year plus food, clothing and lodging, for domestic workers, with housemaids earning anything from £6 to £8, a footman £8 a year and a coachman between £12 and £25 a year. A parish pauper could receive anything between a few pence or a few shillings a week and one could pay halfpenny an hour for cheap child labour. To keep a family, the household would have to bring in some £40 per annum, or for the families who wanted to live more comfortably, £100 a year, and those who wanted some luxury, £500. A waterman would charge six pence to take you from Westminster Bridge to London Bridge and a barber would charge you the same to shave you and dress your wig. The salary of the First Lord of the Treasury was £4,000, so he could afford 80,000 shaves a year or 80,000 trips to London Bridge…luxury! Carpenters' wages however, of which there were several in Denmark Street, rose slowly from 2s 6d a day to 5 shillings a day.

 *George III shilling and George III halfpenny*

By the middle of the 1800s a skilled engineer was in such demand they could command 7s 6d a day or £110 a year, but that wasn't much more than the previous century. If you weren't troubled by the need for sartorial elegance, for two pence a night you could get a shared bed in a lodging house. Unfurnished rooms could cost 1 shilling and sixpence, depending on the area, or you could rent a property from £10 a year upwards. By the mid-1800s a family needed £50 a year simply to get by and if a man wanted to look smart, a good suit would set him back somewhere in the region of £8, or a work suit, £2. You could buy one that fitted reasonably well from Denmark Street tailor Robert Holiday Ready during the first half of the 1820s, but after 1825 who can say, as he made his will on 28th June 1825, which is available at Kew Records office in case you feel lucky and a pile of unclaimed money has accumulated. The same year a man calling himself the Revd. R. Smith, not only obtained the chapel in Denmark Street by false pretences, but also pretended to adopt the two children of a tradesman, promising to take them into care and look after them. In reality he was an itinerant juggler (in more ways than one, obviously) and made the children dance in the street while he performed his tricks and took money. They were eventually returned to their parents, but being the juggler he was, the mysterious reverend disappeared without being brought to book for his crimes.

Bad Boys

In October 1827, John Barry and Samuel Griffiths were indicted for breaking into the dwelling- of William Jackman at St Giles-in-the-Fields and stealing a pairs of shoes worth four shillings and sixpence. In court Jackman, of 60 St Giles High Street said: 'On the 12th October about 6 or 7 o'clock in the evening I was at home...the prisoners were brought into my shop by the witnesses, who charged them with breaking my glass and taking a pair of shoes of the window...' John Boston, a porter who lived at 59 Tottenham Court Road was one of the witnesses: 'I was on the opposite side of the way to Mr. Jackman's house, in company with Roberts, and saw the two prisoners in company, standing near the window. I observed Barry press his thumb against the window several times...he left and Griffiths remained at the scene. Barry returned and I heard the glass shoved in. Griffiths took something out...Barry ran down the street and they joined each other at the end of Denmark Street. We laid hold of them and out of Griffiths' apron I took these shoes.' Roberts, a painter and glazier, corroborated Boston's account of the proceedings. William Jackman identified the shoes as being his property, but in Barry's written defence, he said that he had been playing with his little sister in Denmark Street when Griffiths had come up and spoken to him: 'I saw no shoes in his hand, nor did I know he had committed the robbery. I am innocent. I unfortunately was committed to the House of Correction for three months and had only been out a week; the constable who took me thought I must be guilty because I spoke to Griffiths who had also been in the House of Correction with me, in the same yard, but I am innocent and have kept myself innocent of robbery ever since I have been out of prison.' John Barry and Samuel Griffiths were both sentenced to death, with the Jury recommending mercy as they were both only...twelve years old.

In 1839, Twenty-seven-year-old John Thomas Cummins was indicted for stealing mail and bank notes posted by Joseph Scrivener, a traveller for Denmark Street soap-boilers, Woolley and Marahalh, in March of that year. Scrivener gave evidence as did various post office workers. The prisoner approached letter carrier, William Buckingham, on two occasions in Charlotte Street, purporting to be from Woolley and Marahalh and procuring letters intended for them. Two of the Denmark Street soap-boilers, Benjamin Zacharia Woolley and Edward Woolley gave evidence against the prisoner. The defendant's brother-in-law also gave evidence, stating, rather bizarrely that the prisoner had told him that he was off to start a new job as the Superintendent of Police, in New Brazil. He did get to go abroad though; Cummins was transported for fourteen years. He was placed on the 507 ton ship the *Canton*. She was later wrecked in 1848, sailing from Sydney to China.

That same year, Harriett Newsum of Denmark Street was in court to give evidence against Mary Rudge, who was alleged to have stolen a cap, gown, shifts, a handkerchief and a petticoat from the premises. Newsum told the court: 'I am the wife of Samuel newsum; he is at sea...I live in Denmark-Street; the prisoner was recommended to assist me as a milliner...I entrusted her with the care of my house....the next evening I saw her coming towards my house...I found my handkerchief on her; I had missed all the articles stated but nothing more....there were articles of much greater value there...I have found her honest before.' A cap and bundle were found at her lodgings and pawnbroker Robert Linwood told the court: 'I am a pawnbroker. I have a gown pawned by the prisoner...she has been in the habit of coming for the prosecutrix.' In her defence, Mary Rudge said, 'The prosecutrix allowed me to wear her clothes.' Mary Rudge was found Not Guilty. It was such a fine line between being acquitted and being transported. In another case, five years later, one prisoner was found Guilty and transported for fifteen years, another was found

Guilty but no punishment given, while the other was told that he was free to go. James Shaw and Frederick Shaw, who also lived in Denmark Street were up before the court, with a third man, Frederick Radford, on a charge of stealing leaves of gold, gold dust, 230 brushes, 25 packets of metal and 36 shells from the house of Jacob Worster, an oil and colour man of New Compton Street. Worster insisted that he'd padlocked his door the night before and when he'd come downstairs in the morning, 'It was wide open and the padlock was on the ground...I got into the shop and found a great number of the drawers taken out of their nest....the prisoners, the Shaws, come to my house for gold-books...I buy gold-books, and sell them...this is part of the property I lost that night.'

Frederick Shaw's servant, Mary Ann Moore, told the court that Radford had come there (Denmark Street) with a blue bag. 'He asked if Mr. Shaw was at home...I said no, but James was at home. He said, 'James, I can't sell these brushes, will you buy them.'' She said that James offered him 25 shillings and that William the apprentice was also there at the time. She also answered the question as to the living arrangements as she was part of the household but separated from her husband. She swore that she lived as a servant not as a mistress. Henry Dowell, a carpenter who lived next door to the Shaws said, 'I was standing at my door...James Shaw came to me...he said, 'I have had a few words with my father' and asked me if I would come and help him to carry some things...he took me up to his bedroom...took out some gas-pipes, a brass lamp, and a blue bag...' James Shaw was found Guilty and transported for 15 years, Radford was found Guilty but there was no charge against his name, but Frederick Shaw was found Not Guilty. Radford was transported and ended up in St. Marks, Tasmania, where he married Eliza Davey who bore him two sons.

Frederick Radford and Frederick Shaw were also indicted for stealing 110 rings, 73 brooches, 16 lockets, 44 swivels and an assortment of watch-keys, jewel-boxes, seals, tubes and chains for which 28-year-old Radford was found Guilty and transported for ten years and Frederick Shaw was found Not Guilty. Frederick Shaw was indicted a *third* time, on this occasion for 'burglariously breaking and entering the dwelling-house of Caroline Jones with intent to steal a tankard, spoons, a cup, neck-chains, a necklace, a purse, candlesticks, a sauce tureen, five guineas and a sovereign...and a greatcoat, value 2 shillings.' Frederick Shaw, yet again, was found Not Guilty. But the justice system still hadn't finished with him as he was indicted once again, this time for 'feloniously receiving....2 gas branches, value £3 3 shillings, 1 gas standard and burner, value 12 shillings and two lamp-burners, value £1 10 shillings - the goods of James Slater.' Slater stated to the court, 'I am a gas fitter and brass-manufacturer and live in Denmark-street. About the 8th or 9th June I lost from 20 to 22 pounds worth of property, which was kept in a store-room at the top of the house...the two gas braches, two burners and these two gas-pipes are part of the property I lost.' William Pocock (PC F 81) said that he had, 'Searched the prisoner's premises on the 1st of March and found this property under the drawers of the press bedstead...I found 112 brushes under the bed in the drawer, and in a paper parcel between the bed and the wall, two balls of string and twenty-eight brushes.' Surely this time Frederick would be found Guilty and sentenced? His son had been transported, his friend had been transported and the intrepid PC F 81 had now as good as nailed him. But no, yet again the gods of Denmark Street smiled upon old Fred...who presumably kept the stolen goods!

It was a tough existence for many, with even those trying to make an honest living feeling the pinch. Soap manufacturers and dealers, William and Edward Cleaver had had their business in the street from at least 1816, but in 1839, after over twenty-three years of endeavour, they went out of business. With businesses struggling, and poverty, disease and infant mortality rife, maybe some felt they had little to lose by taking to a life of crime. Disease pays no heed to one's position in life, high-born or humble. Cholera killed thousands in the area during the 1840s, with residents writing to the *Times*, 'We live in muck and filth. We ain't got no priviz, no dust bins, no drains, no water-splies, and no drain or suer in the hole place.' Charles Dickens captured the atmosphere of the area around St Giles and Denmark Street. in *The Old Curiosity Shop*.

> 'How many people may there be in London who, if we had brought them deviously and blindfold to this street fifty paces from the Station House and within call of St. Giles's church, would know it for a not remote part of the city in which their lives are passed? How many who, amidst this compound of sickening smells, these heaps of filth, these tumbling houses with all their vile contents, animate and inanimate, slimily overflowing into the black road, would believe that they breathe this air?'

In February 1832, it was reported that the first London deaths caused by cholera had occurred in St Giles, those of Mary Platt, the wife of Edward Platt, a chimney sweep, and Margaret Martin, the wife of an out of work tailor. Twenty-four-year-old Jeremy Keef miraculously recovered, but the violent cramps, vomiting and purging generally brought death. It was initially believed that the disease was airborne. That September a local man, J. Pidduck had a letter published, under the heading; *Treatment of Malignant Cholera in the Parish of St. Giles, London,* addressed to the secretary of the Board of Trade, describing a long and complex method for dealing with Cholera.

The high mortality rate among infants and the regular outbreaks of cholera, encouraged those who could to move out of London, or even move abroad. Sophia Comley was born at 3 Denmark Street in 1840 and married Stephen Fuller, three years her senior, in 1857. They had five daughters and two sons while living in London and moved to Australia in the mid-1860s where they had another four sons and two daughters. Some of the children died in infancy. William Fuller lived the longest from 1866-1929. Sophia passed away in Sydney, New South Wales in 1908.

During another Cholera outbreak in 1849, 285 people died in St. Giles and in 1854 another 115. In August 1854 there was a major outbreak in Soho and by the time it had run its course, with over 600 dying within a month, Dr. John Snow had gathered enough evidence to prove that the disease was waterborne. He'd mapped the cases and noticed many grouped around the pump at Broad Street in Soho. After organising for it to be disconnected the cases of Cholera dropped severely. Places of work with their own water supply were relatively unaffected.

Things were about to change though, as that decade saw a beginning to the clearance of the slums when New Oxford Street was driven through the St Giles Rookery. In 1851 there were still almost 40,000 souls crammed into what were the worst conditions imaginable, but sewers were beginning to be laid, breweries and workshops started to use that area as their base and the residential population began to dwindle. The population would have been one less if John Marabello had been a better shot.

In 1844 Charles Joseph Reynolds, a printseller from Denmark Street was at the Old Bailey as a witness to a shooting. Forty-eight-year-old Marabello was accused of, 'feloniously assaulting Jospeh Lever, and with a certain loaded pistol shooting at him with intent to murder him.' He was also charged with stating his intent to maim and to do him grievous bodily harm. The pair had apparently a 'trifling dispute' about some fixtures on a property that Lever had sold to Marabello.

Reynolds, the printseller told the court, 'On the 26th of Jan., near one o'clock in the afternoon, I was passing along Silver-street, and saw the prosecutor entering the passage, followed by the prisoner—seeing them running I was somewhat surprised—I followed, and the prisoner fired the pistol—the prosecutor had retreated towards the yard door, before that—he closed the door on him, and the pistol was discharged by the prisoner—I saw the pistol in his hand—I just laid my hand on him, and a policeman came in—I went to the yard door, and said, "The prisoner is in custody," and then followed to the station—the pistol was fired as the door was in the very act of closing—to the best of my belief the prisoner was about three yards from the door, two or three yards, I did not measure.' Marabello was found Guilty of the charge of 'grievous bodily harm' and transported for fifteen years.

Although there were many 'lone wolves', like Marbello, it was still an area worked by criminal gangs headed up by 'thief-trainers', Charles King being one of the most notorious. Among his gang of professional pick-pockets was thirteen-year-old John Reeves who stole some £100 of property in one week alone. That's almost £10,000 in today's money. An easier way to make money, although nowhere near as much, was to get your dog to do the work.

Despite history relating that that the first modern dog show took place in Newcastle-upon-Tyne in 1859, it seems that the first canine gathering was in fact in Denmark Street in 1852. Charles Aistrop, former proprietor of the Westminster Pit in Duck Lane, pioneered the Toy Dog Club, England's second official dog club. He launched his *Fancy Dog Show* in a Denmark Street Tavern, with crowds lining up to see exotic breeds such as Bulldogs, Black and Tan Terriers, Italian Greyhounds, Chinese Pugs, Skye Terriers and Blenheim Spaniels.

The first National Dog Show wouldn't take place for another seven years, but it proved to be so popular that by the end of the 1860s the show was attracting over 700 dogs and 20,000 paying visitors. When the show went to London there were an incredible 100,000 visitors. It was the manager of Spratt's dog food, Charles Cruft,, who took it to new levels, but it started in Denmark Street, or possibly Little Denmark Street as there was a tavern there, the Eight Bells.

Two other likely lads, older but clearly no wiser than John Reeves, may have taken off at high speed down Denmark Street, but succeeded in getting away with nothing but a heavy gaol sentence for their trouble. On 19th July 1879 cab driver Augustus Jack was driving in St Giles at about 2.00am when he saw a man lying in the road and two man bending over him. He told the court 'I stopped my horse and the man called out, "Cabby! Cabby! Help me!"…the two men then rose off him and turned down Denmark Street a few yards.' Richard Richardson told the jury that he was a surveyor from Camden Town and while he was walking past St Giles church near the end of Denmark Street he felt: 'Something like the report of a pistol in my right ear, but I do not know what it was and I fell to the ground…I saw no-one…I then saw two men unbuttoning my coat…I have a slight recollection of Riley, but I cannot swear to him…I had five pounds ten shillings in my trousers pocket, but missed nothing but an ivory two-foot rule…was five or six minutes on the ground…a cabman came up and called 'Stop thief'…I think the cab had a grey horse.' The men were chased by James Irving, a leather-dresser from Cloth Fair and kept them in sight until a policeman arrived. There were apparently some four or five people giving chase despite the lateness of the hour. Policeman E 139, George Matthews told the court, 'I heard cries of 'Stop thief' and saw the prisoners running down Denmark Street…I never lost sight of them until they were taken…I took Barry.' Policeman E 495, John Fudge concurred that at no time did they lose sight of the prisoners. A third policeman, John Littleboy, E 495, said: 'I saw Riley running as fast as he could…I ran after him about twenty yards and caught him…he was alone…I held him until the other constable came, when he was taken to the station and charged with assaulting Mr. Richardson…he made no reply.'

One can get a feel for the area behind Denmark Street from this 1886 watercolour by F. Calvert (*left*), the view being towards Flitcroft Street which runs up to join Denmark Street at the church. The Georgian houses that once stood at the end of Stacey Street are shown as is the old Shelton's Charity School on the left, which still stands today. The establishment was built with money left by a St Giles vestryman, William Shelton, in his will. Behind the cart is an 18th century courtyard called Eight Bells Yard, a site on which the main leper hospital residential building, the Mansion, or Capital, Place stood for centuries. By 1888, Denmark Street was a mixture of jewellers, gunsmiths, invalid chair makers, silversmiths, sword cutlers, restaurants, a coach works, a public house at No.27 and a barrel shed behind nos. 1, 2 and 3.

It's not surprising that some authors used the street as a setting for bad deeds in their books. In the Mary Elizabeth Braddon's 1890 novel, *One Life, One Love,* Robert Hattrell, a man of means, position and considerable strength is lured into a 'shabby London lodging', in Denmark Street by a messenger. On his way to a business meeting to buy the land next to River Lawn, his house near Henley, he is carrying

£4,000 in cash in his breast pocket and is stabbed to death in the street by an unknown assailant. Braddon (1835-1915) who was born at No. 2 Frith Street, off Soho Square, a stone's throw from Denmark Street, was best-known for her sensational 1962 novel, *Lady Audley's Secret* and for founding the *Belgravia* magazine. Possibly not the magazine of choice for the five hundred inmates that were in the workhouse serving St. Giles in 1881, which was presided over by thirty-seven-year-old Chas Rowland Elles and his wife, Elizabeth. There was more fiction based in Denmark Street in 1881; in the book *Sherlock Holmes and John Watson: 50 New Ways the World's Most Legendary Partnership Might Have Begun.*

In the chapter *Nursery Rhyme* with the sub-title *Denmark Street 1881,* two men as yet unknown to each other, Sherlock Holmes and John Watson, are browsing in a small, dusty music store in the street, run by a Madame Vilranda, when Holmes is called upon to suggest some suitable music for the other customer, looking to purchase something for a young lady. Holmes suggests Vivaldi's Four Seasons and presents Watson with *Spring* as a gift, Holmes picks up a violin and demonstrates the piece, with Watson and Madam Vilranda joining in vocally. Asked his name, he writes a note: 'Play well for your God-father, he is very proud of you, Your humble servant, Sherlock Holmes.' Making his usual uncanny deductions, he determined the relationship between Watson and his god-daughter with consummate ease, his occupation, marital status *et al.* Watson is suitably impressed and says: 'Let me buy you a coffee Mr. Holmes...' And so began their fictional partnership...in Denmark Street.

During this time, the 1880s, Charing Cross Road was built, along the line of Hog Lane, running from Shaftesbury Avenue in the South to the intersection with Oxford Street and Tottenham Court Road and as industry increased, Denmark Street became something of a centre for small industries. In 1888 there was a silver caster at No. 26 and a sword cutler at No. 5, and also the latter half of the century architects Sir Arthur Blomfield and the Gothic Revival architect, William Butterfield, made some alterations to St Giles-in-the-Fields in 1875 and 1896. Butterfield came up with a design the previous year for the extension of the Chancel.

In 1887 the social commentator Charles Booth undertook a survey which included Denmark Street, with school board representatives visiting individual dwellings and enquiring about occupations, the number of rooms in the house, the number of children, number of adults and the social status of the family. It was no longer easy to be invisible.

Although the old St. Giles Rookery had long gone, there was still plenty of immoral, illegal and criminal activity at the tail end of the century in Denmark Street and the immediate vicinity to keep the local police force busy. From police notebooks of 1898, we know that Denmark Street and the St. Giles area was patrolled at different times by police constables, Albert Gunn, Robert Turner E. Tait. G Moir and Inspector Tyldesley. The notebooks make mention of 'Prostitutes and skilled workers' in Denmark Street and that the local prostitutes are a mixture of English, French, German and Belgian. Also mentioned are the 'Foreign bullies [pimps] living on Phoenix Street.' Also noted is the amount of 're-building of public houses in the sub-division' and the local rents. But gradually the old haunts were being demolised, building and alleyways in the area were disappearing and roads were being widened.

Charing Cross Road, as we've heard, was originally Hog Lane, a 'Highway of immemorial antiquity', described in 1720 as 'very ordinary' and 'a place not over well built or inhabited.' The street numbers now stop at no.11 on the south side and begin at no 18 on the north side. In a 1977 music magazine, no. 126 Charing Cross Road was given equal billing with no.17 Denmark Street. On the south corner is 120 Charing Cross Road, presumably the site of 12 Denmark Street. As there is no recent history on them, it seems that 13-16 Denmark Street were demolished when the old Hog Lane, or later Crown Street, was reconstructed as the much wider Charing Cross Road. This is borne out by the fact that the existing Crown Street buildings, nos 16-24, 36, 40-44, 46-50 48, 52, 64, 66, and 68, were all even nos. They were re-numbered with the creation of Charing Cross Road.

Eight of Denmark Street's twenty properties, completed by 1691, have survived into the 21st century and it retains the unique distinction of being the only street in London to have 17th Century terraced facades on both sides. Once on the edge of an infamous and sprawling slum, this area was also a centre for the printing and distribution of ballad sheets, also known as 'broadsides, which were then sold far

and wide by itinerant hawkers. The 20th century successor to the broadside trade was the publication of sheet music, the first publisher to set up in the Denmark Street being Lawrence Wright, also a songwriter, at No. 11 in 1908.

A 1927 selection of lawrence Wright Songs.

I Write The Songs

During the 1920s Denmark Street began to get a reputation for being London's Tin Pan Alley, the nickname having been borrowed from the area around New York's West 28th Street (*below*). At the beginning of the 1900s the songwriter and publisher, Harry von Tilzer had an office in the New York thoroughfare, and they say the sound of his piano gave rise to the street's nickname. Monroe H. Rosenfeld who was writing an article on songwriters, heard the sound, likened it to a tin pan and gave his article the headline, *Tin Pan Alley*.

The street also became popular with London's Japanese, their national club having over 400 members in the 1920s. By the 1930s several of them had set up shop in Denmark Street, not as publishers, but as hairdressers, jewellers, restaurateurs and hoteliers. So Tin Pan Alley, as it was rapidly becoming known, was not only home to the music publishers and songwriters, but also several Chinese and Japanese restaurants, which led to the short thoroughfare also being known as 'Little Tokyo'. The eateries also became the haunts of the music industry moguls. The coming of the BBC in the early 1920s, bringing in first radio and then television, created more outlets and more show windows for the British songwriters and publishers and the move from silent films to 'talkies' provided another enormous boost for a growing industry.

On with
the dance

Gay, high spirited dance music, straight from the best
orchestras, may be yours this Christmas. Get a Mullard
Speaker for your radio—it reproduces so perfectly that
the band might be in your own room.

With the Mullard full-wave high tension supply unit, you
get all the high tension power you need by simply switching
on the electric current and the Mullard low tension
Battery Charger keeps your accumulator at full strength.

Write now for free booklet " How to Get Better Radio."

Mullard
MASTER · RADIO

It means
profit
for you

Naturally you want to sell a first-
class set. There's goodwill in it!
And also — because your profits won't
thrive on sentiment — you want a
first-class seller. In the Mullard "M.B.
Three" you have both. It's the finest
proposition on the battery market.

The
M.B. THREE 8 GNS

PRICE EIGHT GNS. INCLUSIVE OF ALL BATTERIES
OR 43/9 DOWN AND 13/4 MONTHLY FOR ELEVEN MONTHS

The Mullard Wireless Service Co. Ltd., Mullard House, 127, Charing Cross Road, London, W.C.2.

Anyone making music wanted to be in or around Denmark Street and one of those businesses was the Mullard Radio valve Company. It was founded in 1920 by UK radio pioneer Captain Stanley R. Mullard, (born 1883). The company produced components, including valves and transistors, as well as radio and television sets. The company was originally financed by the Radio Communication Co., a bacon producer and a firm of East India merchants. They moved from Charing Cross Road to Denmark Street, where they were based at 'Mullard House, Denmark Street, WC2 Gerrard 9668. They published their own quarterly magazine and in 1927 the company was bought by Philips, who retained the Mullard brand and name. Two years later Stanley Mullard resigned as Managing Director but continued as Chairman. At the 1938 Radiolympia, Mullard displayed a laboratory demonstration fifteen-inch television, returning the following year with two commercial televisions, the show being cut short by the outbreak of war with Germany. In 1948, the Mullard Wireless Service Co officially changed its name to Mullard Electronic products, to reflect the company's expansion into industrial, scientific and

communications activities. In 1957 Philip Mullard set up the Mullard
Radio Astronomy Observatory at Cambridge University and in 1966
the Mullard Space Science laboratory in Holmbury St. Mary. A Paul
Robeson fan and champion amateur golfer, Stanley Mullard MBE
died in 1977.

Alongside the street's churchgoers, musicians, publishers,
songwriters and restaurateurs, there were the troublemakers. From the
1920s through to the 1950s and beyond, Soho and the nearby areas
were subject to organised gangs, with names like Jack Spot and Billy
Hill striking fear into people's hearts. A typical instance of violence
occurred in January 1931 with a fight taking place outside the Pheonix
Club in Little Denmark Street. Harry White, a nattily dressed
cockney, heavy smoker and drinker, and Eddie Fleisher (Fletcher)
attacked the manager Casimir Raczynski and a chap called Fred
Roache as they left the club. White and Fletcher were charged for it.
The fact that mild-mannered and diminutive Stanley King had been
drinking at the same club one night in May 1936, probably saved him
from the hangman's noose. His wife, Constance May Hinds, who
worked locally as the prostitute 'Dutch Leah' was found in their flat
at 66 Old Compton Street, strangled and with her head beaten in with
a rusty flat iron. It was the area's fifth murder in six months and of
course it was being sensationalised by the press who reported that
police were searching for a new 'Jack the Ripper' dubbing him 'The
Soho Strangler'. Twenty-three-year-old Dutch Leah had been raised
in a criminal family, married twice by the age of eighteen, she had
eight convictions for prostitution and was an alcoholic. On being
questioned, her husband Stanley King stated that he'd been at the club
in Little Denmark Street from 11.15-3.30 and had walked back down
the road to find their door locked. Fearing the worst, he said he broke
the door down. There was only one key, which was still in the
possession of the dead woman, and with the flat being on the second

floor with no other means of leaving, apart from a 25 foot drop on to the pavement, the police were baffled. Did King need to break the door down, or was he the killer? Maybe he simply assumed he would be the prime suspect and broke the door down in an attempt to create an alibi. The so-called 'Soho Strangler' who murdered Dutch Leah and possibly others was never found.

War

On the evening of 9th October 1940, a number of bombs fell in the vicinity of Denmark Street, mainly at the back of the church and a few yards south on the corner of Stacey Street (*pictured left*) and New Compton Street. Many houses were badly damaged, but 62 New Compton Street took a direct hit. That is now the site of the Pheonix Garden. The buildings that were damaged dated from the 1770s, when the road was named Stidwell Street after local landowner Sir Richard Stiddolph. It was renamed New Compton Street in 1775. The Stacey Street buildings dated from the 17th century, known than as Brown's Gardens. Brown was a local gardener who rented a plot on the edge of the churchyard. The name Stacey however comes from the earlier 19th century when the street was a footpath and James Stacey owned two houses on either side. It was re-named after Stacey in 1878. At least two businesses were destroyed on the night of the raid; Printers P.G.Savage & Son and Edward James' Garage

.

Showing the clearance of the bombed Stacey Street site. Now the Phoenix Garden.

By February 1941 the bomb site had been cleared and was used as a car park until it became the Phoenix Garden in 1984. The following picture has the Phoenix Garden overlaid on an old depiction of the leper hospital.

The present site of the Phoenix Garden shown within a plan of St. Giles Leper Hospital and precincts

Originally the garden was a part of the orchard attached to the leper hospital, but eventually built over in the 1900s. It's run by a local committee of volunteers and is open to the public from 7.30 am until dusk. The garden won a *Shell Better Britain Campaign Award in* 1985 and has won first prize for *Best Environmental Garden in the Camden in Bloom* competition, six times from 2004-2010 inclusive. Part of the wall to the garden is listed by English Heritage and is listed as being in the conservation area of Denmark Street.

Looking west up New Compton Street: 3rd September 1941

Further clearance work of the Stacey street bombsite, c. 1941

St Giles Church escaped the worst of the bombing by a matter of yards but lost most of its Victorian glass. During 1952 and 1953 the church underwent a major restoration. John Betjeman described it as, 'One of the most successful post-war church restorations.' It was designated a Grade I listed building in 1951.

Some footage exists to remind us of what an important, thriving street this was, important for our culture, entertainment and economy. The earliest clip dates from 1938 and features Lawrence Wright the street's first publisher and singer Judy Shirley.

The Times They Are a Changing

The beginning of 1947 was a grim time for Tin Pan Alley with US industry paper, Billboard printing this report from London:

'The coal crisis and the continuing severe weather here has practically brought the music business (along with industry generally) to a standstill. No printer is permitted to turn out sheet music and there hasn't been a single sheet printed since the crisis began. English music men anticipate that the situation is likely to last at least another couple of weeks and wonder what will happen if it runs longer than that. Along Denmark Street, in publisher's offices, staff work with their overcoats on...wear heavy slacks and boots and work by candlelight a good part of the day. Record making, of course, has also come to a complete halt and this adds another blow to the biz. Since even when operating at full capacity about 50 per cent of the disks tuned out must be sent out of the country in order to get foreign currency into England.'

As if the weather and fuel crisis wasn't enough, there also appeared to be a payola crisis in the UK music industry, with the King's Counsellor 'conferring with leading music men.' The US press again taking a report from London: 'the entire payola system here has been aggravated to a considerable extent by several severe and increasing blows suffered by the music business in the past year or more. The BBC is using practically no pop dance bands and the record situation is far from good. The payola continues rampant here and according to some music men has reached greater proportions than at any time in the past.' The BBC and the music publishers were looking to set up a committee to investigate any illegal activity, but a similar committee in the States had never proved to have been an effective deterrent to payola.

An increasingly effective and legal way to help sell your song, without resorting to payola, was to create a story that would interest the media. In 1949 a Pathe newsreel, entitled *Tin Pan Alley Wants It Straight*, showed comedians Arthur Askey and Charlie Chester joining in a PR stunt after song publisher Eddie Rogers put out a song about a pig with a curly tail. Rogers offered a £1,000 reward to anyone who could produce a straight-tailed pig. Hundreds of people gathered in the street as two farmers tried their luck. The tail wasn't straight enough for the judges so no money changed hands. In 1964, Rogers would publish a book, *Whatever Happened to Tin Pan Alley?* The older publishers saw the coming of the Beatles as the end of an era, the next generation saw it as the start of an era.

There is also a short documentary film which features the publishers, songwriters, singers and arrangers from Denmark Street., in January 1951. This was shown in cinemas to show audiences how new songs were written, performed and hits created. The song used as an example in this film is *Last Night's Kisses,* a number written by Sam Brown, Jimmy Kennedy and Ray Hartley. There are several shots of the old publishers' signs in the street, including Southern House, Baxter & Beverly Music, Lawrence Wright Music, Leeds Music, Sun Music Publishers, 20th Century Music, Campbell Connelly Music and Peter Maurice. The short film is full of singers, publishers and songwriters of the period, such as Billy Cotton, The Beverley Sisters, The Five Smith Brothers, Johnny Johnson, Tommie Connor, Mantovani, Joe Loss, Petula Clark, Joe 'piano' Henderson, Eric Winstone, Anne Shelton, Geraldo and Lew Stone.

One of the lesser-known publishers whose sign could be seen in the film was that of Baxter and Beverley. In the edition of the British Songwriter & Dance Band Journal dated 6th May 1947, a small article featured Don Adams, who wrote *Hammersmith Jive* and Dave Beverley, as part of the 'Three B's,' wrote *Don't Tell A Soul,* who, they said, were out of work songwriters looking for jobs. Any jobs, as long as they could have time off to write. The other 'two Bs', Bobby Bond and Monty Baxter they said, were 'still pounding the Alley for more successes.' Bond and Baxter had songs published at the time by Lawrence Wright and Noel Gay, including the popular *Confetti on the Pavement*. Within a year though, Beverley and Baxter Music Publishers were up and running in Denmark Street. One of their popular songs was *Our Anniversary Day*, published in 1949. In 1950, through A & B Music Company c/o Radiomusic Publications of 6, Denmark Street Monty Baxter claimed the copyright on a song called *Up and Down on the Round 'a' bout*.

One of the most successful singers in the UK charts during the 1950s was Ruby Murray, who features in another short piece of film of her singing *Bambino*, entitled *Birth of a Record*, shot in Tin Pan Alley during 1955. In that year alone she had seven top ten hits. There was other, slightly more unorthodox, entertainment on hand, such as an escapologist (*below*), who kept people amused around the corner in the Charing Cross Road.

7.   LONDON LIFE : An Entertainer escapes from a bound sack in Charing Cross Road.

By the 1940s many of London's music publishers were located here and business thrived. The geographical concentration had a sound economic rationale. Professional singers, who in those days rarely wrote their own material, would make the rounds of the publishers looking for hit songs, so it made sense that they were all in the same street. Before the start of Buddy Holly and the Crickets' only UK Tour, in March 1958, their equipment was still being shipped over and Buddy was in need of a guitar to use in the meantime. He continued to use it on the tour bus and in hotels as they travelled. Des

O'Connor, the compere for the tour, took Buddy down to Denmark Street where he bought a 1956 Hofner President Archtop guitar which he gave to Des at the end of the tour. The guitar, serial number 2559, is now owned by the Buddy Holly Educational Foundation and is in the Buddy Holly Museum in Lubbock, Texas.

Buddy Holly's 1956 Hofner President, Photo courtesy the Buddy Holly Educational Foundation.

By the early 1960s Denmark Street was the bustling, expanding centre of music industry, packed with publishers, recording studios, musical instrument shops, equipment retailers and cafés where you might just bump into someone who could change your life. For eighty years this was the street that made British music a force to be reckoned with around the world.

As well as the big-name publishers and successful songwriters, there were many people working with them behind the scenes, like Winifred Young (*right*). Winifred was the sister of infamous child poisoner, Graham Young, who would poison dozens of his family, friends and acquaintances, killing his stepmother and two workmates. One morning in November 1961, as his twenty-two-year-old sister Winifred was preparing to head off to Denmark Street, Graham gave her a cup of tea, but while on the train she was taken ill and began hallucinating. When she eventually staggered into the music publishers where she worked, they realised something was seriously wrong and sent her to Middlesex Hospital, where it was discovered that she was suffering from belladonna poisoning. Winifred survived, but others weren't so lucky. Her brother was committed to Broadmoor but released in 1971 only to poison another 70 people, killing two of them. The rest of his days, until his death in 1990 were spent in Parkhurst. In 1973 Winifred wrote a book about her brother, *Obsessive Poisoner. The Strange Story of Graham Young,* in which she refers to his loneliness and depression, apparently once telling her, 'There's a terrible coldness inside me.' He also referred to himself as

'Your friendly neighbourhood Frankenstein.' Mary Shelley, who wrote *Frankenstein*, having been on Denmark Street, 150 years before Winifred.

In 1964, while the seventeen-year-old Young was languishing in Broadmoor, Mike Hennessey published a book simply called *Tin Pan Alley* featuring some of the stars of the day on the cover. Too early for David Bowie to feature, but he was captured on film a year later, purely by chance, walking down Tin Pan Alley to the Gioconda café. Bowie smiled but said nothing. Twelve years later the Sex Pistols gave an interview in the street where they didn't smile and said

slightly more than nothing.

1972 saw the release of the film *Whatever Happened to Tin Pan Alley*, directed by Brain Lewis. Among those appearing were Pete Townshend, Marc Bolan, Anne Shelton, Heinz, Cliff Richard, Larry Parnes, George Martin, Mick Jagger, Adam Faith, Paul Jones, Dick James, Issy Bonn and songwriters Nicky Chinn and Mike Chapman and Tommie Connor.

In 2016 we filmed a TV series called Tin Pan Alley, which was not only a competition to find some great unsung British song writers, but also a way of re-connecting our lyricists and composers with the industry. Where hopefuls would once come to Denmark Street with the dream of being signed to a publisher and getting their songs covered, they could now send songs to Tin Pan Alley the TV series. We had over 700 good songs submitted with DJs, producers, publishers, singers, musicians and record labels taking part in the voting. The final 12 became part of the series and were whittled down by our five Execs, who gave constructive and inspirational advice. The Execs were songwriters Lamont Dozier and Cathy Dennis, Singer/writer David Grant, producer/songwriter Chris Neil and promotion man Judd Lander. The eight-part series also included many stories behind hit songs, told by such writers as Barry Mason, Don Black, Mike Batt and Dave Hill from Slade, all a part of the original Tin Pan Alley, and Graham Gouldman, Gary Kemp, Lamont Dozier and Cathy Dennis. The series also featured many tales from Tin Pan Alley's glory days. Supported by PRS for Music, whose Chairman, Guy Fletched started out in Denmark Street at the age of fifteen, the six finalists and the subsequent winner, Nikki Murray (aka One Lone Boy) were presented with their awards at PRS Head Quarters by Spandau Ballet's Gary Kemp. The eight-part series aired on Showbiz TV on Sky with the special from Jamaica featuring the winner recording there, being shown at a later date.

Part 2

Living by Numbers

No.1

In 1919, Wellmon's was at No.1 Denmark Street, offering, among other music, pantomime numbers including *Old Farmer Brown, Dear Old Dad* and *Big Ben Chimes.*

Harry Malcolm Wellmon (*right*) was an African-American conductor and composer who was born in North Carolina in 1883. He began as a variety performer in Harlem and from 1907 worked in London where he became well established as a composer for music hall acts and later became one of the early publishers in Denmark Street. In 1907 he and Louis Laval composed the score for *Pick of the Bunch* which toured the UK. Wellmon also contributed *Lily of Bermuda* to the touring show two years later. He wrote songs for artists such as Jessie Weston, Frank Cumminger and he wrote *The Good Old British Isles* with Dick Carlish, for Victoria Monks. Carlish, born Richard Wienskowitz was formerly a member of Fred Karno's troupe and after his partnership with Wellmon broke up he became a club manager, most famously for Kate Mayrick's at 43 Club in Gerrard Street, Soho.

Wellmon had a studio at 47 Oxford Street and also worked out of Shapiro Von Tilzer Music at 100 Charing Cross Road, returning to London late in 1910 after a year's sojourn in the States. His son, Malcolm Harry Wellmon, was born in Southsea in 1911 through an affair with confectioner Lilian Riley. Returning from a second trip to the States he formed the act Carlisle and Wellmon. The pair treaded the boards together until their final appearance at the Lewisham Hippodrome in December 1913. Wellmon had now moved his studio to 2 Gosfield Street. From March 1926 he formed an act with L.C. Glass, registering in London, for the draft two years later in 1918. In April 1919 he married Lavinia Elizabeth Jeffs, born in Stoney Stanton, Leicestershire, at St. Giles Registry Office and set up his business at No.1 Denmark Street in partnership with V. Swift. Over the next two years he conducted orchestras across Europe and in Bombay, and he and Lavinia, whose stage name was Odette Jeffs, later performing as a duo in the Netherlands, France and South America. Lavinia had five siblings, including William, a year younger than her, who was killed in action fighting with the Leicestershire Regiment in October 1914.

In July 1921, when he was thirty-nine years old, Wellmon filed an application for a passport extension which was supported by George W. Mitchell of 18 Cavendish Square, who'd known Wellmon for ten years. Wellmon told the authorities, 'The only explanation I have to offer for my continued foreign residence is that having been a music hall artist for years, I came abroad as such to fill theatrical engagements at various places in the British Isles and France, and of late to publish songs of my own composition.' He wrote *Sweet Dreams* with Walter Smart in 1903, and often collaborated, but his main song-writing and Music Hall stage partner was George H. Carlisle, born in Minneapolis, Minnesota in 1883.

George Carlisle

A 1921 review in *Musical America* described Wellmon thus:

'...a superbly vigorous conductor in the uniform of a Brazilian general, wearing dazzling white gloves and green shoes, leads this heterogeneous instrumental ensemble. He uses no score, and at times marches straight into his orchestra to stimulate some player who seems to lag; at others, when all is going as it should, he lowers his baton, and, hands behind his back, looks at the public with eyes twinkling with satisfaction.'

Wellmon returned to New York alone in 1935 and died in Manhattan ten years later.

1-3 Denmark Street has now been owned by the government department for over seventy years. Work and Pensions is based there. It has, however, a decidedly grisly past, from the period when it was being used as a job centre, at one time specialising in catering vacancies. One of their employees has gone down in the annals of crime as one of the most notorious British serial killers of all-time. Dennis Nilsen was born in Fraserburgh, Scotland in 1945. He served in the army and then briefly in the Metropolitan Police. In 1974 he found work as a civil servant and was posted to the job centre at 1-3 Denmark Street, his role being to find work for unskilled labourers. He was promoted to Acting Executive Officer and remained in Denmark Street until June 1982. For one of the Christmas parties something large enough to make a copious amount of hot punch was needed. Nilsen said that he just the thing at home and brought in a large cooking pot. It was the very pot in which the man who became known as the *Muswell Hill Murderer* had boiled the body parts of young men who he'd murdered. His ritual, following a killing, would be to bathe and dress the victims' bodies, which he would then retain. All his victims were murdered by strangulation, sometimes accompanied by drowning. The remains he would burn on a bonfire or attempt to flush down the toilet. His crimes were discovered by a Dyno-Rod employee, Michael Cattran, who found fleshy material in a drain, that he reported to his supervisor, Gary Wheeler. Returning to the property at 23 Cranley Gardens, Muswell Hill, Cattran and Wheeler discovered flesh and bones in a pipe leading from the top flat of the house. The mortuary confirmed that the bones were indeed human, one piece of flesh, from a neck, showing a ligature mark. On being visited by Detective Chief Inspector Peter Jay and two of his colleagues, in 1983, Nilsen eventually admitted his crimes, stating: 'It's a long story; it goes back a long time. I'll tell you everything. I

want to get it off my chest. Not here…at the police station.' He confessed to killing 12-15 men between 1978 and the date of his being apprehended, most of whom were killed during the time Nilsen worked in Denmark Street. He was convicted of six counts of murder and two of attempted murder at the Old Bailey and sentenced to life imprisonment in November 1983. And there he remained until May 2018 when he passed away at HMP Full Sutton maximum security prison in Yorkshire.

Now the television company, Studio Lambert, are based at 1-3 Denmark Street as well as in Los Angeles. They are part of the global production group, All3Media and were launched in 1988 by Stephen Lambert, creator of many well-known global formats, including the award-winning *Gogglebox, Undercover Boss* and *Four in a Bed.* All3Media occupy the upper floor offices, the ground floor in 2016 became a branch of Fernandez & Wells, where tourists and locals sit and sip coffee and eat croissants, probably unaware of the grisly past of one of its former occupants.

No. 4

By the 1930s, the basement of No. 4, was the Nanking restaurant, which was presided over by Fung Saw, whose clientele comprised the street's publishers and writers as well as young Indian politicians. In 1932 an article in *The Queenslander (quoted below)* commented that Demark Street was almost completely given over to Chinese and Japanese restaurants. It was an ideal time for the Japanese to be working away from their own country as Japan was experiencing a deep economic downturn, mainly due to the government's deflationary policy and the fallout from the Wall Street Crash of 1929, which created a severe negative impact on the Japanese economy. On top of that, political and intellectual thinking, partly due to the influence of Marxism, was shifting from economic liberalism towards a state managed economy.

'Undoubtedly the most amusing of the places is the Nanking, presided over by Mr. Fung Saw. Mr Fung is something of a politician, and to his restaurant come many of the more youthful budding Parliamentarians. These, together with composers and songwriters, their publishers and film artists, comprise the chief of Mr. Fung's clientele. The hall of feasting is reached by long, steep steps, which lead to an exceptionally large, light and lofty basement. There is another and mere prosaic entrance through a hall door on the ground floor, but somehow no-one ever seems to notice it, and so we descend the more picturesque steps. Inside, the decorations are reminiscent of a Chinese junk, and the walls are decorated in vermillion and in greens and yellows, which only a Chinese artist is able to use to Oriental perfection. On the opposite side of the road are two Japanese restaurants, and just around the corner we can enter the banqueting hall of Wah Yeng, who contents himself with catering, to the exclusion of everything else. Mr. Yeng explained that he had a large back room, which he reserved for Chinese businessmen, but as Chinese merchants do not so often come to London the hall at the back is usually thrown open to all.'

From the 1870s many English Universities began to admit Indian students, many of whom would spearhead a political awakening and began to discuss the question of possible liberation for their country. By the mid-1930s after nearly two centuries of British domination, Indian nationalism filled the hearts of many who were fuelled by the success of the Bolshevik revolution of 1917. Revolution, socialism and Marxism were increasingly on the agenda for many young intellectuals. Existing customs were questioned and there was an increasing call for liberation. Sajjad Zaheer's Urdu novel, *A Night in London,* featured underground revolutionaries, angered by repressive British policies in India. London was fast becoming a hotbed of radical anti-colonial activity.

Many London-based Indian activists met at No.4 Denmark Street, including Jyotimaya Ghosh, Syed Sajjad Zaheer, Pramod Sengupta, MD Taseer and Mulk Raj Anand, their meetings leading to the formation, on the premises, of the left wing anti-imperialist Indian Progressive Writers' Association on November 24th 1934. The group was supported by several literary figures, Oxford University's Ralph Fox was cited by Zaheer as being particularly influential in encouraging the formal organisation of the group in London. Fox, who regularly travelled to, and worked in, Russia, was a leading member of the Communist Party of Great Britain, but just three years later would die in a hail of machine-gun bullets fighting with the International Brigades in the Spanish Civil War. The group's draft manifesto stated, 'Radical changes are taking place in Indian Society. We believe that the new literature of India must deal with the basic problems of our existence today…the problems of hunger and poverty, social backwardness and political subjection. All that drags us down to passivity, inaction and the un-reason we reject as reactionary. All that arouses in us the political spirit, which examines institutions and customs in the light of reason, which helps us to act, to organize ourselves, to transform, we accept as progressive.'

The group, mainly comprising Oxford, Cambridge and London university students, met twice a month, despite the views they expounded provoking hostility in their home country and their writings being banned due to their political radicalism. In 1935 Zaheer (*right*) returned to India to develop the organisation there and to campaign for Independence and social equality. The first meeting took place in Lucknow in April 1936, but some members such as Ahmed Ali were keen to strengthen the group's links with communism, splitting and effectively weakening the organisation.

Born into an affluent Muslim family in Lucknow in 1905, Zaheer spent almost ten years in Britain, gaining a master's degree at Oxford before going into the law at Lincoln's Inn. His collection of short stories and his novel were deemed to be inflammatory and critical of the culture of his country and Indian society in general. The stories, in which he'd been aided by Ahmed Ali, Rashid Jahan and Zafar Mahmud, were banned in India.

In September 1946 Zaheer was sworn in to the new Indian cabinet taking the oath at New Delhi and becoming Minister for Law, Post and Air.

Having been ruled by the East India Company from 1757-1858 and the British Raj from 1858, the Indian Independence Bill came into force at the stroke of midnight on August 15th 1947. The pressure group that had assembled at No 4 Denmark Street with that aim, thirteen years earlier, had achieved their goal. Zaheer remained a communist and a radical, later being jailed for being involved in a Soviet plot to overthrow the first Prime Minister of Pakistan.

The association of young Indian activists that had been founded in the building where the Rolling Stones and Black Sabbath would make their debut albums, officially ended on January 1st 1956. Zaheer, whose father had been knighted for services to the Raj, died in 1973.

The Whitehall Studio film casting agency was based in the building which was connected to the short-lived Whitehall Films in Borehamwood, which meant the company would have been at No.4 in 1928/29. With an incredible lack of timing, Chilean actor/director Adelqui Millar (1891-1956), born Adelqui Miglia, started Whitehall Films, converting an old pre-fabricated aircraft hangar with no sound-proofing, beside a railway line to create Whitehall Studios. He made the silent movie *Life* there late in 1928, although it was mainly shot on location in Spain, with another silent film, *The Inseparables*, being shot at the studio the following March. Not a problem for silent movies but this was just as talking pictures came in - a bit like investing heavily in canals as the railways were making inroads. The noise and vibration from the passing locomotives were less than ideal for sound recording, resulting in Millar only directing the two silent films at the studios before the company was wound up in 1929. A soupcon of film-making jeopardy was added to the set-up, as someone would have to be positioned on the roof to ring a bell if a train was approaching so that they could stop filming, or at least try to minimise the noise. Brilliant.

Millar had already been involved in twenty-five films before setting up Whitehall, so had been steeped in the silent movie culture. The complex was purchased in 1930 by Audible Filmcraft for £15,000. In 1934 the building was leased by Consolidated Films, becoming Consolidated Studios, changing to J.H. Studios and M.P. Studios during the mid-1930s. Following requisition in WWII, J. Arthur Rank bought it, renaming it the Gate Studios and using it for shooting religious films until 1954. The last film produced there was *John Wesley* in 1954. Despite a campaign to save the buildings, no listing was forthcoming and its twenty-five-year life as a film studio started by Adelqui Millar and Whitehall Films came to an untimely end in 2006. When the building was demolished and the site redeveloped for housing. One can only wonder who auditioned here in their Denmark Street offices, hoping to be the next Greta Garbo or Clara Bow.

Songwriter and publisher, Jos. Geo. Gilbert, aka Joe Gilbert, was also based at No.4. Joe wrote or co-wrote many classics from the late 1920s onwards and his songs are still being released on compilation albums in the 2000s. Among his earliest successes to emerge from Tin Pan Alley were *When You Played the Organ and I sang the Rosary* in 1927 and *Sweet Suzanne*, covered by Rudy Vallee in 1929. In 1930, Gilbert and Lawrence Wright, Tin Pan Alley's first publisher, aka Horatio Nicholls, wrote *Amy* the tribute song to aviation pioneer Amy Johnson, after her historic flight from England to Australia. Gilbert had continued success during the 1930s, co-writing with the likes of Edgar Leslie, Bob Fisher, Nat Lewis and penning the top-selling *On Sunshine Bay*, a hit for Joe Loss in 1946. Gilbert again collaborated with Horatio Nicholls on *A Californian Serenade* made famous by Jack Hylton, who also recorded Gilbert's *Let's Be Sweethearts Again.* Jack Hylton and his Orchestra also covered various other songs co-written by Gilbert, including *Moonlight Avenue* and *I Want to be Alone with Mary Brown.* US singing heart-throb Guy Mitchell also covered *Let's Be Sweethearts Again* in the 1950s, while Vera Lynn sang Gilbert's *I'm Sending My Blessings* and Anne Shelton recorded *It's Never Too Late to Mend.* Another of his fifties successes was *Me and Jane in a Plane,* covered by The Temperance Seven in the 1960s (who also did a version of

Gilbert's *Miss Elizabeth Brown*) and the Pasadena Roof Orchestra in the 1970s. In the late 1920's *Me and Jane in a Plane* had been part of the industry's first great publicity stunt, when Jack Hylton flew his band over Blackpool playing Joe Gilbert's song. Published by Gilbert's Demark Street neighbour, Lawrence Wright, the song sold over 5,000 copies an hour at Wright's seafront booth, following Hylton's stunt. Maybe the first real PR 'spin'. Gilbert died in 1973.

The publishers and writers had non-musical neighbours as well, including, in 1950, wine and spirit Merchant George Charlton Yearsley Morton, who had previously been a Commercial Traveller. Grosvenor Music were also based at no.4 that same year.

One of the best-known businesses at No.4 was Regent Sound Studios, founded by violinist Ralph Elman in the late 1950s. Elman sold it to James Baring, eccentric heir to Baring's Bank, in 1961. Baring was a major music fan who knew and got to know many top musicians. The Rolling Stones first album was recorded here after rehearsing at Tin Pan Alley studios across the street, spread over ten days between January 3rd and February 25th 1964. The album's opening track and single, *Not Fade Away* was recorded on 10th January and *Good Times, Bad Times,* the subsequent B side of *It's All Over Now,* on 25th February. The sound-proofing was basic and improvised, as Keith Richards remembered: 'We did our early records on a 2-track Revox in a room insulated with egg cartons at Regent Sound. It was like a little demo in Tin Pan Alley…we used to think, Oh, this is a recording studio, huh? This is what they're like. A tiny little back room. Under

those primitive conditions it was easy to make the kind of sound we got on our first album and early singles.'

(left) Mick Jagger during the recording of the first Rolling Stones album at Regent Sound.

The Rolling Stones' manager, Andrew Loog Oldham got visiting Americans Phil Spector and Gene Pitney down to the studio with Spector and Pitney contributing to the track *Walking the Do*g, on maracas and piano respectively. The group also recorded *Little Red Rooster*, at Regent Sound on September 2nd 1964.

The Rolling Stones recording their first album at Regent Sound in 1964 with Andrew Loog Oldham.

The Rolling Stones outside the Tin Pan Alley Club

Regent Sound in 1962. The Rolling Stones, David Bowie, Slade, Jimi Hendrix, The Beatles, Black Sabbath and Tom Jones...they would all come.

So Barings were a part of Tin Pan Alley over thirty years before the business operations of their trader Nick Leeson generated losses of 827 million pounds and brought about the collapse of the family company which had been trading since 1762. The great-grandparents of Diana, Princess of Wales, were the 6th Earl Spencer and Margaret Baring, daughter of the 1st Baron Revelstoke making her a relation of Regents Sounds' James Cecil Baring, who became 6th Baron

Revelstoke on the death of his brother in 2005. The man who brought many of the great names of the 1960s to Regent Sound died seven years later in 2012.

Andrew Loog Oldham saunters down Tin Pan Alley in 1964. The side of the street would indicate a Rolling Stones rehearsal, or a trip to Julie's café, rather than a recording.

Andrew Loog Oldham referred to Tin Pan Alley in his memoirs as: 'Short, shabby Denmark Street, just off Charing Cross Road, an inhospitable place, full of brutish men. The wooden hanging signs that denoted the five or six publishers per square foot swayed in the afternoon breeze, eerily reminding one of the Shylocks and pawnbrokers, while the storefront windows were flooded with the sheet music of the day. The piano copies were fronted by 8x10 glossy shots of young, tousled men with eight-quid guitars and crucifixes, worried 30-ish crooners in cardigans and sucking on pipes a la Bing Crosby, and/or wasp-waisted, flair-skirted, peroxide-topped, smiling damsels of song.'

Loog Oldham had first come to Denmark Street in the late 1950s in a failed attempt to sell a song he'd written called *Boomerang Rock.* At least Loog Oldham came back.

(Below, left) Slade at the time they made their first single, You Better Run, at Regent Sound. (right) Regent Sound demo of Hedgehoppers Anonymous' hit It's Good News Week.

Margo and the Marvettes from Co. Down (*below*) parked in Tin Pan Alley in an age before traffic wardens and yellow lines, and when it was cool for one of the group to smoke a pipe. Shel Talmy produced three singles for them, but without major success. Margo Burns changed her recording name many times, becoming Maggie Brown, Liza Dulittle, Sherri Weine and Sherry Cantrell, which also failed to captivate the record buyers on a large scale.

Also here in 1964 was one Dave Gilmour, playing guitar with Cambridge band, Jokers Wild, along with Saxophonist Dick Parry. The group recorded a privately-pressed, one-sided studio album at Regent Sound, a tape of which is in the British Library Sound Archive. They also recorded a UK cover version of Sam and Dave's *Hold on I'm Comin,* with Jonathan King producing, but the original was released in the UK and Jokers Wild's version never saw the light of day. Gilmour would replace Syd Barrett in Pink Floyd and Parry would later play sessions for the group and support Gilmour on a solo tour. The Jokers Wild drummer, Willie Wilson later drummed on Syd Barrett's album *The Madcap Laughs* and was surrogate drummer for the live shows and soundtrack for *The Wall*. For several years during the 1970s, he was a member of Sutherland Brothers and Quiver. Joker's Wild bass player Rick Wills later played with Bad Company and Foreigner.

The Tom Cats from Ealing, who had previously been The Playboys and The Thoughts and went on to become July, in Tin Pan Alley. Across the road is an Oriole Records van.

Tin Pan Alley may have been the street where doors and opportunities could open, but not everybody made it... not everybody had the wherewithal. As well as the major names that recorded at Regent Sound there were hundreds and hundreds of groups and singers whose dreams came to an end somewhere along the trail. Reading group Vernon Bliss and the Blue Stars recorded here in 1963, and in 1964 the Dynamites from Carmarthen in West Wales drove up to Regent Sound and back the same day and recorded three tracks including a version of Johnnie Ray's *Cry.* Group member Charles later wrote: 'Why only three tracks? We were paying for the recording time and ran out of money.' Another typical example of many thousands of groups who never achieved the success they dreamed of were the Firebrands from Somerset, a group that also made three demos there in in 1966, Mel from the band recalled: 'I remember how tiny the studio was. I believe there was a very small water fountain in the studio. Although out band never made the big time, I still have the demo discs as an everlasting memory of those great times in the sixties.' Fronted by singer Ian Harris, blues band The Earth, formerly

Conviction, recorded an album here with Alan Parsons on lead guitar. A limited edition of the LP was released forty-seven years later through Record Collector magazine.

(Above) The Liberators, just before their manager Reg Calvert, renamed them Pinkerton's Assorted Colours. The photograph was

taken opposite Reg's office at No.7 Denmark Street
Sound, in September 1965, with assorted fans in front o
Ford Thames van, across the road from Regent Sound
1965. Stuart Colman who would join the following yea
string of hits for Shakin' Stevens and a No1 for Cliff Richard and the
Young Ones with a re-make of Livin' Doll.

In October 1967 Jimi Hendrix, Mitch Mitchell and Noel Redding rehearsed and laid down demos at the studio. The volume of the Jimi Hendrix Experience was so much louder than any previous artists, that the Labour Exchange next door lodged a complaint. Jimi's riffs meant that they could no longer hear themselves speak. Jimi appeared to be cool about it saying, 'Ok guys we've had a good rehearsal, we'd better find somewhere else to make our noise.' When Black Sabbath recorded *Paranoid* here there was no record of a complaint from the neighbours, so Jimi was clearly cranking his amp up to eleven, years before Spinal Tap. Sabbath went into the studio with producer Rodger Bain and engineer Tom Allom and laid down their debut album in one day, starting at 10am and finishing at 10pm, costing them £600. It was mixed the following day and had to be done quickly as the record label had given them a tight budget. The studio saw many other artists coming through the door over the years, to lay down demos or make masters, including The Who, Elton John, The Bee Gees, Mott the Hoople, Amen Corner, The Downliners Sect, David Bowie & the Lower Third, The Equals, Sandie Shaw, John Martyn, Herman's Hermits, The Troggs, Davy Graham and Slade, who recorded *You Better Run* here. Later the Eagles would rehearse at Regent Sound for their *On the Border* sessions. Regent Sound opened a second studio in 1968.

Tom Jones recorded *It's Not Unusual* at Regent Sound, learning the song, which had been written by his manager Gordon Mills and Les

.eed, in the car on the way to the studio. The song was basically a demo for Sandie Shaw. Tom remembered that they were running late and only had thirty minutes left of their session time. 'Gordon and Les Reed did the vocal backing...when they played it back I said, "Gordon this is it, this is it." He said, "Nah it's a pop song, it's for Sandie Shaw." I said, "Gordon, I can feel it. This is a hit song and you know it is."' Luckily for Tom, Sandie turned it down, it was re-recorded and became Tom's first hit.

In the late 1960s Kassner Music bought the studio and in the 2000s the basement became The Alley Cat Club, still a venue where musicians perform live in a retro atmosphere. The musical instrument shop upstairs still retains a pluralised version of the original name, Regent Sounds.

In 1963 George Harrison came to the street to buy an acoustic guitar to play on the recording of the Beatles version of *Til There Was You* for their debut album. Four years later he was back...with John, Paul and Ringo. The first two recording sessions for *Fixing a Hole* from the album Sgt Pepper's Lonely Hearts Club Band took place at Regent Sound's sister studio, at University Street, Tottenham Court Road, on the night of 9th February 1967, as Abbey Road Studios weren't available. It was a piece of history, as this was the first time the group had recorded at a studio other than Abbey Road for EMI. Unusually, the lead vocal was laid down at the same time as the rhythm track. It was also unusual because Jesus was at the session. Paul McCartney was about to head to the studio when someone rang the bell on his gate, announcing himself as 'Jesus Christ'. Paul, rather taken aback, admitted him: 'I thought, well it probably isn't, but if it is I'm not going to be the one to turn him away. So I gave him a cup of tea and we chatted...I said, 'I've got to go to this session, but if you promise to be very quiet and just sit in a corner, you can come, so he did...I introduced him to the guys and they said, 'Who's this?' I said, 'It's Jesus Christ.' But that was it...the last we ever saw of Jesus.'

The reel to reel magnetic tapes on which every artist recorded could bring their own problems, as CBS Tape operator David Hahn learned to his dismay one day in 1971. He was asked to take a 16-track tape of The Tremeloes *Too Late to Be Saved* across to Regent Sound, and was told on no account to take the tube. Reckoning that he could save most of the £2 he'd been given for a taxi by taking the tube to Tottenham Court Road for a shilling, he delivered the tape and headed back to CBS assuming there was no way anyone was ever going to find out. His boss yelled at him for taking the tube, but as Hahn thought there was no way he could know that, he lied to him several times over. He only confessed after he was told that the sound on the tape was dropping out because it had been wiped by the spinning magnets under the floor of the tube train. The £2 was duly returned, a lesson learned and dismissal narrowly avoided. Although not so well-known as the artists they recorded, among the engineers that were an integral part of the studio were, Bill Farley, Glyn Jones, Jimmy Spencely, Adrian Ibbotson, Eddie Kramer and Ron Pickup.

On the first floor of No.4 Jimmy and Steve, the Clark Brothers, ran their Dance School. Brought up in the Southern States during the depression, as children they slept in one bed with their three sisters and another brother. They were so poor that their father, unable to afford presents at Christmas, fired his gun in the garden and told the children that Father Christmas had committed suicide. Jimmy and Steve became self-taught dancers who created their own style, who got their break when tap dancer Bill 'Bojangles' Robinson appeared near them. The Steve's teacher told Robinson that she had a boy who fancied himself as a dancer. He danced for Mr. Bojangles, with the result that he and Jimmy got to perform with him at the Cotton Club in Harlem, where Duke Ellington and Count Basie had got their breaks. Their next piece of luck was when Frank Sinatra suggested that the guys who had the show *Hellzapoppin* took it to England when it transferred there. Decent of Frank, but hey, the Clarks *were* the cousins of Sammy Davis Junior. The show ran for a year at the Casino (now the Prince Edward Theatre) and for another year at the Shaftesbury Theatre. While here, the Clark Brothers were asked to dance at Windsor Castle for King George VI and decided that they felt so welcome in London that they'd make it their base. They toured the UK and Europe, appeared in the film *Killer Diller* with Nat King Cole and played Las Vegas and New York. In 1952, the Grade Organisation invited them back to the UK and to what became their second home, the London Palladium.

They went on to appear in many Variety shows on TV, as well as *Sunday Night at the London Palladium*, including *The Good Old Days, The Black & White Minstrel Show* and *The Russel Harty Show*. The brothers noticed that as more singers were being booked for variety shows, musicals and pantomimes, they needed to be able to dance. To that end Jimmy and Steve opened the Clark Brothers dance school and even persuaded Princess Margaret, who they'd met at the Churchill Club, to perform the opening ceremony. They called it the University of Show Business, and among their clients were Cliff Richard, Dickie Henderson, Roy Castle and even Ronnie and Reggie Kray, who later admitted that they went to dancing classes with the Clarks to try and improve his social graces. Reggie remembered: 'It was run by the Clark Brothers who, at that time, were ranked among the world's greatest tap dancers…Ron became a friend of theirs and we organised a big party for them at the old Queen's Hall in Commercial Road, to make them feel at home.' Among the guests with Ronnie and Reggie Kray were the MP Tom Driburg, Joan Littlewood and world-renowned boxers Len Harvey and Ted 'Kid' Lewis. Reggie recalled, 'We were very close to the Clark Brothers in those days.' On their very last night of freedom, hours before they were arrested by the police the Krays were at the Astor Club, where Ronnie made the Clarks dance till they almost dropped.

Jimmy and Steve were at the piano with Max Bygraves when he wrote *You Need Hands*; worked on the harmonies and performed it with him on stage in the show *Swinging in the Lane*. The Clarks also danced with Margot Fonteyn and Rudolf Nureyev and appeared on the Royal Variety show as the Beatles and Marlene Dietrich in 1963. After the show, the Queen Mother said to Bernard Delfont on being introduced to the Clark Brothers, 'I don't understand how they keep dancing so fast for so long.' Jimmy Clark passed away in 2009 and Steve in 2017, but the room where they taught the gangsters and pop stars to dance is still there, echoing to different feet.

Another one-time occupant of no.4 was the publishing company, Essex Music; founded by David Platz, who had been sent with his sister to England from Germany for safety at the start of WWII. Born in Hanover in 1929, he left school at the age of fourteen, his guardian having found him a position at Southern Music in Denmark Street. He became the manager of the Latin-American recording section. But despite working his way up the ranks, he was thought too young at twenty-eight to be considered for the vacant MD's job so he went off to front a new company, Essex Music with American publisher Howie Richmond. Initially working out of Denmark Place, the company soon moved to No. 4 Denmark Street. Platz helped Andrew Loog Oldham with the Rolling Stones early career and his publishing company was joined by the likes of Procol Harum, The Who, The Moody Blues, David Bowie, Johnny Dankworth, Ralph McTell, Marc Bolan and even comic balladeer, Paddy Roberts. Platz was in partnership with Decca producer Denny Cordell, under whom, Tony Visconti was learning his trade, the pair playing Visconti some tracks from Bowie's first album in the office at No.4, hoping he'd produce the next one. Visconti found the album too eclectic, with songs that he felt had no common denominator, commenting, 'This guy's all over the place.' Platz conceded, but insisted that the twenty-year-old singer needed someone to guide him and give him a direction. Visconti agreed to meet him, which was fortunate as David Platz had Bowie waiting in the room next door. Discovering that they had much in common musically, the two young men gelled and spent the afternoon together, ending up in an arty cinema in Chelsea watching Roman Polanski's *A Knife in the Water*. Visconti was still unknown to the public, despite being assistant producer for Joe Cocker, Procol Harum and The Move and having just produced the first Tyrannosaurus Rex album which would be released in 1968. Bowie had so far had been determined but unsuccessful. That meeting in Denmark Street in 1967 led to a long personal and professional friendship which led to Visconti producing thirteen David Bowie albums, including his final parting gift, *Blackstar.*

At one time Platz was a director of over thirty publishing companies. He mentored Anthony Newley and Lesley Bricusse with their musicals, initially acquiring the global rights to *Stop the World, I Want to Get Off* in 1961 and later *The Roar of the Greasepaint...the Smell of the Crowd.* David Platz even had an interest in Lionel Bart's *Oliver.* In 1967 he founded the Bucks Music Groups, later incorporating his new record labels Fly and Cube into the company. Unlike some publishers he didn't cling to the commercial safety of mainstream music, putting his own money up for Black Sabbath to record their debut album, downstairs from his office, at Regent Sound Studios. Platz was also a director of PRS. In 1981 Essex Music changed its name to Westminster Music, retaining the Essex Music name in the US. By 1990 Platz original partners had gone. David Platz died in 1994 and the company continues to be run by his son, Simon, who joined the company in 1984. As well as the aforementioned Bowie, the Rolling Stones and Marc Bolan, the company has also published such artists as Pete Doherty, Carly Simon, Woody Guthrie, Brian Eno, Professor Green, Amanda Ghost and David Arnold. One of the country's most successful writers, Tony Macauley, started his career here.

Born Anthony Instone, in Fulham, London, Macauley started as a song plugger for Essex Music and went on to become a highly-successful songwriter. He has won nine Ivor Novello Awards, won the British Academy of Songwriters Composers and Authors Songwriter of the Year Award twice, in 1970 and 1977, and is the only British person to win the Edwin Forrest Award for outstanding contribution to the America Theatre. As a solo writer he penned many big hits, including *Baby Make It Soon* (Marmalade), *(Last Night) I Didn't Get To Sleep at All* (Fifth Dimension) and Don't *Give Up On Us* (David Soul). With writing partner John Mcleod he wrote *Baby Now That I've Found You* (Foundations), *Let the Heartaches Begin* (Long John Baldry), *Something Here in my Heart* (Paper Dolls), *Smile a Little Smile For Me* (Flying Machine) and *That Same Old Feeling* (Pickettywitch). With Geoff Stephens, Macauley wrote *Lights of Cincinatti* (Scott Walker), *Sorry Suzanne* (The Hollies) and *You Won't Find Another Fool Like Me* (The New Seekers). Macauley also wrote *Build Me up Buttercup* (The Foundations) with Mike D'Abo, *Love Grows (Where My Rosemary Goes)* with Barry Mason, and with Roger Cook and Roger Greenaway he penned *Blame It on the Pony Express* (Johnny Johnson and the Bandwagon), *You're More Than a Number (In my Little Red Book),* (The Drifters) and *Home Lovin' Man* (Andy Williams). Tony Macauley's songs have sold over 52 million copies and he's written eight UK No.1s and 3 US No.1s. In the mid-seventies he won a landmark court case in a publishing dispute, ensuring a better and fairer deal for all future songwriters.

Macauley moved from songwriting to musical theatre, before going on the write thrillers.

From 1995 to 2004, the Helter Skelter bookshop, which specialised in rock music, operated from No.4. Founded by Sean Body in 1995 it sold fanzines, sheet music, books and music-related artwork, the building being specifically chosen because of the Stones recording their debut album here. The shop specialised in Bob Dylan books and fanzines, which at one time accounted for 40% of the turnover. Body died in 2008, but Helter Skelter still exists as a publishing company.

Independent production company Origin Pictures who were launched in 2008 by David Thompson, former head of BBC Films, are based here, making drama for both Film and Television. Among their films are *Woman in Gold, The Awakening, Mandela: Long Walk to Freedom, The First Grader and X + Y, and First Grader.* First Grader productions, formed in 2009, also work out of No.4. But what of the neighbours? What was happening at No.5 while The Stones, The Beatles, David Bowie and the Kray Twins were coming and going next door?

No. 5

No. 5 was built between 1686, a year after James II came to the throne, and 1689. These four years spanned James' short reign, until he was overthrown in 1689 by his Protestant son-in-law, William of Orange.

The building was grade II listed in 1974 and has a blue plaque, commemorating the pioneer of the diving helmet, Augustus Siebe (1788-1872) who lived and worked here.

Born in 1788, Christian Augustus Siebe was a German-born British engineer and former army artillery officer, who emigrated to Britain after the Battle of Waterloo. Siebe was certainly in the right place at the right time as the economy was booming. In 1829 he patented a rotating water pump which sold incredibly well, enabling him to move to No.5 Denmark Street. He married and added considerably to

the street's population by fathering nine children. In the 1830s the Deane brothers asked Siebe to work on a variation of their smoke helmet design for use underwater. Siebe made a helmet fitted to a full-length watertight canvas diving suit, later making it detachable at the suggestion of Colonel Charles Pasley, leader of the Royal Navy team that had worn Siebe's design. This became the standard diving apparel which revolutionise underwater civil engineering, underwater salvage, commercial diving and naval diving. Siebe also invented an ice-making machine, a paper making machine, a rotating water pump and won many medals at the Great exhibition in 1851 and the Paris Exhibition in 1855. He became a British National in 1856, lived and worked at No. 5 and is commemorated by a blue plaque. The company was established as Siebe and Gorman by his son, and his son-in-law, William Augustus Gorman in 1868 as Siebe and Gorman at 5, Denmark Street. Augustus Siebe died at the premises of chronic bronchitis in April 1872, having become known as the 'Godfather of Diving'.

No. 5 wasn't such a lucky address for others. Giles Hemens, an auctioneer and appraiser, was born in 1764 and first married Sarah

Holwell in 1789. After her death he married Eliza Clark. Hemens was at no.5 from 1814, his business card proclaiming, 'Most money for Household Furniture', which included a drawing of Hemens looking rather dapper with wavy blond hair and gavel in hand, looking down on the serried ranks of gentlemen customers. He also advertised his business with tickets inviting the bearer to a free pint of beer at the Hand and Hammer drinking booth in the premature peace celebrations at the Hyde Park Fair in 1814. In 1816 a partnership he had with John Robertson was terminated. Arrested for serious debt, he was incarcerated in Marshalsea prison, where he repeatedly complained about his treatment. He fell out with some of the inmates and was constantly beaten and verbally abused by some of the fellow prisoners. At one point he was dragged down the stairs, kicked about the head, a sack thrown over his head and almost drowned under a water pump. He was eventually released and returned to St. Giles, where he died in 1837.

In a different part of the same premises from as early as the 1840s through to the 1890s Edward Thurkle, Master Cutler, manufactured swords. An 1821 Thurkle sword that sold for £216 at auction in 2011 makes no mention of Denmark Street., but an Infantry officer's sword that exists in one collection dates from 1845 with the blade marked E. Thurkle & Sons Denmark Street-Soho-London. So Thurkle arrived in the street sometime between 1821 and 1845. Another of his pieces, an 1895 Pattern Infantry officer's sword with 'etched blade 33 wire-bound fishskin grip in its leather field service scabbard with frog', came up at auction with an expectation of £140. Some of his blades are marked simply 'E. Thurkle' while others carry the mark, 'E. Thurkle & Sons.' A rare 10th Hussars Cavalry Officer's sword which sold for £875 at auction in 2012 described the 82.5cm blade as being made by J.R. Gaunt & Son Ltd., late Edward Thurkle, Denmark Street, Soho, London. JR Gaunt, founded in 1894, took over

Thurkle's business when it collapsed in 1897 and are still operating from Birmingham.

Over thirty-five years later, the company that would become the world's largest independent publisher, Peer Music, would arrive at No.5.

There would be more cut and thrust in the building during the 1930s as this was Peer Music's first of three addresses on Tin Pan Alley and would be here from 1933-1935. Peer Music was launched in the UK in November of 1932, under the name of Southern Music Publishing

 Co. Ltd., with offices in St. Giles High Street, London WC2. The operation was set up by Ralph Peer I (*pictured* left) and T. H. Ward (Tom Snr.) who was already running a publishing company called Associated Copyrights. Initially Tom Ward was placing the biggest US Peer music songs with other UK publishers although this stopped in the mid 1930's, by which time, 1933, the company had moved into No. 5 Denmark Street, with the running of

Peer Music London passed to Harry Steinberg, who was succeeded in 1935 by Billy Boughton. Tom Ward continued to oversee the London company whilst setting up other European branches before finally retiring in 1970 and having been assisted almost from the start by his son T. F. Ward (Tom Jnr.) who succeeded him on his retirement and remained with the company right through until his death in 1993.

By the late 1930s the London office started acquiring more songs, although it had to wait until 1940 for its first big British hit, *There'll Come Another Day* by Alan Stranks and Pat Pattison. Stranks was also the scriptwriter for the comic strip *PC.49* as well as writing many scripts for *Dan Dare* in the *Eagle* comic. In 1942 Billy Cotton's

former road manager, David Toff (*pictured left*), took over the running of the London office. His family recalled that his reaction to being rung up by divas who expected him to recognize their voices, was to say, 'This is a telephone, not a bloody telescope,' and he'd hang up on them. He formed his own music publishing company in 1956 but retained strong links with Southern having a blanket agreement with them for world rights, except France and America. One of his big successes in the late 1950s was with *The Heart of a Man*. In 1957 a Q&A session that Toff and his wife Barbara did with Doris Day was sent out as a special disc to members of the Doris Day Club.

During the sixties he had success with Fireball XL 5, a hit for Don Spencer. In 1972 Toff became Secretary of the Music Publishers' association for a three-year term, but had to relinquish his publishing interests, which went to Mini-Music and Chappells.

Peer Music though was here from 1933-1935 and at No.24 until WWII during which time they moved to No.8 where they would remain until 1992.

Peer would have hundreds and hundreds of songs that would enter the national hit parade, created by their Denmark Street neighbours, The New Musical Express, born in their old premises to bring us the latest music news and the best-selling disc and sheet music charts. Created by Theodore Ingham, the music paper was launched here on 7th March 1952, having its roots back in the late 1940s, when London music promoter, Maurice Kinn, bought the ailing *Accordion Times and Musical Express* for £1,000. In November 1952 the NME published the first UK singles chart, the brainchild of Percy Dickins, with a top twelve, compiled by Dickins telephoning 20 music shops around the country, and totting up their biggest-selling singles. Billboard had been doing this in the States since 1940, but the only music chart published thus far in the UK only reflected the sales of sheet music. That was about to change. From Denmark Street came the very first chart, headed by Al Martino's *Here in my Heart* and also featuring Bing Crosby, Nat King Cole, George Clooney's aunt, Rosemary Clooney, Max Bygraves, Doris Day and Vera Lynn, who had an incredible three song in the top 12. Even more extraordinary is that in 2017 she looks set to have a No.1 album which is being released to celebrate her 100th birthday. The publication operated from No.5 until 1964.

The NME editor from 1957 to 1972 was Andy Gray with peak circulation in 1964 of 300,000. The paper also staged the NME Poll Winners Concert from 1953, with Dickie Valentine and Ted Heath winning awards in the first-ever readers' poll. The 1954 concert also featured Johnny Dankworth with Nat King Cole as the compere. The first NME concert to be televised was in 1961 with 15 million watching the likes of Cliff Richard and the Shadows, Connie Francis and Adam Faith, while 1963 had an all-star cast headed by The Beatles. The following year the Beatles were joined by The Rolling Stones, The Hollies, Gerry & the Pacemakers, Roy Orbison, The Shadows and the Dave Clark Five. The last NME Poll Winners' Concert was in 1971. In the late 60s the paper still had a healthy circulation of around 200,000. Although Maurice Kinn sold the paper in 1963 to IPC, he stayed on for another ten years to run it for IPC.

By the early 70s the Melody Maker was gaining ground on the circulation front, but under new editor Alan Smith the NME turned things around and reconnected with music buyers. By 1973/74, now under the editorship of Nick Kent, the paper once again had a healthy circulation. By 2003, three years after the death of Maurice Kinn, the circulation was around 72,000 but by 2014 it had fallen to 15,000. In 2015 it became a free paper and appeared as an on-line publication only from 2018.

One of our most successful lyricists, Don Black, started as an office boy at the New Music Express, often taking down the names of visiting US artists dictated to him by Maurice Kinn, who'd be on the phone getting confirmation that singers such as Johnny Ray or Frankie Laine would be coming over. Keeping close ties with Tin Pan Alley, Don would go on to join David Toff Music as a song plugger, working on such classics as *Que Sera Sera* and *Don't Laugh at Me.* He co-wrote Matt Monro's hit *Walk Away,* a song that impressed composer John Barry enough to ask Don to write the words to the James Bond film *Thunderball.* Don went on to write the lyrics for other Bond film themes, *Diamonds are Forever* and *The Man with the Golden Gun* with Barry, and *Tomorrow never Dies* and *The World is Not Enough,* with David Arnold. As well as working with John Barry, Don has provided lyrics for such eminent composers as Andrew Lloyd Webber, Michael Jackson, Henry Mancini, Elmer Bernstein, Quincy Jones, Jule Styne and many more. For many years he was also Matt Monro's personal manager, writing Monro's *Born Free* with John Barry, which won an Oscar for Best Song. Don also collaborated with Barry on *Out of Africa* and *Dances with Wolves.* Don Black also co-wrote the US No.1s *To Sir, With Love*, *Ben* and the title themes for *True Grit* and *The Italian Job.* Don has had five Oscar nominations. His stage musical credits include, *Dear Anyone, Budgie, Tell Me* on *a Sunday, Aspects of Love, Sunset Boulevard, Bombay Dreams,*

Brighton Rock and *Stephen Ward: The Musical.* In 2007 Don Black was inducted into the Songwriters' Hall of Fame. There have been two major tribute concerts with major artists performing his songs, at the London Palladium in 2008 and the Royal Albert Hall in 2013. From office boy to one of our greatest lyricists. The shadows of Tin Pan Alley are long.

If ever there was a Denmark Street character whose name shouted, 'I'm in show business', it was Max Diamond. Born Bruno Magnoni into an Austrian-Italian family, he worked for several Tin Pan Alley publishers. At the beginning of the Second World War, with feelings against Italians running high, his father Arthur decided to change his name, inspiration striking when he was dealt the King of Diamonds during a poker game at the BBC. As Rex Diamond, Magnoni snr. wrote scripts for Tommy Handley, Will Hay, Elsie and Doris Waters and their brother, Jack Warner. Thus Max got a taste for the business and became an enthusiastic songwriter, but struggled to make a living. After spells as a polish salesman and a private detective, he supplemented his income by working for a publisher: 'Harold Franz of Unit Music Publishing offered me a job there. I had to earn some money, also I wished to learn about the publishing side of the business.'

As well as running his own group, The Four of Diamonds, during 1952/53 Max was doing the first of two stints with Southern Music out on the road in his 1939 Hillman Minx Drophead Coupe plugging such artists as Morecambe and Wise, who were looking for their big break, Dorothy Squires and Ken Dodd. Another artist he worked with before she became famous was Shirley Bassey: 'Len Martin of the famous 'Stand Easy' radio series brought her to my office at Southern Music. He was convinced that she was going to become a star, and when I heard her sing, I shared that conviction.' Max wrote several comedy songs with Dodd, including Where's Me Shirt, The Nikky

Nokky Noo Song and the Diddly Doo Parade. Not lyrically challenging and maybe a tad too personalised to get many covers, but hey, a co-write is a co-write. Max also worked at Rex Music on £12 a week with £6 a week expenses. After two years there with little to show for it, he was asked by Eddie Calvert to join his new publishing company, Gabriel Music. Max was working there in 1956 when a song on which he collaborated with Calvert won a *Sunday People* songwriting competition, netting them the £250 prize. As they were both well-known in the industry, especially Calvert, they used puns of London areas as pseudonyms, Carl Shalton and Ed Monton. After three years the company began to struggle resulting in Max moving on to become Professional Manager at Ed Kassner's Publishing Company and returning to Denmark Street.

His writing partnership with Charlie Drake came after meeting him with Dick Emery at boxer Freddie Mills' Chinese restaurant in the Charing Cross Road. They wrote many songs together, the first success coming with the B side of Charlie's version of *Splish Splash, Starkle Starkle Little Twink*. Max recalled writing one of their biggest hits: 'I was at Kassner Music, sitting in my office one afternoon when Charlie rang and, without preamble or introduction said, 'My Boomerang won't Come Back.' It had been a remark made by one of his sons that had given him the idea. Max and Charlie met the following week, demolished a bottle and half of whisky, wrote the song and called Charlie's record producer, George Martin. George loved it, produced it and within two months it was in the UK top ten and topped the Australian chart for weeks on end. The BBC insisted on cutting the line 'Oh Gawd, I've hit the Flying Doctor,' for their children's programmes, objecting that the word 'Gawd' might not be appropriate for kids to hear. They could, of course, hear it on any other programme! Diamond and Drake also wrote several other songs with Drake, including *Naughty, Hello My Darlings, Charles Drake 007* and *I Bent My Assigai.* Diamond also co-wrote the music and lyrics for Drake's 1964 stage show *The Man in the Moon* and co-wrote *Old Mr. Shadow* with Drake which was featured in the comedian's 1960 film, *Sands of the Desert.* While Max Diamond was at Kassner he plugged the song *Where You Are* which he got recorded by his friend Denis Lotis. Roy Hudd also recorded several of Diamond's song, including the England World Cup celebratory song, *The Day We Won the Cup.* Voted one of the top ten best pluggers, Max Diamond was a familiar character in the street for some three decades, promoting his early songs, plugging for several leading music publishers and later working as a hit songwriter. During the 60s Diamond, whilst also working as a stuntman, moved To Campbell-Connelly at Nos. 10-11. Having worked in the street for Southern Music, Kassner Music and Campbell-Connelly, Max Diamond moved to No. 5 in 1968 to set up Max Diamond Enterprises. At that time he and fellow stuntman Nosher Powell founded the British Jousting Association. In 1972 he was married to Joan Harris in full jousting regalia having rushed from

hospital with a broken arm following a jousting tournament at the Tower of London. The bride also wore medieval dress.

Max Diamond's wedding. A knight to remember.

There are many photographs of Diamond in his full suit of armour as well as a youtube interview circa 1994 when he was still jousting at the age of seventy. He died in Devon in 1999. With diving helmets, sword manufacture and suits of armour, No.5 was its own tin pan alley, but publishers and songwriters also flourished at the premises.

Lorna Music, formed in 1960, was run by Norrie Paramor's brother, Alan, Leslie Lowe and Peter Pavey, the latter joining Lorna Music in 1961 as Copyright & Royalty Manager, and later General & Professional Manager after Les Lowe left the company. Pavey was born in 1924 and served in the Middlesex Regiment from 1942-1947 bizarrely taking his guitar with him to the D-Day landings at the request of his Commanding Officer. Post-war he became a performer before working on the theatrical side of the business. In 1960 he became a songwriter and was invited to write material for Carole Deene, Ricky Valance, Billy Fury, Frank Ifield, Val Doonican and Sacha Distel. He had over eighty-five of his songs recorded. Alan Paramor was no slouch either, having negotiated a deal in New York, in 1962 which secured Charlie Parker Music as an affiliated company to Lorna Music in the UK.

Pavey was involved in UK publishing of Paul Simon material, and the management team of Helen Shapiro, with her long-term manager Alan Paramor. A young singer/songwriter came to see Lorna one day to thank them for using one of his songs, *Carlos Domingues,* on a successful Val Doonican album. Over a cup of tea Paul Simon played Les Lowe some of his songs, including *Sound of Silence* which had been turned down across the road by Mills Music. Impressed, he took him to see Alan Paramor, who signed him to Lorna Music, recorded some songs with him next door at Regent Sound and got him a record deal with Oriole. The song Mills Music turned down has spawned 122 successful cover versions to date, including Disturbed's 2017 version which went double platinum. A good song can always travel through time. Simon's first album, 'The Paul Simon Songbook' was recorded at Levy's studio in New Bond Street in June 1965 and released on

CBS in 1965. Paul Simon was on his way to becoming a globally successful songwriter and a world star, first as one half of Simon and Garfunkel then as a solo artist. The *Bridge Over Troubled Water* album alone sold almost 23 million copies.

As well as writing songs, Peter Pavey also recorded under the pseudonym Partridge Green, releasing an album, *Suburban Serenade* in 1967 and the *Green Cross Code* in 1971. In 1970 Lorna Music became a subsidiary of Novello, with Alan Paramor as their managing director. As the music publishers and songwriters moved out of the street, it seems the film and TV production companies were gradually moving in.

A graduate of King's College, Cambridge, Margery Bone, the MD and founder of Film production Company, Bonafida Films, opened her London office at no. 5 Denmark Street in 2009. The TV drama and film company also retains its original office in Newcastle-upon-Tyne. Margery previously worked for Film Four, Channel Four, Tomboy Films and Thomas Thomas Films. Elwen Rowlands, who worked with Kudos and Ecosse as well as in-house at BBC, Channel Four, ITV and Sky, manages Bonafida Films. Hayley Manning, formerly of Ipso Facto Films, is Head of production and Finance.

The ground floor of No.5 is currently owned by Relentless, who have fashioned it into a creative and musical hub, with a recording studio and a 'blank canvas space' for workshops, screenings and events. It has even hosted the Relentless Kerrang! awards nominations party. Relentless are keen to retain and acknowledge the street's musical heritage: 'We are excited to have a venue that can help provide a platform to aspiring musicians, as well as further establishing the brand as part the British music scene.' Next door at No.6, our musical landscape would be changed dramatically on two occasions.

No. 6

No 6 was built between 1686 and 1689 and is Grade II listed in 1951. The survival of early fabric warrants its Grade II status, a report revealing that 'The building is a rare, well-preserved, example of its type, reflecting the architectural fashions of the late 17th century.' It now has additional iconic heritage, the preservation of which is being discussed, but more of that after the silversmiths, the Japanese and the Beatles.'

From 1848 the property was occupied by silversmith John Wilmin Figg, who was born in Kenton, Middlesex in 1811. He was first listed on the electoral roll for the street in 1835, No. 6 being listed at Goldsmith's Hall as his permanent address. He married Elizabeth, the daughter of a watchmaker at Islington in 1840. Their son John Henry Walter died at No.6 in 1852, at just nine years old. In 1872 Figg's daughter Elizabeth moved out of No.6 after marrying Charles Bryant Payne at St. George's, Hanover Square. Like his son, John Figg would also die in Denmark Street, in 1886, at the age of seventy-five. His estate was valued at £1,761 12 shillings. Now many of his individual creations sell for more than that, this rather splendid sterling silver preserve dish fetching some £5,000. Money for Jam eh?

(Left) £5,000 worth of Figg's silver preserve dish.

Later Figg's would be owned by Smith & Co, church furnishers who made silverware for ecclesiastical clients and whose lineage stretched back to Sheffield in the 1780s. By 1921 lithographers Grosvenor Press were using part of the building and art metal workers Keith & Co were operating from here in 1930. Dance teacher Miss Iris Ross also worked out of here, her rehearsal rooms also being for hire; a little too early for the Krays' Denmark Street dancing lessons, but not too early for the newly-ensconced Japanese folk downstairs to mount the stairs in order to brush up their *Kabuki* or a perform a quick *Bon Odori.*

Oshima Kantaro came to London via Hong Kong in 1926 to study hairdressing and by 1931 had built up a wide range of Japanese and English clients. By 1938, and possibly earlier, he operated from No 6. Denmark Street and for some while shared the building with a fellow Japanese, importer and exporter, Azakami & Co. Fellow Japanese Hoshino was briefly ensconced at No. 7 after a year working across the road at the Tokiwa before returning for a while to japan in 1926. Whilst there he set up a new venture…The Asuho Shokai with Azakami, Sumoge, which saw Hoshimo sending goods from Japan for the other two to sell in London. In April 1928 he returned with his bride Michiko and another Japanese woman Akiko, a prospective bride for Azakami. The two couples lived together but their wives didn't get on and Hishino went to work for while Azakami then set up on his own at No. 6 Denmark Street in the 1930s, selling amongst other things, gramophones, radios, English books and Japanese newspapers. Hoshino saved enough money to open a basement shop next door at No. 7 but he didn't find it easy and he soon gave up the business. If you were more interested in Aristophenes than Murasaki Kishibu, from 1944 until 1964, Mrs Photini Constatinou ran Zeno's Greek Bookshop at No.6, selling Greek poetry, history and literature, before founding the Hellenic Book Service. At one time there were no less than six different businesses running out of the building and registered here. The shop continued to operate here until 1987.

The rear of the building, approached through a small courtyard, was leased by Badfinger's manager, Bill Collins who turned it into music rehearsal studio. Badfinger, used the studio regularly, but following the suicide of lead singer Pete Ham in 1975 at just twenty-eight, Collins began advertising for a new occupant. At the front of the queue, if indeed there was a queue, was Malcolm McLaren, manager of the Sex Pistols. McLaren told bass player Matlock to offer Collins £1,000 for the lease. In the end £650 and a fender Rhodes piano were handed over as the payment. Steve Jones had nowhere to live so began sleeping upstairs, with Cook and Matlock also staying there on occasions along with other early punk alumni. Previously known as The Strand in 1972, featuring Paul Cook and Steve Jones, Lydon and Matlock joined and they became the Sex Pistols, with the group's first gig taking place in November 1975 St Martin's School of Art opposite Denmark Street in the Charing Cross Road.

In 1976 the Pistols engineer, Dave Goodman also moved into No 6, bringing equipment and making the group's first demos, which, knowing Badfinger had recorded here before them, included one of the group's hits, *Come and Get It.* The group would wait for the milkman to arrive in the street at 5.00 am and steal bread, cheese and milk. Matlock later claimed it was 'an investment in punk rock.' It wasn't long before the milkman was safe from their dawn raids as McLaren signed the Pistols to EMI for £40,000 (about £300,000 now) and the band were on £25 a week each. Matlock bought a £400 Rickenbacker from a shop in Denmark Street, which he used on *Anarchy in the UK* and still owns.

Mclaren's kept the space on until 1986, at one point using it as a rehearsal room for Matlock's Rich Kids after he split from the Pistols. At the suggestion of the Pistols' Paul Cook, it became the home of Karen Woodward and Sara Dallin future members of Bananarama.

The graffiti that remains intact on the walls consists of eight caricature/cartoons by John Lydon is considered to be of historic interest, with academics, Dr John Schofield and Dr Paul Graves claiming, 'The tabloid press once claimed that early Beatles recordings discovered at the BBC were the most important archaeological find since Tutankhamun's tomb...the Sex Pistols graffiti in Denmark Street surely ranks alongside this and...to our mind usurps it...the fact that the graffiti could be considered rude, offensive and uncomfortable merely enhances their status and significance.' Just another instance of insurgency in the street of rebellion that included ideological Indian radicals, regicides, Jacobites and arsonists.

From 1968–1983, the upper two storeys of the main building at No.6 were rented by the design company 'Hipgnosis', whose principals, Storm Thorgerson and Aubrey Powell, designed album covers for artists such as Pink Floyd, Led Zeppelin, The Police, ELO, Bad Company, T. Rex, Paul McCartney and Wings, and Genesis. Their first-ever cover was Pink Floyd's *A Saucerful of Secrets.* Thorgerson and Powell were later joined by Peter Christopherson and by the early 80s had diversified into advertising, designing and campaign production. With the advent of the video age, when every release had to have an accompanying and innovative visual, they also moved into video production, working with Robert Plant, Paul Young, Yes and Dave Gilmour. The trio also wrote, produced and directed three feature films, with Powell and Christopherson forming a new company in 1985 and Powell moving more into writing, producing and directing. Storm Thorgerson died in 2013. The new set of creatives currently working at No.6 are the multi-award-winning Roast Beef productions, who specialise in non-fiction films for film and television, with No Tom guitars offering a splendid range of instruments to music lovers of all ages.

No. 7

Another of the Grade II listed buildings in the street, No. 7 also dates from between 1686 to 1689.

The street was popular with the Japanese in the 1920s and 1930s, when Hoshino had a shop at No. 7 and Sakai the tailors were also based in the same building. The business was owned by the same proprietor who had a woollen and gift shop at No.4.

It was listed in 1951 as a Grade II building, the principal reasons being: 'Architectural interest; the building is a rare, well-preserved example of its type, reflecting the architectural fashions of the late 17th century and preceding the patterns of urban terraced housing which followed in subsequent centuries...the building retains its historic floor-plan and much of its original exterior and interior character, with a hierarchy of original panelling, plasterwork and joinery.'

Pianist, conductor and arranger, Gilbert Stacey, who also had his office at No 7, was born in 1895, educated at Lichfield Cathedral and began his musical career there as a solo chorister as well as playing the organ before going on to study at the *Schola Cantorum* in Paris. He was born John Gilbert Stacey Henderson, later adopting the professional name of Gilbert Stacey. After World War I he became musical director for many leading managers, including Max Darewski, Ernest Rolls and Albert de Courville and conducted two Royal Command performances before King George V. He broadcast on the radio service 6BM from Bournemouth, which ran from 1923-1939 and played tea-time music sessions in the restaurant at Beales department store in in the town in 1927 which was relayed on the radio station. He was also the Musical Director for the 1938 film, Bed and Breakfast, composed a miniature for strings, *Bellisima.* His main forte though was as a composer of ballads such as *When Evening Shadows Fall* (1918), *Down at the Gardens in Kew* and *Sweet Lass of London Town.* During World War II he performed with his sextet as well as being a member of the War Reserve Police Force. A devotee of Elgar, he retained an extensive collection of Elgarina at the bookshop in Lewes which he ran in his later life after leaving Denmark Street. Gilbert Stacey died in 1966.

Dix Music was here in from the late 1920s, publishing songs such as Emmie Joyce and Harry Hemsley's *Lather Father Mister Barber*. Hemsley also wrote the long-running theme, *We Are the Ovaltineys*. Dix was owned by record boss Dick Bradley of Tower Records, who by 1946 was looking at a simpler and more commercial way of plugging songs on jukeboxes. In 1963 Tommy Hudson took over as head of Dix Music in the UK. In 1972 EMI bought a package of publishers from M-G-M, which included Dix, Feldman, Robbins and Francis, Day and Hunter.

Also listed as being at No7 in 1951 is the Humphrey Lyttleton band, Humph once having a clandestine recording session in the street with Matt Monro. Humph would later write: 'As a result of the increased demand for our services, we became more ambitious in our activities. We took an office in London, and Lyn Dutton abandoned his daytime job to take up residence there as a full-time manager.'

Born and educated at Eton College, where his father was a housemaster, he was a self-taught trumpeter, who became one of the UK's best-known and best-loved jazz musicians. He made his first appearance at the Hot Clun in London in 1947 and first came to prominence in the late 1940s appearing regularly at the 100 Club in Oxford Street. Signing to British Parlophone in 1949, his biggest hit was *Bad Penny Blues*, the record, engineered by Joe Meek, charting in 1956. He also presented BBC Radio 2's The Best of Jazz for forty years and hosted the panel game, *I'm Sorry I Haven't a Clue*. Lytlleton was also a cartoonist, collaborating with fellow musician Wally Fawkes on the long-running *Flook* series in the *Daily Mail*. Lyttleton died in 2008.

Harold Elton Box and Desmond 'Sonny' Cox set up Cinephonic Music and then Box & Cox Publishing at No. 7 Denmark Street in the 1940s. With Paddy Roberts and Ralph Butler they wrote *Horsey, Horsey,* the 1938 song being successful for Henry Hall, Jack Jackson and Billy Cotton. Another of their durable novelty songs was *I've Got Sixpence.* They published *I've Got a Lovely Bunch of Coconuts* in 1944, which they wrote under their pseudonym of Fred Heatherton with Lewis Ilda. The song was a hit in the US in 1949 for Freddy Martin and his Orchestra with Merv Griffin on vocals and sold over three million copies, with Danny Kaye also having a hit with it the following year. The song also became associated with UK bandleader Billy Cotton, his band's version being featured on both TV and stage. Cotton had his office on the ground floor of No.7 in the 1940s and early 1950s.

Box and Cox, again with Lewis Ilda also wrote the highly successful *Just a Little Fond Affection* first recorded in 1928 by Ray Starita and his Ambassadors and 1944 song *Chocolate Soldier from the USA. Just a Little Fond Affection* was also recorded by Kate Smith, Louis Prima, Issy Bonn and Gene Krupa. With Paddy Roberts they wrote *The Wheel on my Wagon is Broken.* Box and Cox also published *Galway Bay,* which written by Dr. Arthur Colahan in 1947 and popularised by Bing Crosby. The song is referred to in the lyric of the Pogues No.2 UK hit *Fairytale of New York.* In 1949 Box and Cox along with Light Classical composers Eric Coates and Haydn Wood represented the publishers at a meeting with the BBC about broadcasting rights. Songwriter Bill Martin remembered Box and Cox and said that after a hearty lunch, 'They'd always be good for a fiver or a tenner, with a promise that you're go away and write something as successful as I've Got a Lovely Bunch of Coconuts! And that was a good twenty years after the song came out!' Elton John has always said that he took his first name from jazz saxophonist Elton Dean, which is clearly the case, but the first Elton that the young Reg Dwight would have encountered whilst working across the road at Mills Music, was Elton Box.

By the early 1960s the Scottish music publisher Ben Nisbet was heading up Box and Cox. He was friendly with songwriter Jimmy Kennedy, who he asked to write a lyric to a 1921 melody by Viennese composer Robert Stoltz. Kennedy came up with *Blue Weekend,* but Nisbett wasn't keen, after which the Irish writer came up with new words and a different title. The song, *Romeo,* was recorded by Petula Clark and climbed to No.3 in the singles chart. Jimmy Kennedy may have felt that after his thirty years of writing songs, the landscape was changing, but despite he was still cutting it, writing *Never Goodbye,* a hit for Karl Denver, the following year. Even though the Beatles were leading the way in terms of artists writing their own material, they performed, and had roughly recorded, their version of Jimmy Kennedy's co-write, *Red Sails in the Sunset.* As well as being a publisher, Benjamin Strachen Nisbet, born in 1919, was part of the driving force behind Deep Purple and a songwriter. He moved from Box and Cox to Feldman's, wrote the best-selling TV theme song, *White Horses* with Michael Carr and formed his own company, Big Ben Publishing in 1972, and securing the representation to Bob Dylan's new music firm, Rams Horn Music. Nisbet died, aged eighty-nine, in 2008.

The man with the office on the ground floor at No.7 was born William Edward 'Billy' Cotton in 1899 and joined the army at the age

of fifteen and was a drummer boy at Gallipoli in WWI, later becoming a pilot in the Army Flying Corps. He crashed a plane and was nearly killed on the very day that the Royal Air Force was created. After the war he boxed for London Polytechnic, played football for league side Brentford and later played for non-league side, Wimbledon. He worked in a factory and was a bus conductor before playing the drums in a band at Ealing Palais and then fronting the London Savannah Band with singer Alan Breeze. He was an enthusiastic racing driver and attempted to break the land speed record on Southport sands in 1936, clocking up 121.5 mph.

He took part in the 1938 British Grand prix and ended his racing career in 1949, coming fourth in the International Grand Prix at Silverstone. He entertained troops during WWI and then became popular on BBC radio with the Sunday lunch-time's *Billy Cotton Band Show,* with his trademark catch-phrase, '*Wakey Wakey.'* The show ran from 1949 to 1968, transferring successfully to BBC television in 1956, also running for many years. He later appeared in series for ITV and ATV as well as the BBC. In 2016 his great-great-niece, radio presenter Fearne Cotton, presented a documentary on him: *Big Band, Big Man-The Billy Cotton Story*. Fearne is also the daughter-in-law of Rolling Stones guitarist Ronnie Wood.

In a twist of fate No. 7 went from being the base camp of the Cottons, a family of BBC stalwarts, to becoming the headquarters for a pirate radio station. But there is a link between them. Disc Jockey Simon Dee had been broadcasting on the offshore station Radio Caroline before joining what was then the BBC's Light programme. There he caught the ear of Mabel, Billy Cotton's wife and mother of Billy Cotton Jnr., who was so impressed with his style and delivery she suggested him as a *Top of the Pops* presenter. Acting on his mother's hunch, Bill Jnr., gave him a shot on the show and immediately offered him a three-year deal to present his own chat show, *Dee Time*. The trials and tribulations that followed are another story, but at No.7 the BBC flag had been lowered and the skull and crossbones had been raised.

RaCity Sales, the sales office for the Pirate Radio Station, Radio City had their HQ here in the 1960s, based in the offices of the Kings Agency, but connected to Tarpon Investments, based in the Bahamas. Reg Calvert's wife, Dorothy, owned 94% of RaCity's shares and Reg controlled Tarpon. Radio City was based on Shivering Sands, an abandoned WWII army fort in the Thames Estuary. Following the launch of Radio Caroline in 1964, singer and brilliant self-publicist, Screaming Lord Sutch started his own radio station, Radio Sutch, on the fort, broadcasting from the south tower. It was low budget, as the transmitter, from a Handley Page Halifax bomber, was powered by car batteries with a scaffold pole, adorned by a skull and crossbones flag, as the antenna. After a few months, Sutch sold it to manager and promoter Reg Calvert for £5,000. Calvert refurbished, rebuilt and extended the station, installing a more powerful transmitter. He relaunched it as Radio City in September 1964, using the strapline 'Tower of Power'. The DJs included engineer Ray Elvey, Ian MacRae, Chris Cross, Alexander Dee, Dennis 'The Menace' Straney, Johnny Flux and Tom Edwards.

Radio City's home at Shivering Sands.

The RaCity Sales team in Denmark Street was, In effect, Reg Calvert and his secretary Jill Wileman, with part-time help from American student and sometime Radio City DJ, Rick Michaels. They sold airtime to religious organisations for their evangelical programmes, with many local advertisers taking advantage of very competitive rates. For a while they operated on two wavelengths, presumably so the team in Denmark Street could sell twice over, but the scheme wasn't a success. The religious ads that the sales folk brought in that kept the station going included *Radio Bible Class*, *I Have Found the Answer* and *Voice of Prophesy*. Jill Wileman, then in her late twenties, had recently married a guitarist from Calvert stable of artists. She later moved to South Africa. Before Radio City, Calvert was also managing a stable of pop stars who resembled successful artists, his Elvis Presley was 'Eddie Sex' and his Buddy Holly, 'Buddy Britten.' He also discovered David Sutch, re-christened him Screaming Lord Sutch and put him up to stand at a by-election in Stratford-upon-Avon in 1963, the seat having been vacated by disgraced war Minister John Profumo, who'd been at the centre of a major scandal involving prostitutes and spies.

Reg Calvert with his stable of lookalikes and sound-alikes. Tribute acts before their time.

In September 1965 Calvert talked to first Radio Caroline South and then Radio London about a possible merger, but in June 1966 things took a sinister turn, with Major Oliver Smedley, one of Calvert's business associates (in an argument over a transmitter) taking the situation into his own hands. Smedley was no pushover. He'd been a former paratrooper who'd won the Military Cross at the Battle of Normandy in WWII and was now sending a team of riggers, led by a guy called 'Big Alf Bullen,' to take possession of the Shivering Sands fort. Incidentally. Smedley had always been a political freedom fighter and was such a staunch supporter of *Keep Britain Out*, a campaign to ensure that Britain didn't join the European Economic Community, that he resigned from the Liberal Party in 1962. Smedley had also been a member of The Society of Individualists, believing that the government run Milk Marketing Board and the Egg Marketing Board were the enemies of freedom and also forming the Council for the Reduction of Taxation. Smedley was certainly an action man and as such took action against Radio City's Reg Calvert. It was the buccaneer, Calvert, versus the privateer, Smedley.

The evening of the raid on the fort, an irate Calvert went to Smedley's home and allegedly lunged at him with a tear gas pen, or what he claimed was a tear gas pen. Smedley later said, in his defence that he thought Calvert had come to kill him, and during the ensuing argument, Smedley shot and killed Calvert. He was charged with murder but cleared after a verdict of self-defence.

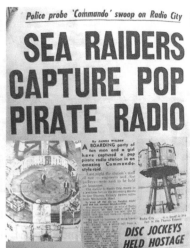

Dorothy Calvert in Denmark Street two days after her husband was killed.

After Reg's death, Dorothy Calvert kept the station going and ran the show, but the increased level of violence led to the eventual shutting down of the pirates the following year. Radio City closed down on 8th February 1967.

Dorothy Calvert died in 2010.

Reg and Dorothy Calvert

By the 1990s, the Tin Pan Alley Club, once the domain of the publishers Box and Cox, was owned by Jimmy Fraser, the nephew of the much-feared gangster, 'Mad' Frankie Fraser, so Frankie and Jimmy were very much part of the Denmark Street scene in the 1990s and 2000s. There would now be far more than just *A Lovely Bunch of Coconuts* to be bought here. Brought up in South-East London, Frankie spent some forty-two years of his life in prison including ten years for his part in the Richardson torture case and five for leading the Parkhurst Riots in 1970. He started out in his late teens as bodyguard to the notorious gangland leader, Billy Hill, taking part in bank robberies and razor attacks, for which he was paid £50 a time. He later became a member of the Richardson, becoming involved with their turf wars against the Kray Twins and their gang. Frankie was nicknamed 'The Dentist' as one of his favourite methods of torturing people was to pull out their teeth with a pair of pliers.

Bizarrely he became something of a celebrity, writing his memoirs, appearing in films and touring a stage show. He ended up living with singer Marilyn Wisbey, the daughter of Great Train Robber, Tom Wisbey, having first met her at Leicester security wing in the late 1960s when she went to visit her father. They re-met and began their love affair in the 'Tin Pan Alley' wine bar in Denmark Street which belonged to Frankie's nephew, Jimmy. Frankie reckoned she was the best thing that ever happened to him; 'She was in there as a singer and she sung that gorgeous song, *Crazy*. Well, having been certified insane three times, I thought, 'Is she taking it out of me?' I went up to her afterwards and said, 'I thought you was having a knock at me.' And she collapsed with laughter. We've been together now eight years and I've never been back to prison.'

Jimmy's Tin Pan Alley bar came under investigation in the early 2000's from the *Sunday People* who reported the Denmark Street haunt as a 'drugs den,' and the police, who had it marked as a centre for the passing of forged bank notes. Police bugged the counter, the toilets and the back room, where it was said that the drug deals were done. It was alleged that the notes were printed in Scotland and then distributed to customers as change at the Tin Pan Alley bar. Jimmy had his uncle, Frankie's prison slippers and pullover on display in pride of place on the wall of the bar. A sign also proclaimed 'welcome to Jimmy Fraser's Tin Pan Alley' and customers were treated to a copious amount of pop memorabilia. Regulars would include actor Ray Winstone, Alex 'Hurricane' Higgins and Wayne Sleep.

Jimmy and Frankie's son Frank Jnr organised a benefit from Denmark Street for Frankie, the last time he came out of prison, which raised over £50,000.

Frankie Fraser

No. 8

By 1830 Thomas Chapman, a manufacturer of invalid beds and chairs had his workshop at No.8 Denmark

Street, that year dissolving his partnership with Noah Morris. A John Alderman was working for Chapman but by 1835 he was being sued under the name of Anthony Austin. It also appears that he used the names of Alderman Austin and William Henry Barrett, and was also a dealer in beer by retail as well as some-time cabinet maker here to Mr. Chapman. Chapman's workshop remained in the street until at least 1843 and may have been connected with the furniture shop that was at No.8 in 1856 and which later moved to the Charing Cross Road and New Oxford Street.

A few years later, George Glenny, a male model would move in to the house. In August 1841 a working artist who used living models on a regular basis wrote to the Art Union Magazine: 'First on the list of male models for strength and muscular development stands George Glenny; I should compare him with the Dancing Fawn, having all the youth and elasticity of that figure; he lives at 8 Denmark-Street. When unemployed professionally, he is to be seen personating a red indian at Catlin's Exhibition, Egyptian Hall, Piccadilly.' There may well have been one or two genuine American Indians in the troupe, but impersonators, like Glenny, were almost certainly hired for the occasion. Glenny could only have played the part of one of four 'genuine' American Indians, *Flying Gull, Moonlight Night, Tobacco* or the *Strong Wind.* He also went with Catlin's show to Windsor Castle, to perform for Queen Victoria and Prince Albert. George Catlin was the outstanding painter of nineteenth century American Indian life, and a flamboyant showman who had a grand design to record 'doomed' Indian cultures for posterity.

How many genuine members of the Ojibbaway Indians (more correctly Ojibwe or Chippewa) were with the troupe and how many actors were brought in by Catlin we may never know. In a street of composers and lyricists we do know that in Henry Wadsworth

Longfellow's epic 1855 poem *The Song of Hiawatha,* there are many toponyms that originate from the Ojibwe language. George Glenny

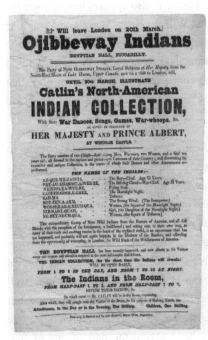

leaves no clue as to how much he was paid for masquerading as a member of the tribe, but it was reported that those that did make the trip were paid a shilling a day, which included several shows a day and being paraded around London.

Was the man from No.8 'Gish-Fe-Gosh-E-Ghee' on the poster, or 'We-Nish-Ka-Wee-Be' or were these the names of real members of the tribe?

The name Iawsaki Moritaro, who lived here some seventy years after George Glenny, however, was real. In 1918 Moritaro opened the Tokiwa Restaurant at 15 Manette Street, off the Charing Cross Road and was joined by his wife Fukue the following year. They opened Tokiwa restaurants in the City in 1922 and Paris in 1923. In 1927 they extended their operations, moving the restaurant to No. 8 Denmark Street., and opening the Tokiwa Hotel at No. 22. They also sold Japanese groceries. In By 1932 they were also running the Tokiwa Travellers Bureau, billing themselves as 'Tourist Agents'. Despite a tenth anniversary party in Denmark Street in the late 1920 to celebrate their success, by 1933 Iwasaki had registered for divorce from Fukue. His new wife gave birth to three children over the next four years.

Meanwhile, the plot thickened and by 1933 the Tokiwa Hotel was in the sole possession of Fukue, who changed the name to Tokiwa House, changing it again the following year to the Yamato Hotel. Fukue then married Akima Katsuji, the couple running the hotel, while her former husband, Iwasaki continued to make a success of the restaurant as well as continuing to run his travel and removal service. His travel service would have organised first class berth on a boat to Japan for around £100.

Lawrence Wright (*right*) was the first publisher in Denmark Street. He had opened a music shop in his home town of Leicester in 1906 at the age of eighteen. He began writing songs and in 1911 set up shop at No.8 Denmark Street. After WWI he moved to No.19 Denmark Street., so for the rest of his story you'll have to move there too.

The first of three addresses for Southern Music on Denmark Street was at No.5, where they had their first UK base from 1933-1935. Peer was founded by Ralph S. Peer a talent scout for the RCA Victor label and was very involved in recording pioneering sessions with early country artists. Peer founded his own company Southern Music in 1928, soon acquiring songs that became standards such as *You Are My Sunshine, Georgia on my Mind* and *Will the Circle be Unbroken.*

At the end of WWII, after a spell at No, 24, Southern Music moved again, this time to a more permanent home, at No. 8. Ralph Peer also moved into Latin-American music and, by 1946, with the help of his London executive, Tom Ward, the company began to grow rapidly. In 1953, with their neighbouring publisher Ed Kassner having picked up the publishing for *Rock Around the Clock* for the UK, Peer weren't slow in obtaining the copyright of the song for Australia.

Major success came in the late 1950's, with Peer in London joining successfully in the scramble for UK and European rights to major US rock 'n' roll hits such as *Long Tall Sally* and benefiting from Peer's US signing Buddy Holly and the Crickets. It was at Southern Music in the States that Buddy Holly met his future wife, Maria Elena Santiago, in June 1958, who was the receptionist for NY executive, Murray Deutch. UK employees in the 40's and 50's included future Essex Music MD David Platz, Leeds/MCA MD Cyril Simons and scriptwriter Barry Took.

Peer was also able to capitalise on the vogue for country music from its own catalogue and that of the Nashville publisher Cedarwood, and for Latin American music in which Peer Music was already the major player worldwide. This prompted the setting up in the London Office of a separate company for this genre, run for many years by Marjorie Murray. The 50's also saw Peer Music as the UK's major printed music distributor, from its 'trade department' within the office, headed by Peter Foss. The London office continued and expanded its business of acquiring UK hits for other peer branches. In 1954 they were listed as Libor-Southern.

The fifties also saw the launch of a background music library operated initially from a separate address by Dennis Berry until the 1970's, and of a light music division incorporating the Liber-Southern catalogue which was run firstly by co-owner Jacques Liber (from 24 Denmark Street) and later by Harry Benson and then Ronnie Bridges who also handled the substantial Peer Music classical music catalogue. An experienced composer and pianist, Bridges had previously been with the Windmill Theatre for nineteen years and would become a director of BASCA. Southern's Max Diamond was reported by Billboard in 1954 as taking over the BF Wood Catalogue. Born Bruno Albert Magnoni, Max Diamond would criss-cross Demark Street over two decades, also working for Ed Kassner and Campbell-Connelly, before setting up on his own at No. 5 which is where we find his intriguing story.

Despite a No.1 with UK copyright *Hoots Mon* in 1958 it was not until the 1960's that Southern's copyrights would become big earners in other countries too, notably the USA. While we are at No.8, an interesting coincidence regarding Denmark Street is the connection between Lord Wharton, on whose land the street was built in the 1680s, and Harry Robinson, whose big hit, *Hoots Mon* and other songs were published by the street's Southern Music almost three hundred years later, in the late 1950s. Lord Wharton wrote the words to Lilliburlero, so technically he was probably the first to compose what amounted to a hit song on the site. Robinson was born Harry Robertson, but changed his name as Decca, for whom he worked as an arranger had made out a cheque out to Harry Robinson and he felt it would just be easier to open a bank account as Robinson. He was also MD for Decca artist Tommy Steele and was a favourite on early TV shows *6.5 Special* and *Oh Boy*, performing as Lord Rockingham's XI and as Musical Director. He worked on such diverse projects as the stage shows *Fings Ain't Wot They Used T'Be, Maggie May* and the West End musical *Elvis*, as well as many Hammer Horror film scores, conducting our UK Eurovision entry in 1961, the Allisons' *Are You Sure*, and arranging for Nick Drake.

In the late 1950s he married Myrtle Olive Felix Arbruthnot, who sang as Ziki Arnot, his wife succeeding as 11th Baroness Wharton in 1990. So the Whartons were back in Denmark Street, built on Lord Wharton's land in the 1680s. Their son, Myles Christopher David Robertson is now the 12th Baron Wharton. Maybe an historic medley of *Lilliburlero* and *Hoots Mon* is on the cards.

Harry Robinson and the future 11th Baroness Wharton on their wedding day.

Following a stint as professional manager, Bob Kingston was appointed MD in London in 1959 and immediately made a point of backing UK songwriters, signing young writers like Geoff Goddard, from Joe Meek's stable, who penned many hits including *Johnny Remember Me, Wild Wind, Tribute to Buddy Holly* and *Just Like Eddie*. Many other songs came via Joe Meek's productions, as both Meek and Goddard were enormous fans of Buddy Holly and loved the idea of being with the same publishing company.

Under the aegis of Bob Kingston, Peer Music played a significant part in the 'UK invasion of America' which had been spearheaded by the Tornados *Telstar*, the first record by a UK group to make No. 1 in the States. *Telstar* was produced by Peer writer Joe Meek and featured one of their copyrights, *Jungle Fever* by Geoff Goddard on the B-side.

John Carter and Ken Lewis were also signed, becoming members of the Ivy League and writing several of their hits as well as penning songs like, *Let's Go to San Francisco, Semi-Detached Suburban Mr. James*.

Geoff Stephens, writer of *Tell Me When, The Crying Game* and *Winchester Cathedral* was another Southern writer and Donovan started his career in their London studios. The 1960's was undoubtedly the 'golden era' for Peer London with Geoff Goddard, Geoff Stephens, Donovan, John Carter and Ken Lewis all writing US number 1 hits.

In 1967 Kingston set up co-publishing deals with two movie production companies as well as starting the company's own label, Spark and publishing the musical *The Likes of Us*, by two newcomers, Andrew Lloyd Webber and Tim Rice. Spark was headed up by

Freddie Poser and seemed a natural progression, as in 1961 Peer London, with its recording studio in the basement of 8 Denmark Street, had become, uniquely amongst UK publishers, an independent record producer, licensing recordings by artists as diverse as Donovan, The Ivy League, Vince Hill and Elmer Gantry's Velvet Opera to existing record labels. It was success in this area that prompted the setting-up in 1967 of Peer's own label Spark Records. Despite a plethora of releases in all genres of music, Spark had a chequered history, enjoying success with Keith Michell, the Sutherland Brothers (as the New Generation) the Band of the Black Watch, and a number of artists associated with leading 'northern soul' club Wigan Casino. Ironically Spark's best period of success came in the mid 1970's shortly before its demise. Many psychedelic pop singles came out on the Spark label from the studios at No. 8 from artists such as Icarus, Just William, Gene Latter, The Fruit Machine, Timothy Blue, and a single by A New Generation, which was the Sutherland Brothers first attempt at a hit, *Smokey Blues Away*. Based on Dvorak's New World Symphony, Spark believed in it enough to take an ad on the whole front page of the New Musical Express, and it was a very good number, but probably what let Spark down at the time was poor distribution. The pre-internet curse of many an indie label taking on the majors. Rather bizarrely Eartha Kitt's version of Donovan's *Hurdy Gurdy Man* also came out on Spark.

At about the same time that Spark was being set up, former Ted Heath singer Bob Britton became the company's professional manager. Also by 1967, Marjorie Murray had moved to become Head of Latin American Music, having joined the firm as a secretary thirteen years earlier and run the company for some time. At the point there was a staff of forty, including Bob England, Marjorie Murray, Dennis Berry, John Underwood, Peter Foss, Betty Wilson and England's son, Barry. Ralph Peer had died in 1960 and for the next twenty years his wife Monique ran the company. Leslie Abbott became MD, followed by Australian, Allan Crawford and then, in 1958 Bob Kingston.

During the 1960s Peer Music had become the first publisher for, amongst others, the Rolling Stones, Andrew Lloyd Webber and Tim Rice, The Pretty Things and Pink Floyd, and acquired songs written by many the UK's major writers of the time, such as Les Reed, Howard Blaikley and Mitch Murray as well as the above. Peer London also had songs in three successive 'Song for Europe' competitions (1969-71), two of them, *Knock Knock Who's There*? and *Jack in the Box* becoming UK Eurovision entries. A good example of how just getting a basic job in the street and getting to know people worked is that of Ken Laws. Fascinated by drums as a boy, he played with a local Cheam band called Prism and on leaving school got a job in the trade department of Southern Music. He later graduated to assistant sound engineer, working with Paul Holland, which brought him closer to the music and musicians. Laws got to work with acts like Elmer Gantry's Velvet Opera, struck up friendships with other sound engineers, picked up the gig of drumming in the musical *Hair* and hung out in the Giaconda Café just along the street. It was there that he got to know Richard Hudson, whom Laws had worked with on the Elmer Gantry project, and John Ford and ended up as a member of Hudson Ford, playing on several of their albums and hit singles such as *Floating in the Wind* and *Burn Baby Burn*. It paid to hang out in the Gioconda.

One of Peer Southern's writers was Glasgow-born Donovan Leitch who grew up in St. Albans and was signed to a management and publishing deal by Geoff Stephens and Peter Eden in 1964, the pair bringing him to Southern Music. Between January 1965 and October 1965 Donovan recorded some forty songs at Southern Music's Studios at No.8, including *Catch the Wind,* with former Shadows bass player, Brian 'Licorice' Locking on bass. It was while recording these demos that Donovan met and became friends with Rolling Stones guitarist, Brian Jones. The song catapulted Donovan into the limelight as it climbed to No.4 in the UK chart. Other songs recorded at Southern include *Why do you Treat Me Like You Do, Josie, The Alamo, Goldwatch Blues, Colours, To Try For the Sun, Universal Soldier, Ballad of a Crystal Man, Candy Man, Jersey Thursday, Sunny Goodge Street, Torquise, Hey Gyp (Dig the Slowness)*. After gaining national fame with five appearances on the TV show *Ready Steady Go,* Donovan went on to become one of the UK's most successful and durable singers and songwriters, with a string of hits that included *Catch the Wind, Colours, Sunshine Superman, Mellow Yellow, There is a Mountain, Jennifer Juniper, Hurdy Gurdy Man* and *Goo Goo Barabajagal.* He had seven top thirty albums in the UK. In the States had a No.1 with *Sunshine Superman,* a No.2 with *Mellow Yellow* and a top five hit with *Hurdy Gurdy Man.* Donovan was one of the Beatles party that famously travelled to India to spend time with the Maharishi Mahesh Yogi. Donovan was inducted into the Rock and Roll Hall of Fame in 2012 and the Songwriters Hall of Fame in 2013. He continues to record and perform, writing a special song, *Tin Pan Alley,* for the unveiling of the blue plaque on the Gioconda in Denmark Street. in 2014. In 2016 he was only the third recipient of The John Lennon Real Love Award.

Another of Peer's most successful writers was the aforementioned Geoff Stephens, who signed with Peer Southern in 1964, his first success being The Applejacks *Tell Me When* co-written with Les Reed. Geoff wrote Dave Berry's big hit, *The Crying Game* and in 1966 formed the New Vaudeville Band for whom he wrote several hits including the Ivor Novello and Grammy award-winning US chart-topper *Winchester Cathedral.* In 1967 he wrote *Semi-Detached Suburban Mr. James* with John Carter and *There's a Kind of Hush* with Les Reed, a hit for Herman's Hermits and later for the Carpenters. Geoff also penned *Sunshine Girl* and *My Sentimental Friend* for Herman's Hermits as well as hits for The Hollies, Lulu and Ken Dodd. The hits kept flowing with *Knock Knock Who's There, Daughter of Darkness, The Lights of Cincinatti, Goodbye Sam, Hello Samantha* and the US No.1 *Daddy Don't You Walk so Fast,* the latter with Peter Callander. During the 1970s there were hits for the Drifters, *Like Sister and Brother,* Sunny, *Doctors Orders,* David Soul, *Silver Lady,* Hot Chocolate, *I'll Put you Together Again* and Dana, *It's Gonna Be a Cold, Cold, Christmas.* Geoff Stephens also won an Ivor Novello Award for The New Seekers song, *You Won't Find Another Fool Like Me.* Geoff collaborated with Don Black on the musical, *Dear Anyone.* In 2000 he was given the Jimmy Kennedy Ivor Novello Award for Services to British Songwriting. In 2002 he received a citation from BMI for 2 million broadcasts of his 1969 song *Smile a Little Smile for Me.* Geoff Stephens is a great example of what Tin Pan Alley was all about; different writers working together in tandem with publishers to provide a variety of artists with hit songs with the pluggers pushing the material through to the radio and TV outlets. Stephens wrote with a wide variety of other Denmark Street creatives, including Les Reed, Don Black, Roger Greenaway, Peter Callander, Barry Mason, Ken Howard, Alan Blaikley, Tony Macauley, Mitch Murray and John Carter.

School friends and writing partners, John Carter and Ken Lewis came from Birmingham to Denmark Street in the early Sixties and signed with Southern Music. While writing they also did many broadcasts for the BBC (*Easy Beat*, etc.), when they formed Carter-Lewis and the Southerners. The group included at one time or another Jimmy Paige and Viv Prince.

Their first hit as writers was *Will I What?* for Mike Sarne, followed by *Can't You Hear My Heartbeat* by Herman's Hermits, which went to No. 1 in the USA.

In the mid-Sixties John and Ken concentrated on providing vocal backing for other artists, and appeared on hits such as *Can't Explain* (The Who), *It's Not Unusual* (Tom Jones), *Out Of Time* (Chris Farlowe). This led to their forming their second group, The Ivy League, with the addition of Perry Ford, with whom had three major hits in the UK with *Funny How Love Can Be*, *Tossing and Turning* and That's *Why I'm Crying*. This led to extensive touring for a year and a half, when John decided to leave in order to concentrate on writing and recording.

John met up with writer Geoff Stephens, who asked him to demo a song Geoff had written, *Winchester Cathedral*. John then did the lead vocal on the finished record, which reached No. 1 on the American charts. About the same time, a joint composition by John and Ken Lewis, *Little Bit o' Soul*, recorded by the Music Explosion, also went to No. 1 in the States. John and Geoff Stephens continued writing together, with hits such as *Semi-detached Suburban Mr James* for Manfred Mann, *My Sentimental Friend, Sleepy Joe* and *Sunshine Girl* for Herman's Hermits, and *Knock, Knock, Who's There?* for Mary Hopkin.

After Ken retired from the Ivy League and the music business in general, John asked his wife, Gill, to write lyrics for his songs. This resulted in a big hit in Europe by Kincade called '*Dreams Are Ten a Penny*. John and Gill also wrote the *Beach Baby* by First Class (produced by John), which went Top 5 in the States. John was approached by George Martin's jingle production company, Air-Edel Associates, to write for them, starting a ten-year career composing music for advertising. Having produced his own material through his publishing and recording companies, he was able to re-compile and release these hits for many years. John teamed up with Salomao Hamzem after hearing him play at open-mic events, and they became friends. They began to play together, which lead to their composing material for a first album. John is still signed to Peer Music.

In 1980 Peer's son, Ralph Peer II, became head of the company, expanding Peer/Southern into nine new countries. By this time the company had enjoyed success with 70s classic *Rock Your Baby* by George McCrae and was enjoying an 80s hot with *Get Down Tonight* by KC and the Sunshine Band. But the pace of local success had slowed. Bob Kingston left in 1977 and between spells at the helm by Tom Ward Jnr. and Peer Hamburg MD Michael Karnstedt, Roy Tempest and later Stuart Ongley as MDs, they saw the company through to 1992 when Nigel Elderton took over.

The 1990s saw a resurgence in the fortunes of Peer Music in London, firstly with Tim Cox and Nigel Swanston- penned hits for Rozalla, produced in Peer's revamped in-house studio, and later, at its new office in at 8-14 Verulam Street WC1, with Urban Cookie Collective, Tony di Bart, Gina G, Sash, Ruff Driverz, Mike Koglin, Echobeatz and Judge Jules, many of them produced in its new studio at Verulam Street. Peer left No.8 in 1992, having effectively being the last publisher on the block. Peer Music in London continues to look after the copyrights of many of the UK's top writers and continues to sign and develop new writers and producers. The company that started as a one man operation now has 32 offices in 28 countries.

There was also a musical mystery at No.8 that began just after WWI and was only solved in 1978.

The Cranz music publishing company was founded in Hamburg in 1814, buying Schreiber publishing in 1879 and taking over the Boehme publishing catalogue in 1886. They opened offices in Brussels in 1883 and London in 1890, moving their HQ to Leipzig in 1897, when August Alwin Cranz took over his father's company. Their writers included Max Bruch, Clara Schumann and Johann Strauss II. They had an office in London which closed during WWII, the company's manuscripts and paperwork being lodged with the BBC. Cranz later opened again in Langham St. and from the late 1949 the music publishers Cranz & Co were at No.8. Southern Music had the premises and at some point had looked after the Cranz manuscripts which maybe is why Cranz subsequently moved there. In 1949 their German office moved to Weisbaden, the year that the composer Havergal Brian was trying to get hold of the score for his work *The Tigers* which he had written between 1917 and 1929 originally as *The Burlesques*, which Cranz had published in 1932. Only when he tried to discover them did he find that the company had moved to Tin Pan Alley without telling him. In the book Aspects of Havergal Brian, it mentions that he wrote on 11th October 1949: 'About the Cranz matter there is silence and I am somewhat surprised that nobody is surprised about it. Cranz of Brussels has not written...although I pointed out to him that when the London firm published the opera I handed to them hundreds of orchestral band parts of the dances and variations which cost me over £100 for the copying. Apart from intervals of lying fallow I've never ceased to write and, apart from the Gothic, no attempt has been made to produce any of the symphonies. Perhaps the Cranz revelation of the loathsome underground operation may deter further large works.'

Trying to locate another work, he wrote a postcard concerning Cranz: 'Apparently their depot at Denmark Street has been handed to Agents at 8 Denmark Street. When I rang up the other day the people at

Denmark Street said they were all at sixes and sevens and Miss Percy of Cranz was ill and 'never comes now to town.' When the contracts with Cranz were made originally, I wrote to a, then well-known, composer and told him what appeared to me to have been a piece of luck. I remember his reply: "Surely…you are not trying to make a friend of your enemy…impossible."' He also wrote of Cranz: '…he gave up and broke all his contracts & I haven't seen him since 1932…he may be dead for all I know…'

His lost work, written for Sir Thomas Beecham, was so important to him, that a well-known medium in Wimbledon reported Havergal Brian's post-death manifestation, bemoaning a lost manuscript! A reward of £500 was offered for it, but it wasn't until 1978 that his burlesque opera, *The Tigers* was discovered in a pile of rubbish in the basement of No.8. Cranz was finally sold to Schott in 1992, who still use the Cranz imprint. The Avalon English School is at now 8 Denmark Street.

No. 9

Built in 1686-9, No. 9 was Grade II listed in 1974.

In the second half of the 1700s, Jacobite Sir John Murray was the occupier of No. 9 until he was 'carried off by a party of strange men'. Sir John Murray of Broughton, 7th Baronet Stanhope was born circa 1718, in Broughton on the Scottish Borders. From 1732 he studied at Edinburgh University moving three years later to the University of Leyden in Holland. He then went to the Stuart Court which was based in Rome in exile, becoming a confidant of Prince Charles. Murray reacquired the ancestral home at Broughton and married Margaret Ferguson, who was also to become famous for serving the Jacobite cause. Murray served as secretary to Charles Edward Stuart (Bonnie Prince Charlie) during the Jacobite rising of 1745 and from then on was addressed as 'Mr. Secretary Murray'. One of his duties was to beg, steal or borrow money for the cause. He was at the Battle of Prestonpans and when the Jacobite forces invaded England, he was sent to negotiate the surrender of Carlisle. The following year Murray allegedly fell ill and hid to avoid arrest, although there were some doubting Thomas's who accused him of desertion. On the day of the Battle of Culloden he had to be carried across Loch Ness to Glanmoriston, where he learned of the rout of the Jacobites. He met

with French ships belatedly bringing financial help, Murray taking possession of the gold that became known as the Loch Arkaig Treasure. Although he attempted to escape to Holland, he was captured at the home of his sister, Veronica Murray Hunter. On July 7th he was sent to the Tower of London and charged with High Treason. He turned King's evidence, his testimony leading to the execution of Simon Fraser, Lord Lovat, chief of the Clan Fraser. Fraser would be the last man in Britain to be executed by beheading. Murray was given a full pardon by the Crown in 1748 after which he chose, not unsurprisingly, to stay in England. Held in contempt and disdain by the Jacobites, they henceforth referred to him as 'Mr. Evidence Murray'. Despite his betrayal, Murray remained a Jacobite, Prince Charles paying him an undercover visit in 1763. The following year though Murray's Broughton estates were sold (along with those of other Jacobite sympathisers) by the Court of Session. In 1775 Broughton burned down and two years after that Sir John Murray passed away. We may never know why the 'party of strange men' bore him off from Denmark Street. Jacobites bent on revenge at him turning King's evidence? Being summoned to secret rendezvous with Bonnie Prince Charlie? Someone trying to get their hands on the Loch Arkaig Treasure? Or maybe something more sinister.

History would repeat itself when No.9 became the Gioconda and musicians would hang out in the hope of being carried off, with their guitar, by a 'party of strange men' as it meant a chance of fame and fortune. The first chart-topping song to be written at the property was penned well over a hundred years before the likes of Bowie, Paul Simon, Ray Davies, Vince Taylor, Marc Bolan and Steve Marriott gathered there and was written by a member of the Rimbault family who were in Denmark Street for decades.

The Rimbaults also helped a struggling German neo-classical painter Johan Zoffany who had arrived in London in 1760, almost destitute, without work and having almost no English. Having spent seven years in Rome though, he was fairly fluent in Italian. Zoffany, was born Johannes Josephus Zaufallij in Frankfurt in 1733 and came to England in 1760, being introduced to and initially working with celebrated clockmaker, Paul Rimbault in St Giles, painting vignettes for his clocks. One of the timepieces painted by Zoffany depicted five men by a forge and a windmill, in which one of the men's arms moved with the minutes and the windmill sails with the hour. Historian and portrait engraver, Francis Alaimet, was also working on the premises in 1763. Between the years of 1760 and 1781, Rimbault had an incredible reputation and Zoffany, who moved in to No. 9 Denmark Street whilst working there, learned well. Rimbault effected an introduction to actor/manager David Garrick, who became Zoffany's first patron. In gratitude, Zoffany painted Rimbault's portrait (*below*).

Within a few years he was enjoying the patronage of George III and his wife Queen Charlotte as well as being popular with the Austrian royal family, whose Empress Maria Theresa made him a Baron. He toyed with a commission for George III's nine living children for so long that three more children, Prince Adolphus, Princess Mary and Princess Sophia were born during the period it took him to paint it. He is said to have exclaimed, 'Oh my soul, this is too much.' A founding member of the new Royal Academy, he painted such actors as David Garrick and became famous for his 'theatrical conversation piece' genre. He is mentioned in the libretto of Gilbert and Sullivan's comic opera *The Pirates of Penzance*, ironic really as he once ate a sailor. The occasion was after a shipwreck off the Andaman Islands when the survivors held a lottery to see who would be eaten, hence Zoffany became the first, and probably only, Royal Academician to have become a cannibal. His works are to be seen in, amongst many other places, the National Gallery, Tate Gallery and the Royal Collection. Zoffany died at Strand-on-the Green in 1810. Paul Rimbault passed Zoffany's portrait to his nephew, Stephen Francis Rimbault who, in the 1820s, hung the painting over the chimney piece in the front parlour at 9, Denmark Street. He, in turn, left it to his son, Edward Francis Rimbault who also lived at No.9. Edward left it to his godson, E.

Rimbault Dibdin, whose daughter, Mrs Alfred Aslett bequeathed it to the Tate Gallery. The fireplace where it hung didn't go to the Tate and remains *in situ*. Two Zoffanys came up for aution at Sothebys in 2011 with an estimate of £6-8 million, not bad for a destitute young man

who spoke no English but found work and support at No.9 Denmark Street. Paul Rimbault made his will in June 1775 and died later that year. In 2012 a 'fine George III mounted ebonised quarter chiming musical table clock' (*right*) made by Paul Rimbault at No.9 sold at auction for £7,000.

Edward F. Rimbault (*below*), the co-founder and secretary of the Antiquarian Musical Society, lived at No.9 in 1842 and for some

years either side. In 1843 he's still listed as residing at No.9 Denmark Street. and described as a Professor of Music. A letter he wrote from Denmark Street in September of that year still exists, requesting a copy of Laing's edition of *Metrical Psalms of Scotland*, from David Laing, though he erroneously writes the address as 8, Denmark Street, Soho Square. Rimbault also posted a notice in the journal, *The Musical World,* announcing the Society's second annual general meeting, which were to be held in the rooms of the Royal Society of Musicians, the same notice also being placed in the *Spectator.* Members were reminded that their annual subscriptions of £1 became due on the day of the meeting and were to be paid to Mr. Chappell of 50, New Bond Street. Rimbault had been born in Soho in 1816, his father Stephen Rimbault being an organist, arranger and composer, who passed on his talents to his son. Also taught by Samuel Wesley and William Crotch, Edward became the organist at the Swiss Church in Soho at the age of sixteen and was later in much demand as a lecturer. He edited many collections of music, arranged contemporary operas, edited and arranged early English music as well as undertaking editorial work for the Percy Society, the Camden Society, the Handel Society and the Motett Society. He was mentioned in *Bent's Literary Advertiser* in February 1842 as being Managing Editor to the latter society and as residing at 9 Denmark Street. H was also mentioned in the *Literary Gazette* as being at the same address in 1841. Rimbault was elected a Fellow of the Society of antiquaries, membership of the Academy of Music in Stockholm, an honorary degree by the University of Oxford in Stockholm and he was offered a teaching position at Harvard. He wrote books on music which were published in 1847, 1855, 1860 and 1865, examining such diverse areas as organ-building, the origin and construction of the pianoforte, the clavichord, the virginal, the harpsichord, madrigals and ballets. He also played the organ for the St. Peter's, Vere St and St John's Wood churches. He possessed a magnificent library, which on his death in 1876 were auctioned by Sotheby, Wilkinson and Hodge, with material going to both the British Library and 600 items being sold to Joseph W. Drexel upon whose death the items were bequeathed to the Lenox Library, a precursor to the New York Public Library. The Drexel Collection, including the 600 items from the man who lived at No.9 Denmark Street now form part of the Music Division of the New York Library for the Performing Arts.

Like his uncle, Stephen Francis Rimbault was also a clock-maker. Born in 1773, his business was originally at Great Andrew's Street St Giles, before he moved to 9, Denmark Street. He was also a composer and organist and was noted for his 'twelve-tuned Dutchmen' clocks that played a dozen tunes with moving figures and decorated backgrounds. His music includes, *The Morn Appears with Beauty Round, Air Russe.* He married Mary Tatem in 1816, the couple having four children, Edward Francis, John Henry, Charles Frederick and Emma Ann. Stephen died in 1837, but three years the whole family were still living at the property; Mary was 50, Edward 23, John 21 Charles 19 and Emma. 14.

In 1830 *The Harmonicon* carried an advertisement placed by Rimbault advertising his manuscript of Handel's *Messiah* and that it could be purchased from him at 'No.9 Denmark-street, or all good music shops.' Mary died sometime in the 1860s, while living with John Henry, who was becoming a highly skilled engraver and would later employ a team of people and be held in great esteem. Henry had one child from his first marriage and eight from his second. Born in Denmark Street, he was to die tragically, close to Big Ben, in 1888. At half-past three one afternoon, the 68-year-old Rimbault was crossing from Parliament-street to Palace-yard and got some 3 ft from the pavement when a cabman shouted out to him. On hearing the warning cry, he hesitated, and a moment later the near side horse of a Kennington Omnibus 'knocked him down with considerable violence and the front wheel passed over his arm.' He was immediately picked up by Constable Kilman and conveyed 'in an insensible condition' to Westminster Hospital. Rimbault, who had sustained a compound comminuted fracture of the right arm as well as injury to the brain, died at the hospital. A verdict of 'accidental death' was recorded.

Lord Wharton, on whose land much of Denmark Street was built, may have written the lyrics to *Lilliburlero,* the country's favourite song of the year in 1681, but the first occupant to have written a song that almost topped the chart must have been Edward Rimbault. In the mid-1800s he wrote a new melody for the old hymn, *Oh Happy Day, that fixed my choice* (based on Acts 8:35) and added a chorus. In 1969 Edwin Hawkins arranged it in a gospel style, only using the Rimbault refrain and omitting all the original verses. Recorded at the Ephesian Church of God in Christ in Berkley, California, with Dorothy Combs Morrison singing the lead. The Edwin Hawkins' Singers took the song to No.2 in the UK, Canada and Ireland, No.1 in France, Germany and the Netherlands and No.4 in the United States. It had now become a gospel standard. The 'B' side was written by Charles Wesley in 1740, *Jesus, Lover of My Soul.* The arrangement of Rimbault's song won Edwin Hawkins a Grammy, was included on the RIAA 'Songs of the Century' list. George Harrison admitted that it had been a primary inspiration for his song, *My Sweet Lord.*

A gold disc and a silver disc presented a song written where gold caster and silver caster John Corbett would be active just a few years later, from 1860 when he was at No.9, until 1900 by which time he was in residence at No. 23.

In 1918 an Italian soldier who fought with the 93rd Infantry was living at No.9. Born in 1886, Amedeo Palombie had lived in South East London before the war and had been married to a lady named Kitty with whom he had a son and a daughter, born in 1912 and 1913 respectively. His unit, the 93rd Infantry were essentially a segregated Division, sent to France in 1917. The 93rd never fought together as a division but were broken up and brigaded with French Army formations and using French equipment while still wearing US uniforms. In April 1918 Palombi married Adelina Marra and was living in Denmark Street, his first wife having either died or the couple having divorced.

The street has never been short of a hairdresser or two and from the 1930s there was a men's barber operating from No.9, no doubt trimming the odd head from Paramount Music publishers who were also based here. The US company was owned by Paramount Pictures and specialised in movie songs, such as *Thanks for the Memory* and

Call Me Irresponsible. It was still a hairdresser's in the late 1950s, trading as Ledenois, with future guitarist Albert Lee as one of its employees.

David Bowie, then still David Jones, recorded an early track here with his group at the time, the Manish Boys. The song, *Hello Stranger* was never released.

David Bowie's look in his Tin Pan Alley days.

David Bowie in the Spring of 1965 randomly caught on cine film by Joe Salama's father heading to the Gioconda. Credit: Joe Salama.

It was at the Gioconda that David Bowie met leather-clad rocker Vince Taylor (Brian Holden), the singer who inspired Bowie's Ziggy Stardust. Taylor's bizarre behaviour pattern intrigued the young Bowie, when he was still David Jones. He found Vince round the corner by Tottenham Court tube station one day with a map spread out on the ground. Perplexed, he asked him what he was doing. Vince told him that he'd marked the places on the map where aliens were going to land and the seeds of Ziggy Stardust was sown. Like Elton, Bowie was determined to be a success and tried various styles of music, before striking it big with *Space Oddity* in 1969. He carried himself like a star well before he became known. He had the drive and attitude as well as the songs. A lethal combination. Vince Taylor, who fronted his group The Playboys, looked every inch the rock star. His stage movements were more frenetic than Elvis, he dressed from head to toe in black leather, had the ultimate rock & roll quaffed back hair style, wore a large Joan of Arc medallion, and the girls and the guys loved him. Born in West London, he never made it in the UK, but unusually became a big star in France, being given a six-year deal with the Barclay label. He later married into the family of the American animator, Joseph Barbera. For all that, he was unpredictable character who inevitably succumbed to his personal demons, dying in 1991 aged fifty-two.

If they weren't in Julie's café across the road, publishers came to the Gioconda for coffee, so songwriters hung out in the hope of getting a

publishing deal and musicians sat for hours hoping to get a gig with a group or some session work. This was *the* meeting place, where you could potentially get access to the important people in the industry without an appointment. All you needed was the price of a tea or coffee. Every young buck hoping to make it turned up here, including David Bowie, Steve Marriott, The Kinks, Marc Bolan, Screaming Lord Sutch, Paul Simon and Jimi Hendrix.

Central Sound Studios was located on the first floor at No.9. David Bowie recorded here, including his early demo *Born of the Night,* with

the Lower Third. The Easybeats recorded here and in 1972, Sweet recorded backing tracks for Top of the Pops.

The control room at Central sound Studios.

It became the Barino before being revived as the Gioconda Dinging Room in 2008 and expanded to the Gioconda Dining Rooms. In 2014 it was renamed the Gioconda and in April that year a blue plaque was erected on the wall of No.9 by the British Plaque Trust to commemorate the songwriters and publishers of Tin Pan Alley.

The unveiling of the Blue Plaque. Left to right Tony Hiller, Mitch Murray, John Carter, Bill Martin, Donovan, Mike Read and Don Black. Credit: British Plaque Trust.

The plaque was unveiled by Donovan who recorded all his early

songs in the street and performed a song he'd written for the ceremony, appropriately titled *Tin Pan Alley*. The occasion was attended by major British songwriters, Don Black, Barry Mason, Mitch Murray, Tony Hiller, Bill Martin, Guy Fletcher and John Carter. A special message was played from Vera Lynn, whose history with the street stretches back to the 1930s.

The current restaurant is the Flat Iron, and still retains the Gioconda name, but spelled Giaconda as it has been for some years.

No. 10

This property was built between 1686-9 and was Grade II listed in 1974.

Dr John Purcell a London Physician who published *A Treatise on Vapours or Hysteric Fits* lived at No. 10 in 1730. Some of Purcell's theories were vague while others were decidedly off-beam. Purcell's thesis was that the cause of 'Vapours' lay not in the nervous system but in the Stomach and Guts. He was also of the opinion that hysteria was passed from mother to daughter and viewed epilepsy and hysteria as two different degrees of the same disease. He also warned of the danger of burying epileptic's alive, and to test whether they were still living suggested to someone, 'hold a very little fine Carded Wool, a feather, or burnt paper before their mouths.'

The property was later occupied, from 1758 to 1771, by the Reverend Dr. John James Majendie, who was appointed English Language tutor to Queen Charlotte after she left Germany in 1761 to marry George III. Charlotte remained his friend and patron, making him her domestic chaplain and tutor to her two eldest sons, the Prince of Wales, the future George IV and and Frederick, Duke of York. Majendie became vicar of Stoke Prior from 1769 to 1783, Prebendary of Netheravon in Salisbury from1752-1783 and Prebendary of the 8th Canonry at Worcester Cathedral from 1769 to 1774. He was appointed to the fifth stall in St George's Chapel, Windsor Castle in 1774 and held the canonry until his death in 1783. His son, Henry William Majendie also served as a royal tutor, to the future William IV, travelling much of the world with him, including visiting New York on board HMS Prince George in 1782, a year before the American War of Independence. In 1785 he was appointed Canon of Windsor, later becoming Bishop of Chester and then Bishop of Bangor, a post he held from 1809 until his death in 1830.

By the beginning of the 1840s, Peter Paris, an 'artificial florist' in his early fifties was at 10 Denmark Street, with his wife Sarah and their four children. They later moved to Hoxton and some of the following generations continued to work as artificial florists. Although the family name appears to have been Read, he was listed as Peter Paris in the 1841 census, when he was at Denmark Street, but by the time of the next census in 1851 he was listed as Pierre Paris. Maybe in support of the recent coup d'etat of the future Napoleon III and the coming of the Second Empire! By 1895 Peter Paris from No.10 had long been covered in real flowers, as had the French Monarchy, but the artificial florist's former home was about to make national news.

On Friday 27th September 1895, the story the papers called *The Soho Tragedy* was played out at No.10. Rose English the 22-year-old daughter of a Coddenham builder was found dead from bullet wounds while her live-in lover Cyril James Hewlett Dutta was unconscious and badly wounded. They were discovered just after midday, lying semi naked on their bed. She had bullet wounds in the left breast and left side and he had two shot wounds to the chest. Blood which had poured from their bodies, saturated the mattress and lay in pools on the floor. A box of cartridges and a miniature revolver were found on the bed. Bullets were also found in Rose English's clothes-box and in the pockets of Dutta's trousers. Correspondence was also discovered which referred to him complaining about being disinherited by his family. Dutta, a medical student at Guy's Hospital who was about to take his BA, was immediately taken to Middlesex hospital where one of the bullets was removed. At Guys he referred to himself as Hewlett, not Dutta.

Dr. Danford Thomas, the Coroner for the Islington area, opened an inquiry at St. Giles Mortuary, into the circumstances attending the death of Rose English. Dr. Thomas had been heavily involved with the 'Jack the Ripper' murders and would later be involved with the Crippen case.

Mrs Annie Bertrawd identified the body as that of her sister, who was a single woman, living with nineteen-year-old Punjabi law student

Cyril Dutta. The deceased was described as a 'Lady's Companion'. Mrs Bertrawd had never heard that either her sister or Mr. Dutta had contemplated suicide. Only the previous Wednesday, the deceased had informed her that Mr Dutta was leaving for Oxford University on the Saturday and she said that they seemed to live happily together. Mrs Gilbert, the landlady of the house in Denmark Street, supposed that on Dutta's departure for Oxford the rooms were to be given up, as he had proposed to stay there for some time. This was seen to be so as Miss English was planning a move to Chelsea.

Rose had lived at the address in Denmark Street for 14 months, being supported by a wealthy grandmother who sent her £10 a week (the equivalent of almost £1,000 a week in 2016). Dutta was the son of a wealthy West Indian Merchant who had disowned him because of his relationship with Rose English.

Dr. George Brown said that Dutta had brought Miss English to him in august suffering from rheumatic swellings and an abscess. On the Monday before the tragedy, on returning from a holiday, Dutta went to see him as it was feared that the abscess was re-forming. The Doctor saw the deceased on the Tuesday and on paying another visit on the Friday was not able to gain admission and feared that his patient may have taken a turn for the worse. The police were called and the door had to be forced.

The police broke open the bedroom door in the presence of the landlady and Dr. Brown. The witness said that she knew of nothing that would have likely led to the tragedy. On the Thursday afternoon the deceased told her that Mr. Dutta's piano was to be removed from Guy's Hospital to the new apartment and that during his time in Oxford they planned to see each other as much as possible. The housekeeper reported that both Dutta and English were out on Thursday night and that all the accused said after the tragedy was

'Rose, oh my God.' A similar testimony was given by the wife of the housekeeper of No.10, who added in reply to the jury that no firearms had ever been seen by her in the rooms occupied by her and Dutta

Dr. Brown admitted that the wounds may have been self-inflicted but it was his opinion was that they were not. Dutta admitted that they'd had words about him going to Oxford. He stated: 'She did not like my leaving. She got the revolver and shot herself. I then shot myself.' On enquiry at the Middlesex Hospital on the Monday night, Dutta was reported to be progressing as favourably as could be expected, the bulletin on him stating: 'He passed a good night, followed by a fair day. He is conscious but not yet allowed to see any of his friends.' Dr. Pepper of St. Mary's Hospital, who conducted the post-mortem examination, said that while her wounds may have been self-inflicted, from his experience it was highly unlikely that this was suicide. The initial enquiry was postponed for a month for the attendance of the hospitalised Dutta. He was still on the danger list having had a slight relapse but had moments of lucidity. Mrs Gilbert who resided at No. 10 was given permission by the house-surgeon to visit Dutta, but the patient declined to see her without giving a reason.

At another Marlborough Street Court appearance, Dutta, already on remand, was up before Mr. Curtis Bennett, charged with causing the death of Rose English at 10 Denmark Street and with attempting to commit suicide. It was revealed that on the Thursday evening, the day before the tragedy, he had appeared at the hospital trying to cash a cheque. He was invited into the secretary's office, but then strangely declined and walked away.

Dutta appeared four times at Marlborough St Court charged with having murdered Rose English on the 27th September 1895. On the fourth occasion the treasury was not represented and Mr. C.O. Humphreys who defended, stated that he had just been informed that the Treasury had not yet decided what course to pursue. Mr. Curtis Bennett said that he would be sitting on Tuesday next and would adjourn the case till that day. In the event of the case being fully gone into, he would take it on the next Wednesday.

A month before her death, the deceased had told her Landlady that she and Cyril were going to Ipswich but it was to be a secret because of Dutta's father. When they had been away for some days the landlady received a telegram from Dutta which read 'Rose is mine.' From that, she said, she had understood that the marriage had taken place. They returned a fortnight before the tragedy and seemed to be on the happiest of terms. The landlady said that she believed that Dutta loved Rose completely and could never do her harm. She thought the girl was distressed at being the cause of the estrangement between Dutta and his father, and that may have induced her to take her life.

Mr and Mrs J English arrived in town from their home in the village of Coddenham, north of Ipswich, two days after the tragedy. They were conducted to St Giles mortuary and neither had trouble recognising their daughter. Mr English made a statement in which he admitted that he knew nothing about their daughter's alleged marriage to Mr Dutta. It transpired that Dutta had been introduced to Guy's Hospital two years earlier by a religious and educational body in the East Indies, at which time he gave his name as Cyril J Hewlett. During his time in England he had been more or less under the eye of Roman Catholic priests as his parents were wealthy Mohammedans who had completely cut him off when he converted to Christianity. From that time he had been under the care of the aforementioned religious organisation from the East Indies, who took pains to secure him a good position in England. It was revealed that he spoke English fairly well, was industrious and well-behaved. He was a diligent student who passed his first examination successfully and qualified for his second examination in anatomy and physiology. An admission ticket for the latter had been presented to him in July, but he'd unusually failed to attend. It was understood that Dutta had been holidaying at Clacton on Sea. All enquiries relating to the alleged marriage at Ipswich drew a blank, but they were undoubtedly there as the presence of the two young people was noticed by the many of the locals '…whose attention was arrested by the exceptionally dark complexion of the man and the elaborate dress of the lady.' Even efforts to establish where they stayed in Ipswich proved fruitless. On Saturday November 30th the Ipswich Journal, Suffolk, Norfolk, Essex and Cambridgeshire Advertiser published a single paragraph with the headline, *Suicide of a Coddenham Girl.* After two months the Treasury had withdrawn from the prosecution of Dutta and he was discharged.

Leslie Rose, Victor Morris and Stanley Rose.

So one Rose departed from No.10 and years later, three Roses would move in. Charles and Stanley Rose set up Rose Brothers, anticipating that their brother Leslie would soon be discharged from military service. The three brothers began to trade in various items, including children's toys, with their sister Clara becoming the company secretary, a position she'd keep for forty-three years. They began in Denmark Street at No.11, soon moving to No.10. In 1920 Stanley Rose brought an old work colleague, A.V. Morris, into the company, with a name change to Rose, Morris & Co. Ltd. Sensing the business was moving slowly, Charles moved abroad, but the business was saved by the humble mouth-organ. Usually made in Germany, they had become increasingly difficult to obtain, but their re-emergence after the war gave the Rose Brothers the opportunity they'd been looking for. Despite a lack of funds, by the 1930s the company had become one of the country's largest stockists of mouthorgans.

As well as selling harmonicas at 4/6d a dozen and the now defunct C-melody saxophone, Rose Morris began selling portable gramophones at 12/6d with a deluxe model at 14/-

1930s Rose Morris gramophones.

Even when radio was in its infancy, a piece of music played simultaneously to thousands of people created a sudden demand, leading Rose Morris to becoming record factors, wholesaling Imperial, Piccadilly, Broadcast and Sterno from 8 shillings a dozen. The company went from strength to strength and in 1960 the company was acquired by Grampian Holdings, with Leslie Rose deciding it was time to leave after forty years while Stanley stayed on. In 1965, Tony Morris, the grandson of A.V. Morris joined at almost the same time that Rose Morris became sole agents for the amplifiers manufactured by one of their customers, Jim Marshall. They had also been the first British distributor for Rickenbacker guitars since 1862, demand for the brand increasing dramatically after John Lennon started playing one. Two years later they opened a retail showroom in Shaftesbury Avenue.

The Soho Love Tragedy was all but forgotten thirty years later, when Campbell Connelly Publishing moved in to this building and to No.11. The company had been founded in 1925 by Jimmy Campbell, born in Newcastle-upon-Tyne in 1903 and Reg Connelly, born in Buckhurst Hill, Essex, in 1895, after they'd had success in the States with *Show Me the Way to Go Home*, written in 1925 with Hal Swain, for which they used the pseudonyms Irving King and Ivor King, They allegedly wrote it on a tiring train journey from London during which they'd had a couple of drinks, hence the lyrics. It was referenced by George Orwell in his 1934 novel *Burmese Days* and by Norman Mailer in his 1948 novel, *The Naked and the Dead.* Brick, one of the main characters in Tennessee Williams *Cat on a Hot Tin Roof* sings this song near the end of the play. It was sung in various films including *Jaws.* The song was recorded in 1926 by thirty-seven-year-old Ohio-born Frank Crumit and subsequently covered and/or performed by many artists including, more recently Emerson, Lake & Palmer, Ozzy Osbourne, Jefferson Starship and Bono. With Ted Shapiro they wrote *If I Had You* the song being covered by many artists including Nat King Cole and Frank Sinatra.

They had another big hit with in the US with Rudy Valee's version of *Goodnight Sweetheart,* a song co-written in 1931 with Ray Noble, with covers by many other artists including Al Bowlly, Guy Lombardo, Bing Crosby and Dean Martin and was also the theme song for the 1990s sitcom *Goodnight Sweetheart.*

Campbell and Connelly also wrote the classic *Try A Little Tenderness* with Harry Woods. A perfect example of how a great song can be expressed in so many different ways and genres. First recorded in 1932 by the Ray Noble Orchestra and later by Ruth Etting, Bing Crosby and Mel Torme. As well as being a favourite with the crooners from the 1930s to the 1950s, it also became a great soul favourite in the mid-1960s, recorded by both Otis Redding and Percy Sledge. Even Three Dog Night had a US hit with their rendition in 1969 and Rod Stewart proved the song's versatility yet again when he recorded his version. Campbell and Connelly also penned the popular singalong songs, *The More We Are Together* and *Jolly Good Company.* They developed relationships with US publishing companies, Harms Inc, Robbins, Famous Music, Shapiro Berstein and De Sylva, Brown and Henderson from whom they purchased the

rights to *Sonny Boy.* They also embraced the growing film industry, teaming up with Gaumont-British and Gainsborough Pictures to bring US songwriters to the UK to write music for their productions. A UK chart from July 1947 shows three Campbell Connelly songs in the sheet music top 20, *Try A Little Tenderness* (in conjunction with Robbins Music), *Anniversary Song* and *Heartaches.*

In the early 1930s Jean Aberbach joined the company as a song plugger, possibly because of his experience with film music and his knowledge of the Paris music scene. He arranged for his brother Julian to join Campbell Connelly in 1932. The Aberbachs appeared to be employed on a commission basis, which offered little security. The brothers soon formed their own company, with Jean staying on for a while at Campbell Connelly in order to bring in the money while

Julian began to build up their own company. By the mid-thirties the brothers had made a fortune from film rights. In 1935 they sold their company SEMI to their US client Ralph Peer. Cyril Gee, after learning how the industry worked with Ascherberg, Hopwood and Crew, ran the Trade Department from 1942, at the age of fourteen, before joining Campbell Connelly in 1952. He stayed until 1954, before moving to Mills Music. Bevan Music Productions, an arm of Campbell Connelly, were also operating from the same building, publishing such songs as *New American Patrol* by Patrick Michael (1944), *My Lady Greensleeves* (1946), Reg Connolly and Reg Shapiro's song *I'll Be Loving* You (1948), *A Tree in the Meadow,* by Billy Reid and *My Favourite Samba* by Edmundo Ros (1950). Among their later successes were *When You're Young and in Love, He'll Have to Go* and *Who Do You Think You Are Kidding Mr. Hitler?* The latter was penned by Jimmy Perry as the theme for the TV series Dad's Army which he co-wrote with David Croft. It was Bud Flanagan's last-ever recording.

Tin Pan Alley songwriter Billy Reid's first successes were with Campbell Connelly. Orchestra leader, accordionist and songwriter, Billy Reid was born William Gordon Reid in 1902. He became one of the most famous bandleaders in London during the 1930s and was one of Decca's top recording stars. When singer Dorothy Squires joined his band, he saw it as an opportunity to write songs especially for her, many of them such as *A Tree in a Meadow, I'm Walking Behind You* and *The Gypsy* becoming hits in the United States. Reid also formed the London Piano-Accordion Band and appeared with Squires in the film *Saturday Night Revue* as well as topping variety bills as 'The Composer and the Voice'. Billy Reid also wrote *Coming Home* for Squires, which was released for VE day in 1945. Reid's songs were covered by many major artists, including Al Jolson, Dinah Shore, Louis Armstrong, Al Martino, Peggy Lee, the Ink Spots,

Margaret Whiting, Eddie Fisher, the latter three artists taking their versions of his songs to No.1 in the United States. The Ink Spots went to No1. With *The Gypsy* in 1946, Margaret Whiting took *A Tree in a Meadow* to the top of the hit parade two years later and in 1953 Eddie Fisher went to No.1 with *I'm Walking Behind You.* Billy Reid became Dorothy Squires' first husband, but his phenomenal success waned with the onset of the 1960s and he went from millionaire songwriter to being penniless and dying in obscurity of kidney disease in 1974.

As Ralph Butler's first hit was with Campbell Connelly, he is here at 10 and 11. Born in 1887, Butler was an active songwriter from the late 1920s to the mid-1950s. His songs were published by several companies on the street publishers on Alley, including Campbell Connelly, Sun Music, Irwin Dash, Lawrence Wright, Noel Gay, Box and Cox and others. He wrote songs such as *Let's All Go to the Music Hall* with Lawrence Wright, aka Horatio Nicholls, the street's first publisher and songwriter. Predominantly a lyricist, Butler's first big success was the million-selling *All By Yourself in the Moonlight,* written under the pseudonym of Jay Wallis in 1929. Butler also wrote *There's a Lovely Lake in London* with Tolchard Evans in 1935 and *Horsey, Horsey* in 1938 with Paddy Roberts, Elton Box and Desmond Cox, which was made famous by Billy Cotton, Jack Jackson and Henry Hall. The song was published by Sun Music at no.23. Butler, Box & Cox also penned *We Went Up Up Up the Mountain.* His collaborations with Richard Armitage (aka Noel Gay) yielded such durable songs as *The Sun Has Got His Hat On, Round the Marble Arch* and a song that Flanagan and Allen made their own, *Run Rabbit Run.* Another song they wrote together in 1944, *We Don't Know where We're Going,* was used in the war scenes in the film *Overlord*. In 1956 George Martin produced Mandy Miller singing Butler and Peter Hart's *Nellie the Elephant,* the song being published by Dash Music and becoming one of the most popular songs on the long-running radio show, *Children's Favourites*. Butler died aged eighty-two in 1969 fifteen years before the song's biggest success. It was unprecedented for someone born in 1887 to write a punk hit, but in 1984 the Toy Dolls version of *Nellie the Elephant* climbed to No. 4 in the chart. Lulu's version from the cartoon series of the same name was released in 1990 and in 2011 Black Lace also recorded a version of the song.

During the 1960s, Max Diamond, Ed Kassner's Chief manager, moved across the street to Campbell Connelly, where he'd remain until setting up his own company in 1968 at No. 5. While at Campbell Connelly he collaborated on at least one song with one of the company's writers, Bob Halfin.

Born Lazarus Isaac Halfin in London's East End, he became known for writing successful Scottish songs, including *Lonely Stornaway, The Heart of Scotland, That's Why I'll Never Leave Scotland* and *Lassie from the Isles,* for such eminent Scottish artists as Calum Kennedy, and the Alexander Brothers. Working out of Campbell Connelly, Halfin co-wrote Max Bygraves' 1955 hit *You're a Pink Toothbrush I'm a Blue Toothbrush*, which Max claimed sold three million…toothbrushes. Halfin co-wrote *The Shake*, covered by such artists as The Bonzo Dog Doo Dah Band and the Temperance Seven, with pianist Bill McGuffie and Campbell Connelly's Max Diamond who co-wrote some of Charlie Drake's hits. Halfin and McGuffie also wrote other material together. It seems that by the mid-60s, Halfin had switched publishers, signing with Ascherberg, Hopwood and Crew. His son Ross Halfin is a successful and highly-respected photographer who has worked with many top artists.

Also at the same address was Irwin Dash Music, who'd had his first success in 1911, composing and publishing *Blue Ribbon Rag*. Dash was from Philadelphia and during the 1920s wrote several successful songs including *It's a Man, It's a Man* in 1923 and *Hinky Dinky Parlay Voo* in 1924, collaborating with Irving Mills, Jimmie McHugh and Al Dubin. Later that decade he accompanied Josephine Trix of the Trix Sisters on recordings of *Magnolia* and *Ain't That Too Bad.* By the 1930s he was in London and working out of No.10 with Reg Connelly from Campbell Connelly helping him to establish a London base. From here he published several albums of popular songs and dance music and classics like Ross Parker and Hughie Charles' *We'll Meet Again* and *There'll Always Be An England,* as well as collaborating with Parker on songs such as *I Love You* for the Squadronaires and *Blue Ribbon Gal.* Dash appeared to be big on Blue Ribbons.

Ross Parker (*left*) was born Albert Rostron Parker in Manchester in 1914, and his first hit was in 1938 when *The Girl in the Blue Bonnet* got to No. 15 on the Billboard chart. His next US hit was the following year: *I Won't Tell a Soul (I Love You)* which hit No.1 on Billboard for Andy Kirk and his Twelve Clouds of Joy. He collaborated with Hughie Charles on the US No.1 as he did on *We'll Meet Again, There'll Always be an England* and *Blue Skies are Around the Corner.* Hughie Charles was born Charles Hugh Owen Ferry in Stockport, 1907. *We'll Meet Again* has had a colossal number of covers, including such artists as Vera Lynn, The Byrds, the Turtles, Russ Conway, Peggy Lee, PJ Proby, Johnny Cash, The Ink Spots, Chris Barber, Ruby and the Romantics and the Chordettes. *There'll Always be an England* was covered by Glyn Davies, his version being featured in the Carroll Levis' film, *Discoveries*, and more famously by Alfred Piccaver. Ross and Charles continued to write patriotic songs during WWII. Ross Parker also collaborated with another Tin Pan Alley writer, Tommie Connor, and wrote such songs as *Home is where the Heart is* and *Hey Neighbour*. In 1956 Parker was asked to write a song specifically to launch rising star Shirley Bassey, for whom he penned *Burn My Candle,* but the song was banned by the BBC for its sexually explicit lyrics. Ross Parker died in 1974 having written chart hits from 1938 to 1970. Hughie Charles died in 1995.

Tommie Connor (*right*), another writer whose first success came with Irwin Dash, quite rightly said, 'No more fascinating or romantic a career than song writing exists.' Born in London's West End in 1904, Tommie

Connor had his first success as a songwriter in the early 1930s with *My Home Town* and *It's My Mother's Birthday Today*. During that decade he penned many classics including the 1937 Christmas Classic *the Little Boy That Santa Claus Forgot* (written with Michael Carr and Jimmy Leach), (*Underneath) The Spreading Chestnut Tree* and *The Biggest Aspidistra in the World.* He wrote prolifically during the war years, with Vera Lynn covering two of his songs. She also famously recorded a song for which Tommie Connor penned the English lyrics in 1944, *Lili Marlene.* The original German lyrics had been written during WWI to which music had been added in 1938. Following the much-covered, *Lili Marlene,* five years later Connor wrote *The Wedding of Lili Marlene.* The 1940s also brought him covers by such artists as Gracie Fields and Anne Shelton

In 1952 Tommie penned both the words and music for what turned out to be another perennial Christmas hit, *I Saw Mommy Kissing Santa Claus,* a song covered by many artists including 13-year-old

Jimmy Boyd, who took it to No.1 in America, the song becoming one of the most-played Christmas songs ever on US radio. The song has also been recorded by such artists as Amy Winehouse, The Ronettes, The Beverley Sisters, Teresa Brewer, The Jackson 5 Andy Williams and even Pinky and Perky. The song didn't suit everybody though, as the Archdiocese of the Boston Roman Catholic Church got the song banned on Boston radio, claiming its 'sexual nature' soured the season. Columbia Records appealed to the Council of Churches, who agreed to lift the ban. In the early 50s there were more covers of Connor's songs, by Phil Tate, Joe Loss, The Radio Revellers and Josef Locke and in 1947 Connor wrote *The Wedding of the Royal Princess*, to celebrate the marriage of the future Queen Elizabeth to Prince Philip. 1955 saw Alma Cogan take his *Never Do a Tango with an Eskimo* into the UK top ten. Being of Irish descent it was only fitting that Val Doonican made a success of Connor's comic song *O'Rafferty's Motor Car.* Connor also wrote the lyrics for the song, *The Story of a Soldier* from the 1966 film, *The Good, the Bad and the Ugly* and two years later penned the patriotic *I'm Backing Britain*, the song being released by Bruce Forsyth. He starred as himself in the 1973 TV Movie, *Whatever Happened to Tin Pan Alley?* with Marc Bolan, Issy Bonn and Heinz. An incredible number of his songs have featured in films and TV shows. Tommie died in 1993.

No. 11

Watchmaker Gabriel Wirgman was resident at No.11 from the mid-1770s, trading as Moriset and Wirgman, jewellers and goldworkers. Wirgman, baptised in Sweden in 1738, married Mary Upjohn thirty years later at St Pancras Parish Church. Moving his business from Red Lion Street to Denmark Street in the 1770s. He still operated from No.11 until at least 1779 and was possibly still there until his death in 1791.

In the early 1800s there was a jewellers at No.11 but the partnership between John Samson and Randal Kennesley was dissolved by mutual consent in 1816. James Samson is also listed as being at No. 11 in 1818. In 1819 Samson and Charles Boden, trading as jewellers at the same address, also dissolved their partnership by mutual consent, but the 1823 directories still list Samson and Boden as trading as goldsmiths and jewellers at No.11. Mary Samson and Son were still trading there until at least 1843.

No, 11 is currently The Early Music Shop, selling early music and heritage instruments, including shawms, crumhorns, harps, lutes and spinets. Also working from the same building is Ricall Music Licencing, a sync music licensing service for advertising, film, TV and video.

Menlo Park Music are on the fourth floor at no. 11, named after Christopher Taylor and John Gresswell's band Menlo Park, who formed the company in 2003. They provide music for adverts, films, television, fashion, scores and compositions and have won numerous awards including a BAFTA and an Oscar nomination.

No. 12

In the 1730s, there was a James Dixon living at no.12 who was a witness to the will of one-time carpenter, Thomas Ellis, gentleman, of Richmond St. Soho. In the next decade Gedeon Macaire was living and working in the property. Born in Geneva, Switzerland in 1745, Macaire came to England in 1775, four years later entering a mark at Goldsmith's Hall in partnership with Mary Aveline, a case-maker from No.5 Denmark Street. Macaire married Ann Lamaitre in Soho in 1783 and notified a change of address to 12 Denmark Street the following year. Both their children, Gideon Paul and Jane Mary, were born there in 1784 and 1787 respectively. The family were still there in 1793, Macaire dying that year and being buried at St Giles-in-the-Fields. That same year, his widow, Ann Macaire/Lemaitre entered a mark at Goldsmith's Hall with a Peter Desvignes in partnership from 13 Denmark Street. All very respectable, but No.13 was soon to become a focal point for treason.

For a period during the first half of the 1840s, publisher and print dealer Ernest Gambart (1814-1902) worked out of No.12. The man that would become known as the greatest of all Victorian art dealers, began his career in Courtrai, Belgium, working in his father's printing, binding and book-selling business. By 1833 he had established his own print and paper-making firm in Paris, before moving to London in 1840. Two years later he formed a partnership known as Gambart & Junin, specializing in importing continental prints, the expansion of the company necessitating a move from Denmark Street to Berners Street. Known for being scrupulously fair, he became a popular figure with the establishment, mixing with the good and the great and giving lavish parties. In 1846 Gambart was granted British citizenship. Possibly Gambart's most famous publication was William Henry Simmons' engraving of Holman Hunt's *Light of the World.* On his retirement in 1870 he passed the business on to his nephew, Leon Lefevre, the company surviving today as the Lefevre Gallery in Bruton Street. Member of the Royal Victorian Order in 1898

No. 13

In the period around 1827, schoolteacher Daniel M'auliff was residing at No. 13, but back to the intrigue that would dominate the family that moved next door from No.12.

In 1793 Ann Macaire (nee Lemaitre) entered a mark at Goldsmith's Hall with a Peter Desvignes in partnership from 13 Denmark Street.

Her nephew, Paul, also came to work there, alongside his cousin, but there was trouble ahead.

Paul Thomas Lemaitre was born in 1776, to John and Frances Lemaitre and he grew up at a time when the guillotine was being put to use with frequency in France. When he was seventeen Louis XVI lost his head on the other side of the channel and there was a growing concern that the violence emanating from the 'swinish multitude' might reach England. There had already been two attempts on the life of George III, but neither were politically motivated nor connected to anarchist movements, with both would-be assassins ending up in Bethlem Hospital instead of the gallows. Nevertheless, the fear of revolution was in the air. In the midst of this uncertain atmosphere, the Austrians had invented a terrifying new weapon, the Girandoni Air Rifle, which could shoot 20 lead balls without reloading and could kill from a distance of 150 yards without the smoke or noise of a normal rifle. That made it easier for those intent on assassination, as did the new air rifle that could shoot a poisoned dart even further. No longer was there such a risk of being caught. The deed could be done silently and from a great distance. The era of the sniper had been born. Not surprisingly the government was keen to crack down on any potential dissenters or those preaching any form of anarchy. It was a dangerous time to be a supporter of anti-governmental or anti-royalist causes. At the State opening of Parliament an unruly rabble attacked George III's carriage, demanding bread and yelling such slogans as 'Down with George' and 'No King.' In the melee one of the carriage windows got smashed and the government took action. They rounded up three members of the London Corresponding Society, claiming that an attempt had been made on the King's life with a high-powered air gun, the poison dart having been shot from some distance and missing the King by inches, with the assailant making good his escape. The Government claimed that they had placed a spy within the London Corresponding Society and that this group were at the very core of the assassination attempt.

The London Corresponding Society were an organisation of artisans and working men dedicated to the cause of the reform of Parliament and universal suffrage; who met and published pamphlets expounding their cause. One of their leaders, James Parkinson, wrote tracts to that end, published under the name of 'Old Hubert'. Three members of what became known as the 'Pop-Gun Plot' conspiracy were arrested; John Smith, George Higgins and Paul Thomas Lemaitre, the latter being taken at 13 Denmark Street for his part in the plot to kill the King. A fourth member, Robert Crossfield, was arrested much later. Lemaitre would be tried for 'treasonable practices'. It was revealed that there had been a planned convention in 1793 with the aim of bringing about 'The British Convention of Delegates of the People associated to obtain Universal Suffrage and Annual Parliaments.' The Convention never actually took place, as twelve of the leading lights were arrested for 'high treason', but it was said that the 'London Corresponding Society' and Lemaitre as a very visible member were deeply interested in it. The Government decided that desperate times called for desperate measures and in May 1794 passed an 'Act to empower His Majesty to secure and detain such persons as His Majesty shall suspect are conspiring against his person and government.'

John Smith and George Higgins were repeatedly questioned by the Privy Council and subsequently acquitted, but the youngest member of the Society came out of it badly. It was reported that, 'The unfortunate Paul Thomas Lemaitre, aged eighteen, appears to have suffered worst. Arrested while working as a gold watch case maker at his cousin's house, 13 Denmark Street, Soho, he was charged with 'treasonable practices' as being a 'delegate' of the London

Corresponding Society, as being in connexion with Smith, to assassinate the King by means of a poison arrow! Arrested Saturday evening, the 27th September 1794, he was for the next three days examined closely by the Privy Council.' Various accounts revealed that Lemaitre, despite his youth, was an active and prominent member of the London Corresponding Society. In his booklet Lemaitre wrote: 'On Saturday, September 27th 1794, between the hours of seven and eight in the evening, a man knocked at the door of my cousin's house, and being informed I was within, signalled to six or seven more persons, who with him rushed into the house...Townsend emphatically called the 'Swell trap of Bow Street Office', at their head. Metcalf the spy bringing up the rear...I was only answered by oaths, and dragged down so forcibly that I was compelled to inform them that I had some knowledge of walking alone...They appeared now to be about to search for my papers, which made me demand, in a peremptory tone, a sight of the warrant: and Townsend in return claps a pistol to my head and says, 'Damn my blood I will blow your brains out if you say another word.''

Lemaitre was taken to Bridewell Prison while, back at 13 Denmark Street, the house was being ransacked and his cousin pushed forcibly down stairs. Townsend and his men confiscated some marbles, a tube and a gun. Lemaitre later claimed that the tube was part of a telescope and the gun a model. The next day the accused appeared before the Privy Council and was questioned by the Lord Chancellor.

The following is from Paul Lemaitre's pamphlet.

Q: Where do you live?
A: No. 13 Denmark Street, Soho.
Q: What trade are you of?
A: Gold watch case maker.

Q: Are you in business for yourself?

A: No.

Q: What age are you?

A: Just eighteen.

Q: Where do you work?

A: At the same place where I live.

Q: Whom do you work with?

A: My cousin, Mrs Ann Macaire and Mr. Peter Desvignes.

Despite his tender years Lemaitre wasn't afraid of being cockily witty.

Q: Have you ever been abroad?

A: No.

Q: Have you ever travelled?

A: Never farther than Richmond, and other small places about the same distance.

He also fought his quarter, complaining that he hadn't eaten for 24 hours, mentioning his rights and often refusing to answer questions.

Q: Are you a member of the London Corresponding Society?

A: I must again refuse answering any questions until I see by what authority I have bene brought here. I have not yet seen any other than that of pistols, and when I demanded, last night, to a sight of my warrant a pistol was put to my head and my hands were bound....I do declare I will not answer another word until you comply with my request.

Despite being informed on being arrested that the charge was 'highway robbery', the court showed him a warrant that declared the charges against him to be 'treasonable practices'. Even then he argued that it wasn't a legal warrant as they had his initials the wrong way around. He displayed all the confidence and arrogance that Oscar Wilde would two hundred years later, even when questioned by a forceful William Pitt the Younger. Lemaitre often let his gaze wander through the window to an adjacent tennis court. When questioned whether he had any friend who could identify his handwriting, he responded: 'Having no-one who is a judge of writing and knows my hand-writing, I must decline.'

A lack of humility possibly didn't help his cause, but they had to be seen to make an example out of someone and so Lemaitre was imprisoned. He was the first person to be sent to the newly rebuilt gaol at Coldbath Fields, Clerkenwell, or as he called it, the 'British Bastille.' LeMaitre wrote several letters to the Lords of the Privy Council in 1795 from the House of Correction, who finally agreed to his release on the 9th May 1795, the lad

BIRD'S-EYE VIEW OF COLDBATH FIELDS PRISON.

having remained incarcerated for 32 weeks, during which time his mother died of grief,. Back at No. 13 Denmark Street he reflected on his situation:

'Restored again to society, to my relations and friends, the scenes, in which I had been so material a sufferer seemed to me like a dream. I could scarce believe, when sitting at my place at the work-shop, that I had been taken from that very work-shop, carried before the Privy Council and examined by a set of men supposed, from their stations, to be much superior in their wisdom to their neighbours; that, after this, I have been confined in dismal cells, being subject to the tyranny of a jailer, and charged with the guilt of high treason. All this appeared like a tale in the Arabian Nights. I was to have killed the King with a poisoned arrow. Fools! What poison have we efficacious enough for this purpose...what end could it answer to take away his life? George the Fourth would have succeeded George the Third...if a young man under twenty could harbour the design of killing the King, what a shocking age we must live in...'

Lemaitre published a work on the alleged conspiracy in 1795 titled, *High Treason! Narrative of the arrest, examinations, before the Privy Council, and imprisonment of P.T. L. accused of being a Party in the Pop-Gun Plot, or a pretended Plot to kill the King etc.*

Aſſaſſination of the King!

OR, THE

Pop-Gun Plot Unravelled;

CONTAINING AN ACCOUNT OF THE APPREHENSION, TREAT-
MENT IN PRISON, AND REPEATED EXAMINATIONS

BEFORE THE PRIVY COUNCIL,

OF

JOHN SMITH AND GEORGE HIGGINS,

ON A CHARGE OF

HIGH TREASON:

The frontispiece for Paul Lemaitre's book published in 1795.

As an appendix to the affair, the young Lemaitre wrote with wisdom beyond his years:

'The steady purpose of my soul is not at all affected by my imprisonment....let is show the hirelings of a profligate administration that if great men, noble personages, high born politicians can chop and change about at random, to get a ribband, a pension, a place or a title, we of the Swinish Multitude have still some principles left in us, that we can act for the public good without their mean and mercenary motives, that to honest men, spies are no terror, to brave men dungeons no control, that we have only one purpose in view, to obtain our rights, the freedom of election and annual parliaments, and that in pursuing these rights we are not instigated by a spirit of faction, but a true desire to serve the best interests of our country. When liberty is established on this basis, we shall hear no more of espionage, of idle alarms, or imaginary plots to overthrow the state or to kill the king....we shall be one nation intent on securing to each man the uncontrouled exercise of his abilities and industry, and instead of interfering in the private concerns of other countries, and wasting the blood and treasures of our own in foolish schemes and ambition, by which a few only are benefitted, we shall learn to set a due value on our own rights, to respect those of our neighbours, we shall be in reality, what it is intended we ought to be by our constitution- A FREE AND HAPPY PEOPLE.'

His days of incarceration weren't over though. In 1798 he was committed to trail at Newgate prison where he had been sent on the order of the Secretary of State on charges of treasonable practices. There is no verdict on record, which could ominously point to there being no trial, but records show that he was transferred to Reading Gaol in August 1799. The Times newspaper of 16th December 1800 reported that Lemaitre had angrily petitioned the House of Commons that while he was in gaol on a charge a high treason, absolutely no evidence had been produced against him. He complained that while in Coldbath Fields, for a second time, he had suffered much bodily injury and was now confined to Reading. He lost the vote in the House to decide whether his petition should be accepted. By 1801 he was again at liberty, as he married Caroline Coe in September of that year and entered a mark as a case maker the following year at Goldsmith's Hall. Lemaitre and Caroline had four children and he was a member of the Cordwainers Company by 1808 and the Clockmakers Company between 1815 and 1824. Widowed, he married Elizabeth Woodhams in 1825 and had two more children. After a variety of jobs, he worked with his son Frederick as watchmakers in 1828, but by 1832, he was in Guyana at Berbice, as an Assistant protector of Slaves, the year after it had been merged with Demerara-Essequibo to form the new crown colony of British Guiana which became Guyana in 1966.

Lemaitre survived being shipwrecked in Pevensey Bay in 1833 and lived to a good age, being listed as a Colonial Civil Servant living in Hammersmith in 1851 and as retired in 1861. Lemaitre died in 1864, aged eighty-seven, having been on an extraordinary journey since that life-changing knock on the door of 13 Denmark Street in 1794.

No. 14

Until his death in 1845, Alexander Strathern operated at No.14 as a baker, the business presumably being purchased or taken over by one Gottleib Weiss who ran the business until 1866. Within a few years the house would seemingly disappear under the new Charing Cross Road which was opened in 1887.

No. 15

The appropriately named Joshua Flies worked out of No.15 as a tailor and habit maker in the early 1840s. This address would also appear to be lost under the redevelopment of Charing Cross Road, depending on whether what is now Wunjo guitars at 126, Charing Cross Road once had two or three entrances on to Denmark Street.

No. 16

It's doubtful that head honcho Terry Slater or any of the folk at Robbins Music at 1-6 Denmark Place, realised that one of their copyrights, in a roundabout way, was inspired by a young man who visited Denmark Street in 1844. Robbins published what was to become a highly durable song, written by singer Peggy Lee for a 1958 film. As well as being one of America's most popular singers of the era, Lee was also a prolific songwriter, having written a US No.1, *Manana*, and many other successful numbers. She provided four songs for the film *Tom Thumb*, starring Russ Tamblyn, Terry-Thomas and Peter Sellers, one of which was *Tom Thumb's Tune*. The storyline is about a couple of rogues who try to exploit Tom for their own gain. Whilst he may not have been a rogue as such, it has a ring of P.T. Barnum bringing his self-styled Tom Thumb to England in 1844, where Denmark Street became part of their story.

General Tom Thumb was brought to London in the spring of 1844 by showman and businessman, Phineas Taylor 'P.T.' Barnum, his half fifth cousin twice-removed. Born Charles Sherwood Stratton in 1838 in Connecticut, he never grew to more than 102 cm, but Barnum sensed that he could make money from the boy. He taught him to sing, dance, mime and impersonate famous people, and took him on extensive tours of Europe raking money in from the pocket-sized entertainer. On his first visit to London, he met Queen Victoria, Prince Albert, the Prince of Wales and the Duke of Wellington at Buckingham Palace, the Queen taking his hand and showing him around. Her Majesty asked him to perform a song and he sang '*Yankee Doodle*' for her. He also dined with Baroness Rothschild and other eminent London Society folk as well as making his debut at the Princess's Theatre at no.73 Oxford Street. The numbering changed so No. 73 is now No. 150, the site later becoming Woolworth, then HMV and now Sports Direct. So if you bought your CDs in that branch of HMV, you were on the very spot where Tom Thumb sang his songs in 1845. Barnum then showed off his protege on at the Egyptian Hall, Piccadilly, cannily pretending that the seven-year-old boy was actually eleven. The Princess's Theatre was a just a few minutes' stroll from Denmark Street, so maybe its proximity meant that Barnum and 'Tom' took a walk and came across a nearby company would build a suitable carriage for the boy, at No.16. As reported in the Illustrated London news on August 31st 1844, the equipage for General Tom Thumb was made at 16 Denmark Street, by Mr. Beaton:

'Mr. S. Beaton, of No. 16, Denmark-street, Soho, has just built for his Generalship an elegant dress chariot, suitable to the dimensions of the hero. The body of the chariot is twenty inches high, and eleven inches wide. It is completely furnished in the richest lining, lace, lamps, blinds, and plate glass windows, spring &c. The colour of the body is an intense blue, elegantly picked out in white; the wheels are blue and red….upon the door panel are emblazoned the General's arms, Brittania and the Goddess of Liberty supported by the British Lion and the American Eagle; crest the rising sun and the British and American Flags; the motto 'Go-a-Head.' The crest is also repeated on the body and on the harness, made by Messrs Fillingham of Whitechapel-Road. The box is furnished with a superb crimson hammer-cloth, elegantly trimmed, with a silver star and red and green flowers. The Carriage will be drawn by a pair of Shetland-ponies which have been purchased off Mr. Batty, of Astley's Royal Amphitheatre. Two lads have been engaged as coachman and footman; they wear liveries of sky-blue coats, and with aguilettes tipped with silver; red breeches with silver garters and buckles; buttons, plated, cocked hats and wigs; the footman provided with a cane. The whole turn-out cost between £300 and £400. The carriage has been exhibited, gratuitously in the drawing room of the manufacturer, it is, really, a very elegant affair, and highly credible to the taste and skill of the builder.'

General Tom Thumb's Carriage. Made in Denmark Street 1844.

John Hennessey and John Langley were working as cabinet makers from the same address, so they may well have had a hand in the making of the carriage, but their partnership lasted only a little while longer. A year later, a copy of the London Gazette for July declared: 'Notice is hereby given the Co-partnership lately existing between John Hennessey and John Langley carrying on business at no. 16 Denmark Street, in the Parish of St Giles-in-the-Fields, in the County of Middlesex, of cabinet and chair makers under the firm of Hennessey and Langley was this day dissolved by mutual consent, being the 30th day of July 1845.' There was also another coachmaker at the other end of the street to Beaton; Robert Costello, who operated from No.1.

P.T.Barnum and General Tom Thumb

General Tom Thumb made his final appearance in England in 1878, dying just five years later at the age of forty-five. The contrast between the opulent carriage that would have cost £25-35,000 in today's money sitting in Seaton's drawing room at No. 16 and the circumstances of the occupants who were there forty-seven years later couldn't have been sharper. In 1881, forty-one-year-old Henry Sharp, an out of work porter, lived at No. 16 with his wife Sarah, a laundress. Born in 1865, Henry and his wife appeared to have three of their children living with them, sixteen-year-old Henry, who was employed at the Lead Works, John, fourteen and Charles, twelve - both still at school. A hundred years on and the premises would be full of young hopefuls not only looking for guitars, but also for a manager/publisher/agent who could do for them what P.T. Barnum did for 'General Tom Thumb'. For most though, there would be no ornate carriage and liveried footmen, but an unreliable 15cwt Commer or Bedford van, shared with three or four other group members and a roadie. But possibly Henry and his family pre-empted the street's musical future over eighty years earlier, having five Sharps in one flat.

No. 17

In 1843 William Sounes, a dye-sinker and engraver, late of 17 Denmark Street was languishing in London's Debtors Prison and later Louis Braun print seller German painter famous for his battle scenes, who died in 1916, occupied the premises. Braun's son, Hanns, born 1886, was a top athlete who would take silver and bronze medal at the London Olympics in 1908 for the 1600 metre relay and 800 metres respectively. Hanns also took the silver in the 400 metres at the Stockholm Olympics in 1912. He became a fighter pilot and died fighting for his country a month before the end of WW1. He was inducted into Germany's Sports Hall of Fame in 2008

No. 18

Where the hairdressers, Constantinou Brothers, now concentrate on the outside of clients' heads, the radical reformers that began here a hundred and sixty-five years ago were more concerned with the inner workings of the cranium.

The Denmark Street area was a stronghold for the O'Brienites, the followers of the Chartist, Bronterre O'Brien, who formed the National Reform League in 1849. They were believers in artisan radicalism and big on land reform, with settlements also being established in the States. The Chartists six-point People's Charter included demands for universal manhood suffrage, a secret ballot and payment for MPs.

Once again, the country rose up to demand a vote for the ordinary working man.

In 1850, O'Brien (*right*) leased an empty chapel at 18 Denmark Street and renamed it the Eclectic Institute/Eclectic Hall. It opened its doors to the public in January 1851 and would be the permanent home for the National Reform League for the next quarter of a century. O'Brien was so frustrated that London's working men were unable to comprehend  advanced Socialist principles, he transformed the Hall into an educational institution, where the more advanced students taught the beginners, and there were 'Eclectic Young Men's Educational Classes' and classes in 'English grammar and composition, French, mathematics and sciences.' O'Brien also delivered weekday lectures and Sunday discourses at no. 18 on the finer points of his philosophy. Like most Chartists, O'Brien believed that adult education programmes, libraries and a fluency in literature were essential to political liberation. By the early 1850s O'Brien's health began to deteriorate, as did his relationship with reform leaders, with the result that the NRL leadership was gradually passing into the hands of his disciples. The activities at the Eclectic Hall drew the attention of Karl Marx, who in 1852, alerted Frederick Engels to the appearance there of the poet, novelists and Chartist, Ernest Jones. Even after the death of O'Brien in 1864 the O'Brienites continued to hold their meetings at the Eclectic Hall, Denmark Street, two of the leading lights being Charles and James Murray who were inspired by the message of O'Brien's 1830s book, Poor Man's Guardian which flew the flag for currency reform and land nationalisation. The O'Brienites front man in Denmark Street was John Radford, who wrote in the *National Reformer in* 1869:

'The O'Brienite principles are eagerly sought after and enquired into and the people generally speak approvingly of the aims and objects of the new colonists. Labour is recognised as the only true dignity and there are no merchant millionaires or aristocratic blockhead princes in the locality to devour the people's industry.'

The O'Brienites also played an important part in the First International that also met in the Eclectic Hall. Also known as the International Working Men's Association, First International was formed in 1864 by Secretary of the London Trades Council, George Odger, Henri Tolain and the historian Edward Spencer Beesley, to support the working man, fight capitalism and establish a socialist society. Odger, First International's first, and only, president, has a blue plaque erected to him at his home in St Giles High Street. The plaque is now on the wall of St Giles-in-the-Fields Church a few yards from where he held his meeting as no.18. A republican club established during the radical revival that followed the outbreak of the Paris Commune in 1871 would later use the hall. It was formed in the wake of France's defeat in the Franco-German war and the collapse of Napoleon III's Second Empire.

No. 19

After WWI, Lawrence Wright moved his publishing company from No.8 to No 19. Writing under both his own name and that of Horatio

Nicholls, he penned over six hundred songs. In 1927, while visiting the States with Jack Hylton's wife Ennis, he wrote a new song, *Shepherd of the Hills.* Desperate to get it arranged immediately, he got Ennis to sing it on a transatlantic phone call so one of his Demark Street arrangers, Leighton Lucas, could score it for a show at the Alhambra that evening. The cost of the phone call was £350, but songs were big money and bandleaders could command some £700 a week. Lawrence Wright was certainly moving into the modern age as two years later his composition *You're In My Heart* became the first song to be sent across the Atlantic by Marconi photo-radio. One of his most successful songs, written with Edgar Leslie, was *Among My Souvenirs*, covered by everyone from Frank Sinatra to Judy Garland. On an old Pathe News clip, Lawrence Wright can be seen writing in his office and playing piano as Judy Shirley sings his new 1938 song 'I'*m Saving the Last Waltz for You*.

Lawrence Wright and some of his stars, toasting his new protege, Julie Andrews. They have alcohol...Julie has tea!

Wright founded the Melody Maker here at No. 19 in 1926, primarily as a magazine for dance band musicians, with whole page adverts costing £10 a page and classifieds a shilling a line. This was the year they also started to review gramophone records. The periodical's first editor was Edgar Jackson, who would later lose his entire, and highly valuable record collection to a land mine, during the London Blitz in 1941. Edgar Jackson died in 1967. Noel Gay Organisation would later move here, but their main story is at No. 24.

After being sacked by Mills Music, Eric Hall started work here in 1965, packing parcels and taking the tea urn to Julie's café on the corner of Denmark Street. Former member of the Raindrops vocal group Len Beadle also joined Lawrence Wright as professional manager in 1965 having previously written songs for artists such as Adam Faith and Gene Pitney. In 1968 he was poached by ATV Music, wrote the theme to *Rupert the Bear,* and remained with the company for nine years until moving to CBS's publishing company, April Music.

No. 20

No. 20 is another property that was built in 1686-9 and was Grade II listed in 1974. It included 16 Denmark Place, a former warehouse for No. 20. It was also another building taken over by the 'Little Tokyo' Japanese community between the wars.

Yamanka Chushi came to London with his cousins in 1924, married a 20-year-old English girl, Winifred Cornell, and initially set up as a jeweller in New Bond Street, targeting English customers. A linchpin of the Japanese community, he moved his premises to No. 20 Denmark Street in the mid-thirties, added cameras, books, watches and even golf clubs to his merchandise, and also began selling to Japanese clientele. Starting out as Yamanko & Co he later changed his trading name to Chushier. Chushi and Winifred had three children, one boy fighting for the Japanese Navy in World War II and the other for the Royal Navy. Their daughter, Joyce, later commented, 'When I was growing up, yes, my father must have been pretty well-to-do...they had a cook, a housekeeper, a live-in maid, a weekly gardener, a nanny after I was born and somebody who came to do the sewing once a month.'

Despite being part of the Japanese community in Denmark Street and embracing his adopted country, Chushi appears to have been deported at the beginning of World War II. He and his wife never lived together again. Winifred died in London in 1972.

Winifred and Yamanka Chushi with their children.

The building was soon to house a publisher who would become a major player in the music industry. In 1894, Isadore Minsky emigrated to the United States from Ukraine with his parents and brother Jacob, Isadore later reworking their names to Irving and Jack Mills. After their father died Irving took a number of jobs until he married Beatrice Wilensky, moved to Philadelphia and started to work for publisher Leo Fiest. Jack was working for the publishing firm of Joseph McCarthy and Fred Fisher. In 1919, the brothers founded Jack Mills Music, which they would rename Mills Music in 1928. The Mills brothers discovered many great songwriters

including Hoagy Carmichael, Sammy Fain and Dorothy Fields. Irving also put his own group together, with Tommy Dorsey, Jimmy Dorsey and other top musicians, some line-ups included Glenn Miller and Benny Goodman.

Irving Mills

Irving signed Duke Ellington in 1925 and managed him from 1926 to 1939. In owning 50% of Duke Ellington Inc., his name appeared on songs that became standards such as *Mood Indigo* and *It Don't mean a Thing (If it Ain't Got That Swing)*. Irving Mills was also one of the first to record black and white musicians together on such tracks as Duke Ellington's *St. Louis Blues*. Despite a limited vocabulary, Irving was an impressive lyricist, co-writing *Minnie the Moocher* with Cab Calloway. He also formed an all-female orchestra in 1934, formed subsidiary companies, record labels and became the head of the American Record Company, which became Columbia Records. When radio became popular he went to the stations, a pianist in two, singing and promoting his songs. In 1948 he acquired Arcadia Music in London, who mainly dealt in film, show and light classical music. He remained active in Music Publishing until he sold Mills Music in 1965. Irving Mills passing away at the age of ninety-one in 1985, being survived by four sons, one daughter, and 56 grandchildren and great-grandchildren!

Renate 'Mickie' Schuller and her brother came to England from Germany at the tail end of 1938 on the boat train to Southampton. Initially living with their grandparents, their parents joined three months later, although her father, Adolf, was interned on the Isle of Man for a year. She picked up English very quickly and left school in 1950 with her sights set on the music industry. A friend of her parents knew the head of Mills Music, Harry Ralton, but he could never remember her name and called her Mickie after Mickey Mouse. Ralton, born in 1907, was also a songwriter, composing with the likes of Tommie Connor. In 1953, when Ralton died, Fred Jackson, a former commando, took over command, Mickie becoming his secretary.

Mills Music (far right) in 1955 with Lawrence Wright next door.

In April 1955 Jack Mills sailed to England to meet with Jackson and inspect the Mills premises. When Jackson left, Mickie Schuller took over as Head of the Light Orchestral and Music Department. Mickie Schuller broke new ground by becoming Britain's first-ever female song plugger, which meant that she was responsible for getting anything on the Arcadia/Mills catalogues played or performed by Orchestra leaders, radio stations or artists. Mickie later described the importance of plugging the radio and TV shows, 'To get it played on *Two-Way Family Favourites* or *Housewives Choice* for radio and the television disc spots would be *Off the Record* and the *Jack Jackson Show*.' Through her work she met Matt Monroe, the two of them both in unhappy marriages. They fell in love, married in 1959 and had two children. Matt died in 1985 and Mickie in 2010.

Cyril Gee, who was born Cyril Goldberg, had worked in sheet music from the age of fourteen before joining Campbell-Connelly in 1952 and moving to Mills Music in 1954 as a salesman. He was promoted to General Manager and when Fred Jackson retired in 1958, he became MD of Mills Music Ltd. and BF Wood Music Company at £35 a week. At the same time, it was announced that R. Alan Syrett would remain as a director and Stanley Corrie would be appointed as a new director. The founder Jack Mills said he was 'Extremely pleased with the enthusiasm and confidence given to him by the entire organisation.' Did Mills let offices or PO boxes? Or was the Linton School of Songwriting affiliated in some way?

In Chicago's Popular mechanics magazine in 1956 there was an advertisement which ran: 'EARN money writing words. Tunes, for TV, records, radio. Details free. Linton School of Songwriting, 20 Denmark Street. London W.C.2 England.' The company also advertised in the Musical Times, although you had to send a penny stamp in order to receive details and the Spectator, claiming, 'Famous entertainment stars tell how in a 16 page illustrated booklet, free from

Linton School of songwriting, 20, Denmark Street, W.C.2' By 1961 Linton had moved to Frensham in Surrey.

Another member of the Mills team was Ernest Tomlinson, born into a musical family in Rawtenstall, Lancashire and later becoming head Chorister at Manchester Cathedral in 1939. After serving in WWII he became a Bachelor of Music and was made a Fellow of the Royal College of Organists. On coming to London he worked as a staff arranger for Arcadia and Mills Music, providing scores for radio, television, stage and recording studios. He was organist at a Mayfair Church and formed the Ernest Tomlinson Light Orchestra. In 1984, after discovering that the BBC were about to dispose of their light music archive he took charge of it and founded The Library of Light Orchestral Music, which contains over 50,000 works. Tomlinson won two Ivor Novello Awards and was awarded the MBE in 2012. Tomlinson's younger brother Fred performed the music for Monty Python's Flying Circus.

Composer Carey Blyton, the nephew of children's author Enid Blyton, was music editor at Mills from 1959-1963, having trained as a composer during the 1950s. He went on to become the music editor of Faber and Faber from 1964-1974 and became Benjamin Britten's personal editor. Blyton later wrote *Bananas in Pyjamas* and incidental music for *Dr. Who.*

Cy Payne was among the arrangers at Mills Music, having started in the business in 1950 and was also the Assistant Musical Director for Jack Good's TV Show *Oh Boy!* He later arranged for many other TV shows, including *Come Dancing* and *The Hot Shoe Show,* formed his own orchestra and composed for many films including *Some Like It Cool* and *Out of the Shadow.* He's been MD on tours from Billy Connolly to Patrick Moore and worked with a considerable number of military bands since 1965. Cy and his band still play for the

Sandringham Estate Christmas Party every year. Well over sixty-five years in the business and still performing.

When Eric Hall, the nephew of songwriter Tony Hiller, who had the job of tea boy, was sacked in 1965 by Fred Hartnell, the head of Mills' trade department, for being economical with the truth to secretary Jo Wright, Cyril Gee replaced him with a young lad called Reg Dwight. Reg was suggested to him by the company's professional manager, Pat Sherlock, who knew the lad's father through football connections. Reg's cousin was Roy Dwight, the former Fulham and Nottingham Forest player then playing out his career at Millwall. Dwight won an FA Cup Winner's medal in the 1959 Cup Final, but was famously stretchered off with a broken leg. Reg would become even more famous than his cousin and would also become heavily associated with football, becoming chairman at Watford FC. Reg, who would later re-name himself Elton John, was taken on at £5 a week, but soon began composing his own material. Cyril Gee was surprised, and said to his wife, 'You won't believe this, but even the office boy is writing songs.' Elton would borrow one of the pianos used by the company's arrangers, when they weren't around. In October 1969 he wrote *Your Song,* which would become his first hit single several years later. Elton also mentioned Denmark Street in his 1974 song, *Bitter Fingers.*

Paul Simon went into Mills Music with two songs, *The Sound of Silence* and *Homeward Bound* but had them rejected. Cyril Gee continued to run the company when it later merged with another publisher to become Belwin-Mills.

Some family ties to Tin Pan Alley go back a long way. Plugger turned songwriter, Tony Hiller, followed in the footsteps of his uncle, Joe Hiller, also a plugger turned songwriter, born in 1889 in Spitalfields, London. Joe began his career in 1907 as future Marx Brother Chico

Marx's singing partner, before going on to write lyrics and promoting Irving Berlin's music. Along the way he also worked with the likes of Al Jolson, Eddie Cantor, Perry Como and Groucho Marx. Joe died in 1973, but the family legacy lived on in his nephew Tony.

Born in London in 1926 Tony Hiller was a long-term fixture at Mills Music, joining in the late 1950s and later signing songwriters Roger Cook and Roger Greenaway to the company. Hiller began as one half of song and dance act, The Hiller Brothers, with his brother Irving. They released singles and appeared on stage with dozens of major artists including The Shadows, Gene Vincent, Alma Cogan, Tommy Cooper, The Dallas Boys and Kathy Kirby. 'My brother Irving and I initially joined Mills as record pluggers, as we knew Cyril Gee from trying to push our own songs to him. He just asked us if we fancied working for the company, so we took over from their existing plugger, Pat Sherlock and began pushing songs to radio and TV, particularly representing the Leroy Anderson catalogue. I also went all over the country promoting the Mills Music catalogue to theatre organists.'

Tony Hiller also specialised in writing light orchestral music, *Midnight Tango* being one of his most popular works in that genre and picking up many covers and even being featured in 2008 in Australia's version of *Strictly Come Dancing*, *Dancing with the Stars*. Tony would mix and work with the likes of top songwriters Tommie Connor, Jimmy Kennedy and publisher Jimmy Philips.

'Jimmy was the biggest in Tin Pan Alley throughout the 50s and into the 60s. As pop music took hold I signed such writers such as Marty Wilde and his sometime collaborator, Ronnie Scott and also Perry Ford, later a member of the Ivy League. I plugged our catalogue at the BBC and was writing songs at the same time. We'd rehearse our songs in the graveyard at St Giles Church, before going in to record at either Regent Sound or Central Sound.'

Scott Walker and Matt Monroe remain Tony's favourite singers; he even wrote Matt's last single release, *You Bring out the Best in Me*. Tony Hiller became one of our most successful songwriters with over 500 artists having recorded songs that he has written and co-written, including Elton John, Olivia Newton-John, Andy Williams, Sonny and Cher, The Miracles, Crystal Gayle, Bobby Vinton, The Fortunes, The Osmonds, Glen Campbell and The Hollies. Tony wrote and produced numerous hits for Brotherhood of Man, including the much-covered *United We Stand, Save Your Kisses for me, Angelo* and *Figaro*. Tony must hold the record for having written the most songs for different football clubs; Manchester United FC, Liverpool FC. Everton FC, Crystal Palace FC, Chelsea FC, the Scottish World Cup Squad and the England World Cup Squad of 1986. Tony has also written eight Eurovision songs including the No.1 and song of the year, *Save Your Kisses for Me,* which to date has had an incredible 315 different covers. The fruits of his incredibly impressive career include six Ivor Novello Awards, eight ASCAP Awards and over forty platinum, gold and silver discs. During his long career he has written over 2,000 songs and is still an active songwriter, working his material and enjoying it as much as he ever did; 'I entered this industry when it was a cottage industry and now it's come a full circle and is a cottage industry once again.'

Endless gold discs! Tony Hiller with Brotherhood of Man.

A much-loved figure in Tin Pan Alley and the music industry in general, Tony Hiller passed away in 2018. As well as wring hits himself, Tony also saw potential in two budding songwriters he signed to Mills Music…Roger Cook and Roger Greenaway.

Former members of the Kestrels, Roger Cook and Roger Greenaway became a formidable writing partnership. After Hiller signed them, they had their first hit with *You've Got Your Troubles,* a transatlantic hit for The Fortunes in 1965. That same year they began performing as David and Jonathan, having hits with *Michelle* and their own song, *Lovers of the World Unite.* Their final single as a singing duo and another of their own compositions, *Softly Whispering I Love you* became a big hit in 1971 for The Congregation. Their many other hits, some with collaborators, some not, are too numerous to mention, but among them are *I've Got You On My Mind, When You Are A King & My Baby Loves Lovin'* for White Plains, *Banner Man, Melting Pot & Good Morning Freedom* for Blue Mink, *Long Cool Woman in a Black Dress* and *Gasoline Alley Bred* for the Hollies, *Home Lovin' Man* (Andy Williams), *Something's Gotten Hold of My Heart* (Gene Pitney, and Gene Pitney & Marc Almond), *Something Tells Me (Something's Gonna Happen Tonight)* (Cilla Black) and *A Way of Life* (Family Dogg). In 1969 Roger Cook became lead vocalist, with Madelaine Bell, of Blue Mink, for whom he co-wrote most of their hits, while Roger Greenaway teamed up with Tony Burrows to sing as The Pipkins and was briefly a member of Brotherhood of Man. The New Seekers' *I'd Like to Teach the World to Sing (In Perfect Harmony)* began life as a Cook and Greenaway song called *True Love and Apple Pie*, which they subsequently rewrote with Coca-Cola account executive Bill Backer and Billy Davis, to have it used as a Coca-Cola radio commercial. First aired on American radio in 1970, it was used a year later in their TV commercial, sparking public demand for its release as a single. Reworked, to remove brand references, the single was recorded by the New Seekers and climbed to No.1 in the UK and No.7 in the US in 1972.

Cook and Greenaway were the only writers to be awarded Ivor Novellos two years running for Songwriter/s of the Year. Roger Cook moved to the US in 1975, having more success writing songs like *Talking in Your Sleep* for Crystal Gayle and *Love is on a Roll* for Don Williams. Roger Greenaway then worked with other partners, notably Geoff Stephens, the pair writing successfully for Crystal Gayle, as well as teaming up with Barry Manilow and also writing for Tom Jones. Roger Greenaway took an increasing role in the business side of the industry, becoming Chairman of the Performing Rights Society in 1983 and in 1995 taking charge of the ASCAP office. He also wrote jingles for Allied Carpets, Asda and British Gas. In 1997 Roger Cook was elected to the Nashville Songwriters Hall of Fame. The following year Roger Greenaway was awarded the OBE for services to the music industry and was inducted into the Songwriters Hall of Fame in New York in 2009. The boys from Mills Music did all right for themselves, Tony Hiller having spotted their talent.

The Mills Music building is now Wunjo Guitars.

Roger Cook and Roger Greenaway.

No. 21

Giles Loyer entered a maker's mark at Goldsmith's Hall in 1799 as a gold worker from 21 Denmark Street and was assessed to Land Tax on an unnamed property (Denmark Street) in St Giles-in-the-Fields from 1798-1822. Trade directories for 1811 and 1822 describe him respectively as a goldsmith and engine turner, and gold and silversmith, working from No. 21. Loyer died in 1822, his will being proved for probate on 8th May. Eight years later, The Times newspaper of 15th July 1831 carried the notice of sale of two rose engines, the property of the late Giles Loyer. During his time there, one of his most unusual employees was Mary Ann Talbot.

Talbot, who'd served in the French Revolutionary Wars dressed as a man, worked in Denmark Street from around 1799: 'The money I'd received from his Royal Highness the Duke of York being expended, the idea struck me that if I could obtain a machine similar to the one I'd observed the German use in the prison at St Clare, with which he manufactured the gold-wire, I might obtain a comfortable subsistence. For that purpose I called on Mr Loyer, a jeweller in Denmark Street, St Giles, in order, if possible, to get a machine made from my description. Mr Loyer, from my instructions, soon produced an instrument that in every way answered the purpose. And having informed him of the use for which it was intended he informed me that if I were to manufacture it in his house, he had no doubt he could, from his connections, dispose of enough to keep me constantly employed. I made no objection to his proposal and worked gold wire in various shapes, so much to his satisfaction that I continued in his employ for some time. Mr Loyer kept a number of persons employed, I worked in the same department as some others, among whom was a German, named Heironimo...At the time of my employ with Mr Loyer I put on my seaman's dress and accompanied the procession when their majesties went to St Paul's...I was one of Lord Howe's attendants and rode on the car, and the chains of the bracelets which her majesty wore on the occasion where made by me at Mr Loyer's by order of Messrs Gray and Constable, jewellers of Sackville Street, Piccadilly.'

Born in 1778, she would later claim to be one of the sixteen illegitimate children of Lord William Talbot, Baron of Hensol. Her mother died in childbirth when she was four-years-old resulting in her being brought up by an assortment of guardians, before going to a boarding school in Chester. She fell into the hands of a Mr. Sucker, who was in charge of her inheritance left from her sister. By 1792 at the age of fourteen, she became the mistress of Captain Essex Bowen who enlisted her as his footboy under the pseudonym John Taylor for a voyage to Santo Domingo. The regiment, the 82nd of Foot were diverted to fight in Flanders against the French, where she became a drummer boy in the battle for Valenciennes. In the battle, Bowen was killed and she was wounded by a sabre. From Bowen's letters she discovered that Sucker had squandered her inheritance, so she made the decision to continue working as a male sailor. She eventually deserted, fleeing through Luxembourg into Germany and became a cabin boy on a French ship. When the British navy captured the vessel, she was transferred to the *Brunswick* and serves as a powder monkey. Talbot was

Mary Anne Talbot.
alias
John Taylor.
Foot Boy Drummer Sailor &c &c &c.

wounded again fighting the French in 1794, when grapeshot almost severed her leg.

On recovery, she rejoined and was later captred by the French and spent eighteen months in a dungeon in Dunkirk. She was able to return to London in 1796, where she signed on as a clerk aboard and American merchantman. Circumstances forced her to return to England after the captain's niece declared her love and enthusiasm to get married, unaware that Talbot was female.

In 1797 Mary Ann Talbot was seized by a press gang and forced to reveal her gender. Despite her deception, she received monies howing because of her service and wounds, but on visiting Mr Sucker found that he'd squandered every penny on her inheiteance. He died of a heart attack three days after her visit.

During her time in Denmark Street, she continued to dress in sailor's clothes. It was while she was working in the street that she tried her luck as an acress at Drury Lane but ended up in debtor's prison at Newgate. On her release, she worked as a servant for the publisher Robet S. Kirby, who would later include her tale in his book, *Wonderful Museum and the Surprsing Adventure of Mary Ann Talbot*, in 1809, a year after her death.

Three years before she died, Talbot published her biography, which some challenged due to geographical discrepancies. Whatever the circumstances, she certainly packed a lot into her thirty-four years.

The cross-dressing days at No.21 were long gone when William Clutton moved there in 1837, to operate from there as a Goldsmith. Born in 1788, he married Elizabeth Cox in 1818. One of the witnesses was David Cox, who entered a maker's mark in 1828 at Goldsmith's Hall in partnership with Clutton. The christenings of Clutton's children show him as a jeweller, but he entered another mark, this time alone, from the Rupert Street address where he'd worked with

David Cox. The Goldsmith Hall records show that he moved to 21 Denmark Street in 1837, where he was recorded by the censuses of 1841 and 1851. By the time of the second census he was employing six men and his son William, born in 1826, had become a silversmith. William Clutton died while living at Denmark Street and was buried in 1854. The 1861 census reveals that his sons William and James were still at No. 21, working as goldsmiths and engravers. It would later become the home of gold discs and ravers.

Peter Maurice Music was founded in the 1930s by Belgian-born Old Etonian Peter Maurice Jacques Koch de Gooreynd and later run by Jimmy Phillips who joined from Lawrence Wright. Despite being born into a banking family, Maurice became a songwriter and an inventor. During WWII he would serve as Principal Staff Officer to the Chief of the Secret Service, dealing with issues concerning the armed services, wireless and cryptography.

Peter Maurice would be the first British music publisher to sell an advance catalogue to America. Being a publisher in Denmark Street was all about finding the right songs, being able to hear those that could be a commercial success, signing them and then putting them together with the right artists.

A Nightingale Sang in Berkeley Square, written by Manning Sherwin and Eric Maschwitz just before the outbreak of World War II, was a big song for Peter Maurice Publishing from 1940 to the present day and would provide the company with numerous covers down the years from many great artists, including, Carmen McRae, Glenn Miller, Rod Stewart, Perry Como, Frank Sinatra, Nat King Cole, Stephane Grappelli, Mel Torme, Vera Lynn, Twiggy, Bobby Darin, Harry Connick jnr., and Manhattan Transfer.

> 'That certain night, the night we met,
> There was magic abroad in the air,

> There were angels dining at the Ritz
> And a Nightingale sang in Berkeley Square.'

In 1945 the company published what would prove to be another great catalogue song, *Autumn Leaves,* originally *Les Feuilles Mortes*, with Johnny Mercer writing English lyrics two years later. No apologies for a list of just some of the many covers of the song, which include; Jo Stafford, Nat King Cole, Edith Piaf, Doris Day, Andy Williams, Errol Garner, Frank Sinatra, The Coasters, Patti Page, The Everly Brothers, Joan Baez, Chet Baker, Grace Jones, Chick Corea, Jerry Lee Lewis, Andrea Bocelli, Iggy Pop, Jermaine Jackson, Gene Pitney, Bob Dylan, Bing Crosby, Perry Como, Tom Jones, Benny Goodman, Willie Nelson, Frankie Laine, The Four Seasons, Count Basie, Eric Clapton, Eva Cassidy, Louis Armstrong, Duke Ellington and Susan Boyle. An example of how a great song can cross the genres and the eras. Those songs fed the industry. Only a small percentage of our current songwriters want to make a career out of singing, but they need those that do to record good songs, whoever wrote them. Conversely, many of our singers who regularly chart don't write songs form anyone else to sing but themselves. Unless you're a seriously good writer that can maintain a very high standard, the singing career isn't going to last as long as the singers that simply picked the best songs and sang them.

Success is not always instant. *O Mein Papa* was written in 1939, but didn't become a hit for fourteen years, when Eddie Fisher took it to No.1 in the US and Eddie Calvert took his instrumental version to No.1 in the UK, making it the first chart-topper to be recorded at Abbey Road Studios. Yet another song that was a money-spinner with covers by many artists, including Billy Cotton, Harry James, The Beverley sisters, Billy Vaughn, Guy Mitchell, Ray Anthony, The Everly Brothers, and even Siouxie and the Banshees and Bjork.

In the mid-thirties Wally Ridley joined Peter Maurice, with one of his early successes being *Isle of Capri*. Born in St. Pancras in 1913, Ridley began as an exploitationist (an early term for plugger) in 1928 at Feldman's Publishing, playing their songs on the piano to both radio and music hall artists.

Moving to Peter Maurice, he helped to launch Vera Lynn on her pre-war career and introduced Flanagan and Allen to the song *Home Town*. He also wrote songs, his first collaboration and cover came as a sixteen-year-old when he and sixty-five-year-old writer, Harry Castling, wrote *The One Little Hair on His Head* for Gracie Fields. He also wrote for such artists as Al Bowlly, Nat King Cole and Paul Robeson. He worked with and promoted top songwriters Michael Carr and jimmy Kennedy as well as coaching the young Vera Lynn and found the song *We'll Meet Again* for her. In the early 1950s Wally Ridley wrote and conceived the popular radio series *Educating Archie* with Eric Sykes, which pulled in 20 million listeners a show and made household names of Tony Hancock, Beryl Reid, Eric Sykes and Harry Secombe and Max Bygraves. Wally Ridley later said, 'Max Bygraves stumbled over long lines and so he (Eric Sykes) gave him short, little lines and it worked perfectly. When I made records with Maxie, I did exactly the same thing. I found him songs with short lines that he could punch in and we had lots of hits.'

Ridley then moved to EMI, where his illustrious career was kick-started by acquiring Elvis Presley's *Heartbreak Hotel* for British release. He became a producer for HMV at Abbey Road studios and had many chart hits with such artists as Max Bygraves, Alma Cogan, Johnny Kidd and the Pirates and the Swinging Blue Jeans. He also suggested the song *Bring Me Sunshine* to Morecambe and Wise. It was Ridley who decided to release Elvis Presley's Heartbreak Hotel: 'I released it and HMV got the worst reviews it ever had. The chiefs wanted to sack me for releasing it. Radio Luxembourg wouldn't play it and nor would the BBC.' Wally Ridley died in 2007 at the age of ninety-four.

Early In 1959 Peter Maurice Music merged with Keith Prowse Music to form KPM, essentially publishing library music on their own label. The songs or melodies with commercial potential were licensed to established record labels. Jimmy Phillips discovered Tommy Steele and put him with songwriter Lionel Bart. Adam Faith and Marty Wilde would also regularly turn up at Peter Maurice Music to see if Lionel Bart had any suitable songs for them. Jimmy's son Peter joined his father at Peter Maurice in 1958, later looking after such writers as Tammy Wynette and Phil Coulter. When the company was sold to Rediffusion/KPM he stayed on as general manager and started the KPM library. In 1977 Peter joined ATV/Northern Songs managing the Beatles catalogue as well as the songs of Neil Diamond, and the Pretenders. He left in 1984 to start the Music House music library, later sold to EMI. He retired to Brighton where he lived with former Tin Pan Alley colleague, Kay O'Dwyer, until his death in 2015. Peter Maurice died in 1973.

One of our most successful songwriters would join Keith Prowse in 1934, when his career was already in full swing. During the 1920s, Irish songwriter Jimmy Kennedy, while working as a teacher, made many trips to Denmark Street, but despite having many of his songs rejected, he felt that he was getting closer to the heart of the songwriting industry and learning about the kind of material that publishers and singers were looking for. By 1927 his persistency paid off when he sold two songs for £2 each. Kennedy would later describe those Tin Pan Alley days thus, 'Through the open first floor window the tinkling of a piano filters into the narrow city street. The tune halts suddenly in the middle of a bar, and voices chip in, arguing...but, where are you? In Denmark Street, London's Tin Pan Alley, and a new song is being born. It may sell a million copies; make a fortune for somebody whose name you have never heard, be sung by famous stars, or strummed on pianos in five continents. Or its writer may take to a score of the music-filled first floor rooms in Tin Pan Alley and hear his song played through, discussed, dissected...and walk out with the crumpled sheets of paper back in his pocket. Between those two extremes, lie all the triumphs and heartbreaks, the clinging hopes and dull disappointment of the Alley. Just imagine yourself in a business where 20 minutes work may make a £1,000 for you...or weeks of struggle and concentration mean...NOTHING! Where your empty pockets may compel you to sell outright the results of your labours for a few pounds only to see it make a fortune for someone else.'

He wrote from experience. Despite its success and popularity, one of his songs, *Ukuleles in the Moonlight*, published by Maurice Scott in 1929, made him nothing at all. Despite having written both the words and music, Scott credited himself as the composer and informed Kennedy that the contract he'd naively signed, gave all the writers' earnings to Maurice Scott Music. The number sold 150,000 records and an incredible amount of sheet music. Scott earned some £800 for the song he hadn't written. Kennedy earned £5 for the song he had. Lesson learned.

Jimmy Kennedy was determined and in 1930 he joined Bert Feldman and went on to write *The Teddy Bear's Picnic, My Prayer, Red Sails in the Sunset, Harbour Lights* and *The Hokey Cokey*. In 1934 he jumped ship to Peter Maurice Publishing and began to collaborate with Michael Carr, writing such classics as *South of the Border* and *We're Going to Hang Out the Washing on the Siegfried Line,* the latter written while he was a Captain in the Royal Artillery during WWII. Kennedy became Peter Maurice's most successful songwriter. He and the company's Peter Phillips didn't always see eye to eye, Kennedy often feeling that he had many potential hits that Phillips unexploited and that he wasn't always given a fair crack of the whip with some of the writing credits. He wasn't enthusiastic about Kennedy and Carr's *South of the Border*. Jimmy Kennedy was so incensed that he threatened never to write for the company again unless Phillips promoted it. Not only was it a resounding success, the number of covers were incredible and included Al Bowlly, Ambrose, Joe Loss, Shep Fields, Gene Autry, Beeny Goodman, Tommy Dorsey, Tony Bennett, Perry Como, The Stargazers, Patti Page, Frank Sinatra, Dean Martin, Herb Alpert, Patsy Cline, Connie Francis, Chris Isaacs, The Shadows and Mel Torme. Sensing Phillips' initial reticence in releasing the song, Michael Carr felt that is wasn't going anywhere and sold his share before the song was ever released. *South of the Border* went on to sell over six million records and a million sheet music copies!

Until Lennon and McCartney, Jimmy Kennedy had more hits in the States than any other British songwriter and wrote more than 2,000 songs, surely one of Denmark Street's most prolific sons. *Romeo, Harbour Lights, Istanbul (Not Constantinople), Isle of Capri, Love is like a Violin* and *My Prayer,* are just a small sample of a few more songs from Kennedy's incredible output. In the days when all types of genres appealed to both the media and the record buyers, the clever lyricists like Oscar Hammerstein II, Lorenz Hart, Ira Gershwin and Jimmy Kennedy could flex their muscles and have fun with words. With *Istanbul* he felt that his then collaborator, Nat Simon's melody had a distinctly Turkish feel to it, but the only thing that either of them knew about the country was that the former name for Istanbul was Constantinople. As many great songwriters will tell you, as soon as you have the title, the road opens up before you. Add a few clever rhymes like '*Why did Constantinople get the works/That's nobody's business but the Turks',* and you're away. And songs like that brought covers, a reputation and a livelihood. Not only did *Istanbul* make the top ten in both the UK and the US in 1953, but it was also covered over the next sixty years by dozens of artists from Edmundo Ros and Eartha Kitt, to Bette Midler and They Might Be Giants.

Songs were certainly plugged to artists but covers could also be circumstantial. In 1956, just by chance, Jimmy was walking with his publishing friend Art Gallico, when they ran into Buck Ram in the street. Ram was the manager, arranger and songwriter for the Platters who'd just had three hits including taking *The Great Pretender* to No.1. Ram told them that he had a recording session the following day and needed one more song. Had it been 2016, Ram and the group would have written something themselves, whatever the quality, but this was 1956 and great songwriters were gold dust to artists wanting to have long and successful careers. Art Gallico suggested that *My Prayer*, a song written by Jimmy a while back that had been a big hit for the Ink Spots, would suit The Platters style. The song had also made history by reaching No. 2 in the US chart for Glenn Miller at the same time that Shep Field's was at No.1 with *South of the Border*, a feat that no other British songwriter had ever achieved. The fortuitous meeting and commercial suggestion about My Prayer payed dividends. The Platters recorded it the following day, their version selling over three million copies and keeping Elvis Presley's *Hound Dog* off the No.1 spot for two weeks. The Platters recorded two more Jimmy Kennedy songs, *Red Sails in the Sunset* and *Harbour Lights*. The latter song became the top British sheet music best-seller on 1937, a US No.1 in 1950 and a US top ten hit again in 1960, as well as being recorded by Elvis Presley as it was one of his mother's favourite songs.

The difficulty in Kennedy and Will Grosz (who used the pen name Hugh Williams) writing a follow-up to *Red Sails in the Sunset*, was solved by another fortuitous piece of fate. Driving back one dark night from Portsmouth to his home in Weybridge, Kennedy took a wrong turning, but the car headlights picked out a pub sign at Cosham, The Harbour Lights, enabling him to turn around and get back on the right road: '...a perfect title for a song. Maybe even the one we were looking for. By the time I was home the lyric was half done. The next day I showed it to Will Grosz, who came up with a beautiful and romantic melody.' It was not only the year's best-seller in the US selling over a million copies of the sheet music, but was also covered by dozens of artists in Britain and America including the orchestras of Harry Roy, Ambrose, Roy Fox, Charlie Kunz and Mantovani.

The Harbour Lights at Cosham. The inspiration for Jimmy Kennedy's song.

In 1947 Kennedy became one of the founder members of the Songwriters' Guild, created to protect and advance British songwriting. He and Michael Carr even wrote the Tin Pan Alley Symphony.

Jimmy Kennedy got the OBE in 1983, won two Ivor Novello Awards and in 1997 was posthumously inducted into the Songwriters' Hall of

Fame. At a memorial service for Jimmy Kennedy in 1984, a eulogy was read by Denis Thatcher, husband of the then Primer Minister, Margaret Thatcher, as they'd first met in the army forty years earlier. Kennedy is buried at Staplegrove Church, Taunton, Somerset, the small wood between the church and Staplegrove Scout Hut allegedly the inspiration for his lyrics to *Teddy Bears' Picnic.*

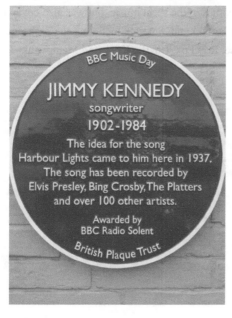

Blue Plaque at the Harbour Lights

One of Jimmy's writing partners, composer Michael Carr, was born Maurice Cohen in Leeds in 1905. After a spell playing small roles in Hollywood films, he settled in London, writing and working in music publishing. Carr co-wrote *We're Going to Hang Out the Washing (On the Siegfried Line),* which he conceived while staying at the Mitre Hotel in Hampton Court. Desperate to write the song, he found Kennedy patrolling a reservoir near Walton-on-Thames and completed the number in the most awkward of circumstances. Carr also wrote two of the Shadows' big hits, *Man of Mystery* (originally the theme to the Edgar Wallace film series) and *Kon-Tiki.* Another of his successful instrumentals was *Lonely Ballerina,* for Mantovani. He also collaborated with Norrie Paramor on another Shadows tune, *The Miracle.* With Ben Nisbet,

Carr wrote the theme to the TV series, *White Horses,* a top ten hit for Jackie Lee. In 2003 it was named the greatest theme song in television history. Among many other songs, Michael Carr wrote, *Dinner for One Please James* and *The Little Boy That Santa Claus Forgot (*with Tommie Connor). Carr also collaborated with other British writers, including Jack Popplewell, Jack Strachey and Eric Maschwitz. Alternative rock band Muse now perform his song *Man of Mystery*. Many of Lionel Bart big hits were also with Peter Maurice.

Stepney-born Lionel Begleiter changed his name to Lionel Bart and started his songwriting career in amateur theatre, as well as writing comedy songs for *The Billy Cotton Band Show.* Both Bart and Cotton frequented Denmark Street., one trying to sell his songs and the other looking for songs. It was in the street that the young Lionel met with publishers and singers and moved into writing pop songs. For Tommy Steele he wrote, *Rock with the Caveman, Handful of Songs, Butterfingers* and *Little White Bull.* Bart either wrote alone or with Mike Pratt and Tommy Steele. Bart's *Living Doll* was a No.1 for Cliff Richard. In 1957 and No.1 again twenty-seven years later. Lionel Bart won two Ivor Novello Awards, another four in 1958 and a further two in 1960, an incredible achievement for someone who could neither read nor write music. He wrote the theme song for the 1963 James Bond film, *From Russia with Love,* a big hit for Matt Monro, *Do You Mind* for Anthony Newley and *Easy Going Me* and *Big Time* for Adam Faith. Working closely with manager Larry Parnes, it was Bart who recommended Parnes should sign up Tommy Steele and Marty Wilde.

Bart also wrote stage musicals, *Lock Up Your Daughters* being the first in 1959, followed by *Fing's Ain't Wot They used To Be* and the phenomenally successful, *Oliver,* which transferred to Broadway and became a highly-grossing film. *Oliver* has sustained its popularity for well over fifty years and has won several Oscars. Bart's next three musicals, *Blitz, Twang* and *La Strada* didn't fare as well, but Lionel Bart was given a special Ivor Novello Award in 1986 for Lifetime Achievement.

The first big successes of writers Bill Martin and Phil Coulter were with Peter Maurice Publishing. As Wylie MacPherson, Bill Martin first came to London's Tin Pan Alley and after knocking on many doors was advised by Cyril Gee at Mills Music to change his name, suggesting Bill Martin. His first song to be released was Tommy Quickly's *Kiss Me Now,* after which he started a writing partnership with Tommy Scott, penning songs for The Bachelors, Twinkle, The Dubliners, Van Morrison and Serge Gainsburg. In 1965 he formed what was to be a long-lasting partnership with composer Phil Coulter, coming up with songs for such artists as Ken Dodd, Geno Washington, Los Bravos, Dave Dee, Dozy, Beaky, Mick and Tich, The Troggs, Mirielle Mathieu, George Harrison, Dick Emery, Tony Blackburn, Cliff Richard, Sandie Shaw and Elvis Presley. Moving from Derry, Northern Ireland, Coulter started working as an arranger and songwriter in Denmark Street which is where they met. Between 1967 and 1976 Martin and Coulter had four No1's in the UK: *Puppet On a String* (Sandie Shaw), *Congratulations* (Cliff Richard), *Back Home (*The England World Cup Squad) and *Forever and Ever* (Slik). Martin remains the only Scottish songwriter to pen four UK No.1s for four different acts. They also had numerous top ten hits including *Shang-a-Lang* (Bay City Rollers) *Fancy Pants* (Kenny) *Requiem* (Slik) and *Surround Yourself With Sorrow* (Cilla Black). Bill and Phil were joint recipients of an Ivor Novello Award for 'Songwriter of the Year'. Martin and Coulter had three chart-toppers in the States, with the Bay City Rollers taking *Dedication* to No.1 on the Billboard Hot 100, Bill Anderson's *Thanks,* on the Country Chart and on the Adult Contemporary Chart, *My Boy* by Elvis Presley. *Puppet on a String* famously won Eurovision in 1967 with *Congratulations* coming second the following year. They formed Martin-Coulter Music, signing such songwriters as Van Morrison, Billy Connolly, Midge Ure and BA Robertson. Martin bought out Coulter in 1983 and later sold the company to EMI. Coulter went on to work with artists like Planxty and Joe Dolan as well as releasing many successful New Age albums as an artist in his own right and was nominated for a Grammy in that category in 2001. In 1983 Bill Martin produced the musical, *JukeBox,* which had a six-month run in London's West End. Martin continued as a songwriter, music publisher and producer with Angus Publications. In 2000, he associated with Sony/ATV Music which sub-publishes his catalogue, while he acquires music catalogues for his partners. In 2009 Bill Martin and Phil Coulter were both awarded the Gold Badge Award for Services to the Music Industry and in 2012 he received the *Sunday Mail's* 'Living Legend Award'. In the 1990s Coulter produced tracks for Boyzone and Sinead O'Connor. Martin and Coulter have won Ivor Novellos and many other awards as well as many Gold, Silver and Platinum discs.

Peter Maurice was a real success story, which would continue with a coming together of Peter Maurice and Keith Prowse at this address.

Keith and Prowse are almost certainly the oldest names to appear in Tin Pan Alley as the alliance between musical composer and instrument maker, Robert Keith (born 1767), and another instrument maker and music publisher William Prowse (born 1801), in 1830 to form Keith, Prowse & Co. Their main thrust was theatre ticketing, which led to them becoming the first ticketing agents for UK air travel, Royal Ascot and Wimbledon tennis. In 1955 the publishing side was sold off to Associated-Rediffusion, one of the early holders of a commercial television franchise. In 1956 the manager of the new set-up, Patrick Howgill, established a music library to work in tandem with TV on a budget of just £5,000 which funded the first 25 78 rpm discs. In 1959 Associated-Rediffusion also bought Peter Maurice

Music which they merged with Keith Prowse Music Publishing to form KPM, standing for Keith Prowse Maurice. EMI bought the KPM Music Group in 1969, adding it to the Francis, Day & Hunter catalogue they'd also purchased.

It was headed up for many years by brothers and Tin Pan Alley legends, Jimmy and Bill Phillips. Writers Jimmy Phillips, Phil Coulter, Keith Mansfield and now head of Peer Music UK, Nigel Elderton, all worked out of KPM at various times. So did Guy Fletcher.

As well as working as a session singer for independent producer Joe Meek, Fletcher also worked in Denmark Street for Keith Prowse from 1964-1966 while his brother Ted ran their commercial studio. Trained as a trumpeter, he began to write songs, meeting Doug Flett in 1966 and signing with the Julian and Jean Aberbach's cousin, Freddy Bienstock at Carlin Music. Fletcher and Flett were the first UK writers to have a song recorded by Elvis Presley with *The Fair's Movin' On* in 1969. Elvis also recorded their songs, *Clean up Your Own Back Yard, Just Pretend* and *Live a Little, Love a Little.* Their first top ten hit was the Hollies' *I Can't Tell the Bottom from the Top,* with hits for Cliff Richard following, including, *With the Eyes of a Child, Power to All Our Friends, Sing a Song of Freedom and Baby* and *You're Dynamite.* Their greatest international success was a No.6 on the Billboard Chart with *Save Me,* with Louise Mandrell in1983. The song was covered by several other US singers. Fletcher and Flett also wrote hits for Ray Charles, Tom Jones, Joe Cocker, the Bay City Rollers, and *Fallen Angel* for Frankie Valli that now features in the musical *Jersey Boys* all over the world.

Guy Fletcher is a former Chairman of PRS for Music where he has been a director since 1998 and has won many awards, including an ASCAP award in the US and an Ivor Novello Award in the

UK, Fletcher has also written TV music, songs, commercials and music for the stage. In 2005, he was honoured in HM The Queen's Birthday Honours List with an OBE for services to British music. In 2016 Guy and his writing partner Doug Flett received gold discs for Elvis' album *The Wonder of You* with The Royal Philharmonic Orchestra, which featured their song, *Just Pretend.* At the end of 2016 Fletcher stepped down after serving two three-year terms as Chairman of PRS for Music. A far cry from his first day when he'd seen a man in an overall churning out sheet music in the basement on a small litho printer. KPM's Chief Engineer and Studio Manager from 176-1978 was Richard Elan, who went on to work on freelance recording projects for their music library.

EMI bought Keith Prowse Publishing in 1969 and retained the name for trading. In 1991 it was bought by former Wembley Stadium owner, Wembley plc which sold Keith Prowse to the company's management in 2002 for £5.5million. In 2004 Compass Group plc acquired the Keith Prowse corporate hospitality business sectors for £20 million with the remaining theatre and tour ticket business being operated by Seatem Group Ltd.

In 1989 Eddie Piller moved into No. 21 and the basement studio next door which had been damaged by the fire of 1980. Over the next few years he recorded Jamiroquai, the Brand New Heavies and Gegory Isaacs there. Moved to Shoreditch in 1992. Pillar's mother had run the Small Faces fan club in the 1960s. Mumford & Sons and Noah & the Whale have since recorded at the studio.

No. 22

The celebrated goldsmith and jeweller, James Morriset, worked in the street from 1773-1778, his partnership with Gabriel Wirgman being dissolved in 1778, with Morriset continuing to work from the premises from 1884-1896 with C. Lukin.

From 1800 to 1821 John Ray and James Montague had an active partnership as goldsmiths and jewellers at No.22 as successors to Morriset. Ray and Montague made presentation swords, freedom boxes, toys, tokens and other items. One of their earliest pieces made in Denmark Street, was a royal gold and enamel small-sword for H.H. Prince William Frederick, 2nd Duke of Gloucester and Duke of Edinburgh (1776-1834) which made £62,400 at auction with Christies. In 1948 another of their swords was bequeathed to the Royal Armouries. It had gold presentation small-sword dating from around 1806-07 and was to have been presented to Admiral Collingwood by the City of London for his role in the Battle of Trafalgar. It's inscribed with letters set with diamonds, reading, 'England Expects Every Man to Do His Duty' on the outside and 'Trafalgar' on the inside. As he never returned, it was presented to his wife in 1810. Ray and Montague made twenty-nine such swords, receiving £210 from the City of London for Collingwood's sword, with another £1.05 to cover the cost of researching the Vice Admiral's coat of arms.

Collingwood's Sword

Another of their swords sold for £220,800 at Sothebys. The weapon, belonging to Captain Philip Bowes Vere Broke, was used during the capture of the American frigate, Chesapeake, off Boston Harbour.

Lt General Sir Rowland Hill's sword for services under Wellington in 1813.

The Victoria and Albert Museum have a sword made by Ray and Montague in the jewellery gallery, room 91 mezzanine, case 80. The shell guard is inscribed to the effect that the sword was presented to Lt. General Sir Rowland Hill in recognition of his services under Wellington at the Battle of Vittoria on 21st June 1813. Their Denmark Street business thrived during the Napoleonic wars, but there was less demand following Waterloo; their last extant work being a dress small-sword presented to Admiral Viscount Exmouth following the attack on Algiers in 1816. The company was dissolved in 1821.

W. Kohler & Co of 22 Denmark Street specialised in satire and humour in Royal and political prints, including lithographs of Queen Victoria, like one from 1843 which depicts her and Prince Albert entering the nursery to see the infant Prince of Wales' wet nurse feeding him alcohol from a bottle. Another, dated 1837, has the view of a ship, Queen Victoria, at sea and when the paper was lifted it revealed a portrait of the Queen herself.

By 1900, another carver and gilder, Edward Court, was in residence at No. 22, his business by then having been established for twenty years. Like the cutlers of Denmark Street, the Japanese were also proud of their ceremonial swords, but how many Uchigatanas and Odachis were wielded by the new residents is lost in the mists of time.

In 1918 Moritaro Iwasaki opened the Tokiwa Restaurant at 15 Manette Street, off Charing Cross Road, and was joined by his wife Fukue the following year. They opened Tokiwa restaurants in the City in 1922 and in Paris in 1923. In 1927 they extended their operations, moving the restaurant to No. 8 Denmark Street., and opening the Tokiwa Hotel at No. 22. They also sold Japanese groceries. By 1932 they were also running the Tokiwa Travellers Bureau, billing themselves as Tourist Agents. Despite a tenth anniversary party in Denmark Street in late 1920 to celebrate their success, by 1933 Iwasaki had registered for divorce from Fukue. His new wife gave birth to three children over the next four years. Meanwhile, the plot thickened and by 1933 the Tokiwa Hotel was in the sole possession of Fukue, who changed the name to Tokiwa House, changing it again the following year to the Yamato Hotel. Fukue then married Akima Katsuji, the couple running the hotel, while her former husband, Iwasaki continued to make a success of the restaurant as well as continuing to run his travel and removal service. On 24th January 1939 he had to travel (to Mansion House Police Court) and he was involved in a removal (he was relieved of £700). He was living around the corner from his business as revealed in the local Marylebone newspaper; 'Moritaro Iwasaki and Yashushi Tomono both of new Oxford Street, were fined £700 each for making false customs declarations concerning imported goods.' That's just under £40,000 each in today's money.

During the 1920s and 1930s the Japanese community had become well-established in the area and integrated successfully into the local community. Many hated the idea of Britain and Japan being at war, some using their positions to try to prevent it from happening. Many went back when they felt that war was inevitable and those that didn't were interned on the Isle of Man or deported to Japan.

As well as starting the New Musical Express, at No.5 Ralph Elman,(*pictured below*) was also here at No 22. Elman ran his own orchestra, Ralph Elman and his Bohemian Players, who were mainly a broadcast band. Born in London in 1907, he was the nephew of Russian violinist Mischa Elman. As well as running his own outfit, he was also the leader of the Ron Goodwin Orchestra, played violin for Burt Bacharach and played violin on the soundtracks for *Thunderbirds, Joe 90* and *Captain Scarlet*. When George Martin resumed working with Ron Goodwin, who he'd produced in 1953, in 1966, Elman was the violinist. This led Martin to use Elman of two Beatles tracks, *Within You, Without You* and *I Am the Walrus.* Back in 1954 he set up one of the first independent in the UK recording studios in the UK, Tin Pan Alley Studios, in the basement of No. 22.

Many groups and artists rehearsed and recorded their demos there before heading across the road to the other studio he founded, Regent Sound, to record the master. The Rolling Stones used it to prepare for their first album and both Manfred Mann and The Small Faces recorded at No 22 in 1964. On the 31st March 1969 The Who's

diary reveals that they were recording here and during a break did a photo session on the roof.

Yes, there were big names associated with the street, with some of the most successful UK artists starting in Tin Pan Alley, but pop music wasn't the only area in which money was being made and careers were being forged. There were publishers, whose business acumen in tandem with creative songwriters brought them success in the UK, US and other territories. There were also jingle writers and the undisputed king of the jingles was Johnny Johnston.

Born John Reine in 1919, Johnston was working for the BBC's light music department by the mid-forties, which resulted in his being asked to form a close harmony quartet for a new comedy half-hour for 1948. He complied by forming the Keynotes who performed the popular radio theme that Johnson had written, for *Take It From Here*, the series running until 1959. The Keynotes made their first recording in 1948 and remained signed to Decca for eight years, often with backing singers like Dickie Valantine, Anne Shelton, Joan Regan and Dave King. Members at various times included Cliff Adams and Pearl Carr. As well as running the group Johnston also wrote songs such as *The Wedding of Lilli Marlene* and *Don't Ringa De Bell*. A busy man, Johnston not only formed the Johnston Brothers in 1949, who also signed to Decca, he put together a third group, The King's Men. The Johnston Brothers had several hits but their first top ten hit was in 1953 with their version of Don Howard's *O Happy Day* (not the gospel song) which stayed in the top ten for two months, peaking at No.4. Two years later their version of *Hernando's Hideaway,* from the movie *The Pyjama Game,* reached No.1 for two weeks before being toppled by Bill Haley's *Rock Around the Clock*. He teamed up with Bill Cotton Jnr., the pair working out of Tin Pan Alley. Johnston also had a publishing company called Michael Reine, which he'd formed with his partner, Mickey Michaels. When Michaels wanted to leave, Cotton borrowed £1,500 from his father and bought her shares, becoming Johnston's partner. Michael Reine Publishing took off, with hits like *Can't Tell a Waltz from a Tango, Bell-Bottom Blues, Friends and Neighbours* and *Never Do a Tango with an Eskimo.* Bill Cotton Jnr. would later leave to join the BBC.

Working out of 22 Denmark Street, Johnston was to make a fortune writing commercial jingles, but at the time there was no commercial channel on radio or television except for Radio Luxembourg, where he and the Keynotes sang for 26 weeks on the *Wisk half-Hour* with Gracie Fields. In the first year of commercial television, Johnston composed, arranged and produced catchy 30 second jingles for such brands as Kleenex Tissues, New Zealand Butter, Stork Margarine and 'Rael-Brook Toplin, the shirt you don't iron.' The latter jingle was brilliant in its simplicity; repeating the one line four times from the root to the third, the fifth and the octave. Within two years he established himself as Johnny Johnston Jingles Ltd. Establishing himself as the 'King of Jingles'. To many, even reading the words evokes the melody for example, 'A million housewives every day pick up a tin of beans and say, "Beanz Meanz Heinz,"' and, 'Softness is a thing called Comfort.' When Bing Crosby sang one of your jingles you know you'd cracked it: 'We're going well, we're going Shell, you can be sure of Shell.'

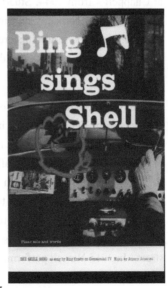

Johnston died in 1998, having written more than 4,500 jingles included one for Birds Eye Peas, the first-ever colour TV commercial, in November 1969.

Johnny Johnston: King of the Jingles

This was certainly a musical property. In August 1974 Frank Coachworth and Stuart Reid moved their new publishing and management company Mautoglade Music Ltd. into No. 22 with Emily Reid handling artist management. Prior to setting up Mautoglade, Coachworth had been at Chappell's from 1944. Stuart Hornell of Hornell Brothers Music later joined the company and the boss of the Chess label is still a director. Mautoglade administered the Jewel catalogue in the UK and published many hit songs, including Tina Charles' 1976 No.1, *I Love to Love*.

Martin Newell, 'The Wild Man of Wivenhoe', front man of the group Cleaners from Venus, recorded in the basement many times between 1986 and 1988:'When I wasn't making records I was helping others to write and record theirs. We often finished work in the small hours so I slept in the control room minder the mixing desk...Captain Sensible, if we were working together, sometimes slept under the grand piano in the main recording room. We often didn't know whether it was light or dark outside as we emerged, frazzled, into the street.' In 2015 Newell performed his 'Golden Afternoon' event at St

Giles-in-the-Fields Church, featuring guitar, piano, poetry, tales of Denmark Street, tea and cake. Perfect

The studio was re-opened in 2013 by Guy Katsav as Denmark Street Studios, but the lease was terminated in June 2016, effectively closing the studio after sixty-two years.

No. 23

John Corbett was a silver and gold caster, whose company was active between 1860, when he was at No.9, and 1900, by which time he'd moved to No.23. While gold was being cast downstairs, upstairs there was poverty, sadness and a horror.

April 1900, Charles Henry Miles was indicted for, and charged at the coroner's inquisition with, the wilful murder of Harry Hartley. Mr. C. Matthews prosecuted and Mr. Sands defended.

Emma Hartley was an eighteen-year-old tailor who lived at 23 Denmark Street with her parents and had known the prisoner, a tinker's labourer, for two years: 'When I moved to 23 Denmark Street in August last, he became intimate with me, and I had a child by him, which was born in the workhouse on August 19th 1899 and was christened Harry Hartley. After its birth I went to live at Denmark Street taking the child with me.' It seems the couple continued to walk out together and Miles paid three shillings a week towards the child's keep until Christmas. Emma Hartley told the court, '...I was not wanting to marry him...he wanted to marry me, but my father would not give his sanction. The connection between us was renewed after the child's birth but it was only walking out.' In February while the couple were visiting her sister and brother-in-law, Emma knocked the pipe out of his mouth: 'I said, "Oh take that thing out of your mouth" and knocked it out of his mouth, because he had hurt himself by smoking...I did not like his smoking a pipe, but I liked him smoking cigarettes...he picked the pipe up off the floor and said, "Mind you and the baby don't go over the Embankment tonight."' She then said that she'd seen him outside her door in Denmark Street on February 14th, but instead of going in to see the baby, he hadn't spoken to her and had walked away. She saw him again on the 17th and managed to get a shilling out of him for the baby, but when she later asked for another sixpence: '...he did not say anything, but struck me on my eye...I said good night and went upstairs...I felt a pain in my eye.' The next day she bumped into him in Denmark Street and he swore at her and demanded to be given the baby; 'I handed the baby to him...he ran away in the direction of St. Giles church and I followed him, but lost sight of him just about the top of Seven Dials. I called after him but he did not stop.' The distraught mother went to one of her brothers-in-law and they went to the prisoner's lodgings before looking around the Charing Cross are: 'I returned home and found a detective there who told me something and I went to Bow Street Police station. I thought he was going to take it as he had done before...it was dressed in this blue frock, black socks, white petticoat, white band and a little white shawl. On March 7th I was taken to the Parish Mortuary at Rotherhithe and saw the naked body of my child.'

Her brother-in-law, Charles Meredith told the court about the incident when the pipe had been knocked out of the prisoner's mouth: 'He said, "You will have to be very careful when you go home tonight, or you and the child might go to the Embankment." I took no notice...he has used bad language to my sister-in-law...he called her a carroty cow...he was always fidgeting about in his chair...' Another witness was school girl Emma Matilda Grinham, who also lived at 23 Denmark Street: 'On Sunday, February 18th I was outside the house with my sister Eliza and saw the prisoner...he kept asking me each time I went outside for errands...I went down several times that evening on errands beginning at 7.30 and three or four times after that, and each time the prisoner was outside the door standing at the lamp-post...he always asked me the same question and I always gave him the same answer...I went up the last time at 10.15 and left him standing there.' Her sister, Eliza, also of 23 Denmark Street, corroborated the story.

Policeman Edgar Adams, 209 E, was on duty near Charing Cross and saw Charles Miles go on to the Embankment from Villiers Street, carrying the baby: 'He seemed exhausted, as if he had been running...he was coming towards me and turned to the left towards the water and I lost sight of him.' Another policeman, Bardell, 112E, said that he'd been standing at the door of the Police station when the prisoner had come up, saying that he wished to give himself up for murder: 'He said to me that he did not know why he did it, he was very fond of the baby, something all of a sudden came to him that he would throw the baby into the Thames, that there was a burning in his head, and probably he should get five years.' On being cross-examined, Bardell said: 'He said that if his mother had been alive it would not have happened...he talked about other things as well...I thought he looked very strange.'

Miles made a statement to Police Inspector William Crawford part of which read, 'I wish to confess that I have just thrown my son, age 7 months into the Thames from the Victoria Embankment. He was dressed in a blue pelisse and cape. Its mother, Miss Emma Hartley, is living at 23 Denmark Street...I took the child out of her arms. I then went down Endell Street to Old Compton Street, to St. Martin's Lane, to Victoria Embankment just past Waterloo Bridge where I threw the baby in the river, and I then came away.' Bardell also said that as far as he was concerned he thought Miles' manner to be rational and that he was perfectly sane. The Court heard that Miles' aunt, Eliza Whitehead, had suffered from delusions and died in a lunatic asylum and his mother, who was admitted to St. Giles Infirmary and used to talk to imaginary people, had died from epilepsy and dementia. John

Landgrove, who found the body, also testified, as did Alexander Grain a medical practitioner of Jamaica Road. Printer's labourer, Richard Leamington spoke up for Miles in Court, as he worked with him and had known him for five years, but admitted: 'He was strange at times, he would dance and skip and laugh when he had work to do...he was sociable...he did not make friends...he sat by himself at times...I did not suspect that he was mad in any way....but he threatened to take his life after his mother's funeral and said that he should go and drown himself or cut his throat. He said he could not afford to keep a wife on fourteen shillings a week.'

It was stated in court that he was a labourer, sending shirts out and seeing that they were all correct and that when he took his glasses off he couldn't see. A printer, James Thomas, told the court; 'I have known the prisoner a good many years...he was very peculiar in his manner, and they used to call him Peluti...he was very cheeky at times and threatened to fight you without any reason.' Emma Hartley's father, William admitted: 'I never struck him, but I pushed him, that was last may when I found out what state my daughter was in.' Divisional Surgeon, George Albert Hammerton told the court that he had been called to Bow Street to see the prisoner: 'He complained of a pain in the head...I thought he was not quite right, but he spoke quite rationally in answer to my questions...I suspected epilepsy; he was very pale and the pupils of his eyes were dilated.' Hammerton had been asked by the inspector if the prisoner was ill, but the surgeon declared that he was fit enough to go before the magistrate.

Miles' employer, John Alfred Hurley told the court that the prisoner had been employed by him since 1897 and that he was simple lad who did not make friends: 'I knew that he was without a father and raised his wages, and the man he worked with quarrelled with him and struck him on the head with a hammer...I had him taken to King's College Hospital...I noticed no difference in him after the affair with the hammer.' A Dr. Scott told the court that he had the prisoner under observation since February 19th: 'He is weak-minded and below the average of intelligence...he complained of pains in his head and giddiness...I found no epilepsy at all...I found no indication of the blow on his head...I think he did know what he was doing, but did not appreciate it to the full extent.' On being cross-examined the Doctor said; 'I should not at any time have felt justified in giving a certificate that he is insane.'

Appearing before Mr Da Butzen, Miles was found Guilty, but insane at the time. He was detained during her Majesties pleasure.

No. 23 was also the one-time HQ of Sun Music Publishing, who published songs like *Ferryboat Serenade* in 1940 and Tommie Connor's *The Knick Knack Song,* recorded by the Merry Macs in 1948 and who you could contact by telephoning Temple Bar 8651/2. It's also a more permanent home to a black-caped, and evidently musical, resident Victorian ghost!

While Consul for the Republic of Haiti from 1939 to 1943, latterly under president Elie Lescott, Reginald Arthur Nicholas Hillyer, lived at No.23. Interesting that the Consul lived in a street with a high ratio of Jewish publishers, and Haiti was responsible for saving some 70 Jewish families (up to 300 lives) during the Holocaust. Almost 300 actually made it to the island, some being able to make a living as doctors, Bakers, shopkeepers and photographers. Even those who weren't going to make it all the way to Haiti, were given Haitian passports, to enable them to flee Germany. Haiti had been neutral until the bombing of Pearl Harbour, after which the country declared war on Japan and then on Italy and Germany and contributed supplies and bases for the US and their allies. Hillyer died in 1956 at his home, Malting Cottage in Dedham, the heart of Constable country. Like his Denmark Street home, his country house was also built in the 1600s and also Grade II lasted.

The office of the press officer and publicist for groups like the Beatles, The Kinks, Manfred Mann and the Walker Brothers, Brian Sommerville was here in the early 60's. Born in 1932, he joined the Royal Navy on leaving school, rising to the rank of Lieutenant Commander. Back in civilian life he worked a film publicist for Theo Cowan and show business correspondent for the Daily Express. Late in 1963 he got to know Brian Epstein, who invited him to become the Beatles publicity manager, but he simply wasn't on the same wavelength of the group who referred to him as 'Old Baldie'. He had in fact only just turned thirty.

Sommerville was with the group when they arrived at New York's Kennedy Airport that historic day in February 1964, to be greeted by thousands of screaming teenagers. He was berated from all angles by journalists who couldn't get a story, photographers who couldn't get a picture, people who claimed they'd paid for an exclusive and correspondents complaining that the police refused them admission to the pressroom. At the Beatles' first gig, in Washington DC, the stage was set up in the middle of the arena so Sommerville had to go on at intervals to help move Ringo's drum kit around to face a different side of the audience.

Sommerville must have thought he was still commanding naval ratings when he admonished George Harrison once for being late. George responded by throwing a jug of orange juice over him for which Sommerville boxed his ears. After the publicist lost his temper with the press in the US, Epstein soon realised the appointment had been a mistake. As well as him not fitting in, Epstein was annoyed at the lavish expense accounts that he was running up. Sommerville was fired prior to the group's tour of Australia and New Zealand, although Sommerville's press statement was that he'd done all he could for the Beatles and they didn't need him anymore and said they were 'ready to fly like birds.' He even put an advertisement in the *Times*: 'Ex-Beatles publicity manager looking for a job.'

Never one to miss a good chance to get his acts a few column inches, Sommerville was checking the Walker Brothers into a hotel in the North of England when he heard someone say that the local bank had been robbed and the police were looking for three men. He telephoned anonymously from his room saying he'd just seen three suspicious-looking men taking rooms at this particular hotel. The local constabulary turned up complete with police vans in which to cart off the offenders, but of course it ended in 'mistaken identity' and a big story in the papers.

Sommerville was also the Kinks' publicist until parting company with them after a showdown with Ray Davies. The group found their publicist eccentric but were bemused when they all checked into the same hotel while playing the Blackpool Opera House and Sommerville burst into their communal bedroom in his silk pyjamas and tried to instigate a pillow fight. Ray Davies thought that he looked like a 'tubby circus clown.' Davies says that, during an argument, he once threw a punch at Sommerville, who apparently squeaked like a mouse and ducked under his desk. Sommerville went on to work with The Who, The Easybeats, Dave Dee, Scott Walker, the Bonzo Dog Doo Dah Band and Manfred Mann, before leaving the industry to become a stipendiary magistrate. Sommerville died in 1994.

The original Forbidden Planet comic shop opened at No.23 in 1978. It was the third dedicated comic shop in the capital and was owned by Nick Landau. Landau, a former sub-editor of the British comics, *Battle* and *2000AD,* went on to form *Titan Entertainment,* a company that distributed imported US comics. One Forbidden Planet fan wrote online: 'I only have to see a glimpse of the Brian Bolland artwork which used to adorn the plastic bags and I'm straight back to the uneven wooden floor, the smell of pulp paper, the shafts of light streaming through the dust which hung in the air.'

No. 24

In 1823 lathe and tool worker Charles Rich had his business at No.24 and nine years later, in 1832, Patrick Sweeney was running his tailoring business from the premises.

Southern Music was here from 1935 to WWII, as was their affiliated company, Libor Music, but the full Southern/Peer story is featured at No.8. There were also film distributers, United Motion Pictures at this address from 1956 and maybe earlier, who distributed 27 films between 1954 and 1963. There was also another major publisher at no.24

Born Reginald Armitage, in Wakefield in 1898, as Noel Gay he started a music publishing company as a vehicle for his show songs and light music. He apparently took his new name after seeing an advertisement on the side of a London bus in 1924, which read 'Noel Coward and Maisie Gay in a New Revue.' A prodigious talent, he studied at the Royal College of Music in London, penned the first-ever song to be used in a British 'talkie' (*Tondeleyo*) in 1929, founded Noel Gay Music in 1938 and moved to No. 24 Denmark Street in 1943. He became one of the most successful composers of the 1930s and 1940s writing such songs as *The Lambeth Walk* and with Ralph Butler, *Run Rabbit Run* and *The Sun Has Got His Hat On*. He also wrote the music for 28 films

and 26 London shows, the most long-running being *Me and My Girl*.

He wrote songs for many major artists, including Gracie Fields, George Formby, Flanagan and Allen, and the Crazy Gang. It was said that he tested his new tunes by imagining Yorkshire mill girls whistling them as they walked home from work.

Bandleader Billy Cotton's office was directly across the road, so his son, Billy Cotton Jnr. knew the street and many of the Tin Pan Alley publishers. Not really knowing what to do when he came out of the army in 1950 he decided on music publishing. He started with Noel Gay, who had been in Soho Square before initially moving to 19, Denmark Street and became a great friend of his father's. When Bill Cotton Jnr. started in the street, sheet music sold at a shilling or two shillings, which, with the distributors taking 7d left either five-pence or one and five-pence for the publisher. Sell 100,000 and you were doing OK. Sell half a million and you were raking it in. That was on top of the income from the Performing Right Society. Have a US hit as well, and you were on top of the world. It was a time when money could be made for both the industry and the economy. Bill Cotton Jnr. went on to work for Chappells with publisher Teddy Hearns, before teaming up with Johnny Johnson and returning to Tin Pan Alley. Johnston, who ran the Keynotes among other groups, was also a music publisher with a company called Michael Reine, which had been formed by Johnson (born John Reine) and his partner, Mickey Michaels. When Michaels wanted to leave, Cotton borrowed £1,500 from his father and bought her shares. Suddenly Michael Reine Publishing took off, with hits like *Can't Tell a Waltz from a Tango, Bell-Bottom Blues, Friends and Neighbours* and *Never Do a Tango with an Eskimo*. It worked well. Bill Jnr published them and Bill Snr. played them on his Sunday lunchtime show! With the advent of commercial television, Bill Jnr.'s partner, Johnny Johnson, began to write jingles for commercials and turned out to be very good at it. Cotton moved on to a highly successful career in BBC TV Light Entertainment, becoming Director-General in the 1980s and receiving an MBE, OBE and Knighthood. He later completed a full circle by returning to Noel Gay as Chairman of their TV section.

Richard Armitage
(aka Noel Gay)

Armitage was awarded a 'Wakefield Star' by his home town. He died in 1954. Sheridan Morley commented that he was 'the closest Britain ever came to a local Irving Berlin.' During the 1960s the agency side represented many music artists, including Russ Conway, Peter and Gordon, The Scaffold, Geoff Love, Paul Jones as well as providing a string of hits for Bernard Cribbins. Noel Gay has remained a family-run business headed up by the founder's son Richard Armitage and then his sons, Alex and Charles, who have continued expanding over the years into other areas of the business.

In 1966 former Harrow schoolboys David Enthoven and John Gaydon joined Noel Gay in their artists' agency department. Having been heavily associated with the Harrow School group, Band of Angels, fronted by Mike D'Abo, music had got into their blood. Their clients at Noel Gay included a comedy trio, Giles, Giles and Fripp. In 1968 the group's guitarist, Robert Fripp invited them to a rehearsal room in the Fulham Palace Road to let them hear his new band, King Crimson performing songs from their uncompleted album *In the Court of the Crimson King.* Having learned the ropes in Tin Pan Alley for two years, they moved on from Noel Gay to set up their own management company. They obtained great deals in the US and UK. It was written that 'Unlike their Tin Pan Alley predecessors, the partners behind EG management looked like rock stars and deployed a raffish charm. They wore leather jackets and cowboy boots and took drugs.' They expanded their roster to include Marc Bolan and Emerson, Lake and Palmer. Then came Roxy Music and a whole lot more. David Enthoven was Robbie Williams manager and saviour for twenty years.

In 1978 Noel Gay celebrated forty years in the industry with a dinner for seventy people, at the same time announcing that one of their top writers, Tony Macauley was heading off to Los Angeles to write with Gladys Knight. The company later moved to No.19 Denmark Street.

My Dear Friend,

It is some time now since I wrote you a personal letter and, as you will see from the address above, it does not come to you through the usual channels of the Russ Conway Fan Club; which brings me to the main point of my letter.

I have always felt that if an artist is fortunate enough to have a Fan Club, it is essential that he should be able to keep in close, personal touch with that Club and its members. This is something I feel very strongly about and for some time now I have been very conscious of the fact that I have not been able to do this. The reason has been the ever increasing amount of work, and the travelling that this work entails; therefore being all over the country and not always up to date with incoming mail etc.

After a considerable amount of very careful thought, I have therefore decided to stop all activities of the fan club in its present form as from the date of this letter.

This raises the very important question of the Club Funds which have been built up by your subscriptions. Mr. Bill Badley informs me that the balance of cash now stands at £23.16s.2d. and I have decided to hand over a cheque for this amount to the National Society for Spastics. Naturally some members may feel they would like to have their membership fee returned, either in whole or apportioned to the time of membership. If so, please write to me at the above address enclosing your membership card, and with the letters B.C.F.C. clearly marked in the top left hand corner of the envelope. In place of the magazine it is my intention to issue a regular news-sheet which will contain a list of my activities and appearances on stage, radio and television, to be printed and despatched from London entirely AT MY OWN EXPENSE. I would ask, however, that any enquiries apart from this be accompanied by a stamped and clearly addressed envelope to help to ensure a prompt reply.

In taking this action I hope to keep a much more personal touch with fans, members or non-members, and I will naturally be able to supervise the printing and distribution of the news-sheet.

In closing, I would appreciate it if members will pass on to me any information they have in regard to the sale of photographs of myself, or any souvenir items which are offered for sale. I strongly disagree with the commercial exploitation of people, young and old alike, who pay out money for such things often than which the artist knows nothing. I have many times discovered photos of me on sale in shops for high prices, and for which my permission has never been given. I will supply a signed photo to anybody at anytime whenever requested entirely FREE OF CHARGE.

Finally, may I say 'Thank You' sincerely, and express my gratitude for your kind interest and the wonderful support you have given me. I do hope you will understand the purpose with which I have made these changes, and bear with me for three or four weeks while I am away from London, until I can completely reorganise the fan club system on my return.

With best wishes always,

Keep smiling,

Russ Conway writes a letter from Denmark Street.

No. 25

There have been tobacconists, bakers and caterers on the site at various times, but carver and figure maker John Wragg worked here from 1789 to 1798. The Museum of London has a letter written by Wragg, from Denmark Street to Horace Walpole's friend Richard French at Derby. French was the owner of a small lay figure, once belonging to the French sculptor, Roubillac, and almost certainly made by him, which Wragg had repaired and referred to as 'Exceeding good work.' He also supplied lay figures to the 3rd Earl Egremont, possibly for use by one of the artists at Petworth. At the age of sixty-seven Wragg had galvanic treatment for a paralytic disorder.

From 1861 until his death in 1875 at the age of sixty-three, Daniel Claridge lived here at No.25. Born in 1812, Daniel was the great-great grandfather of eminent East and Soho photographer, John Claridge.

No. 25 was also the Tin Pan Alley headquarters of two other great publishers, Kassner Music and Leeds Music. Leeds Music was established in the States by Lou Levy with composer Saul Chaplin and lyricist Sammy Cahn in 1935, and was called after a suit that Levy and Cahn took turns at wearing during their hungry years. Levy, who soon became the sole owner of the company, is credited with discovering Cahn, Chaplin, Bob Dylan and Henry Mancini amongst others. He published Mancini's early songs and Bob Dylan's first songbook. Levy either managed, discovered or developed Petula Clark, Bobby Darin, Connie Francis, Buddy Rich, The Andrews Sisters, Charles Aznavour and Eddie Fisher. He supplied the likes of Tom Jones, Frank Sinatra and Petula Clark with hits like *It's Not Unusual*, *Strangers in the Night* and *Downtown*. He also published the Beatles' first US hit, *I Want To Hold Your Hand*. Lou Levy married Maxene of the Andrews Sisters. The couple divorced in 1951 and he later married Julie Levy. Lou has a son, Lou Leeds Levy. Lou Levy served on the board of ASCAP from 1058-1970 and was honoured by ASCAP in 1986 for 'outstanding contributions as a major force in music publishing.'

Hit pianist Joe 'Mr. Piano' Henderson worked out of Leeds Music for a period. Born in Glasgow in 1920, he travelled south, started his own jazz band and served in the forces before doing the rounds of Denmark Street offering his services as pianist to various publishers. The fifteen-year-old Petula Clark and her father came in one day, urgently looking for a song for her BBC TV show that afternoon. Joe found a suitable song, rehearsed it with her and it worked so well that Pet's father, Leslie Clark asked Henderson to be her permanent musical director and accompanist. Petula recalled: 'My father and I went along to the old Leeds song publishing office...and as is the fashion in song publisher's' offices, someone came out to run a selection of songs over on the piano. That 'somebody' happened to be Joe.' Under his direction, Pet Clark made her first record, *Put Your Shoes on Lucy* in 1949. In 1973 Joe remembered the session clearly: 'Each of the songs belonged to different publishers, so I 'phoned them up and asked if they would do the arrangements for us quickly.' Henderson was her MD and pianist from 1947-1960, with Alan A. Freeman working as her producer from 1949 until 1963, until Tony Hatch took over. As well as working out of Denmark Street and touring and recording with Petula Clark, Joe Henderson also regularly competed in the 1960 BBC Light Programme music quiz, *Play the Game,* while he and Petula also had a 26-week radio series, *Pet and Mr. Piano.* Joe and Petula were romantically involved for a couple of years, but when the personal relationship ended, so did the professional relationship, but they remained friends. Henderson won an Ivor Novello Award for his hit number, *Trudy,* the biggest sheet music hit of 1958, while Leeds published Petula's 1960 No.1, *Sailor.*

Cyril Simons, the General Manager of Leeds in the UK had been with Southern Music until 1950 when he moved to join Pickwick Music which later transformed into Leeds. Billboard magazine reported Lou Levy's trip to Denmark Street in 1964 for talks with Cyril Simons and to pass on his thanks to Dick James for the US publishing rights to the Beatles' *I Want To Hold Your Hand.* Simons later signed the Moody Blues and up and coming writers in the area of musical theatre, Tim Rice and Andrew Lloyd Webber. Simons even laid out £1,000 in 1966 to obtain the song rights for John Lennon's father, Fred. In 1985 Cyril Simons was awarded an Ivor Novello for his outstanding contribution to British Music. He died in 2000. Don Angus was the professional manager at Leeds.

After the German invasion of Austria, 19-year-old Ed Kassner (*pictured below*), born 1920 in Austria, escaped through Germany, Belgium and the Netherlands to reach England. He never saw his parents again. They died at Auschwitz. His first job when he arrived in London was working with a milliner in the East End but he was keen to write songs and get into the music business. Regularly looking

through the music papers for an opening, he spotted an advertisement that had been placed by a retired army Captain, Peter Mulrony. Kassner moved into their home in Chelsea, where Mulrony lived with his wife Monica, and the two soon began writing songs and  forming Mayfair Music, to publish their material. Their office in New Oxford Street was wiped out by a doodlebug and as the war intensified, refuges were rounded up and sent abroad.

Kassner was deported as an alien to Australia on the *SS Dunera*, but returned to join the British Army, in which he served as an interpreter attached to a Canadian tank corps regiment in France and Germany. In 1943 he met his future wife, Eileen, at Hammersmith Palais, marrying her a year later. The Kassners set up the Edward Kassner Music Company Ltd. He wrote under the pseudonym of Eddie Cassen, writing what would become his first hit, *How Lucky You Are*, in 1946 while on active duty. After Vera Lynn sang it on the BBC, another publisher offered the Kassners £250 for the rights to the song, but they wisely resisted temptation and the song went to No1. By the early fifties he'd acquired the rights to many top songs recorded by many top singers, including Frank Sinatra, Perry Como and Nat King Cole. He opened a New York office in 1951 and acquired several other publishing companies. One of these, Broadway Music, had the rights to many great songs, such as *I'll Be with you In Apple Blossom Time* and *You Made Me Love You*. Kassner was approached by an ex-marine from Philadelphia with what seemed to many an unlikely song. Against the advice of others, Ed Kassner saw the future and bought the rights to *Rock Around the Clock* for what seems now an incredible $250 dollars. It was featured in the film *Blackboard Jungle* and became one of the most played and most recorded songs of all-time, selling some 170 million copies. In 1955 he formed President Records but had more success with his Seville Record label in the States, with hits such as *Shout! Shout! (Knock Yourself Out)* and *Bobby's Girl*.

Partly inspired by the memory of John F. Kennedy, Ed Kassner reactivated the President label at much the same time as he did a deal with former singing star turned businessman, Larry Page. With Page, Ed Kassner formed Denmark Productions, the deal being that Page found the artists and Kassner got the publishing. Through Page the office in Denmark Street acquired a management and publishing deal with a new group, The Kinks, who would have a string of UK and US hits, topping the UK singles chart on three occasions. Ray Davies remains one of the most innovative and successful UK songwriters.

Regent Sound, across the street from Kassner, was the studio where the Kinks first recorded their classic *You Really Got Me.* The tougher, faster version that would become the single, was recorded a few months later at Pye Studios. The combination of US producer Shel Talmy, Ray Davies' songs and a sharp group, would give them a string of hits. Chicago-born producer Sheldon 'Shel' Talmy had previously been a recording engineer in Los Angeles during the 1950's before graduating to producer and experimenting with new recording techniques. In 1962 he came to London and joined Decca Records as a producer, initially working with acts like the Bachelors. The following year he met Robert Wace at Mills Music in Denmark Street. Wace walked in with a demo of his group the Ravens and asked if anyone wanted to listen to it. Shel put his hand up, listened and agreed to record them. With a name change to the Kinks, Talmy as producer and a ground-breaking single in *You Really Got Me,* the group and especially writer Ray Davies, never looked back. From that point, the Talmy/Kinks hits kept on coming, giving the public such classics as *All Day and All of the Night, Tired of Waiting for You, Dedicated Follower of Fashion, Sunny Afternoon* and *Waterloo Sunset.* Shel Talmy also produced Kink Dave Davies 1967 spin-off hit *Death of a Clown.*

Pete Townshend, the guitar player with West London group the High Numbers was so enamoured of *You Really Got Me*, that he wrote a similar song called *I Can't Explain* and convinced Talmy to produce his group. Recording it with Talmy as The Who, it became their first of many hits, and would help to establish them as one of the major rock bands. Again the combination of an innovative producer and a creative group worked for the record-buying public, with *Anyway,*

Anyhow Anywhere and *My Generation*, *A Legal Matter* and *The Kids Are Alright* becoming classics. Talmy also worked on songs with Davy Jones, before he had success as David Bowie. He also produced the Easybeats' *Friday on my Mind* and formed his own label, Planet, which would be home for groups like The Creation (*Painter Man* and *Making Time*) and The Untamed *(I'll Go Crazy* and *It's Not True*). With Talmy at the controls, The Untamed auditioned for impresario Arthur Howes at Regent Sound Studios. Shel Talmy was also responsible for the music in the 1965 film Be My Guest starring David Hemmings and Steve Marriott. Shel also produced artists such as Roy Harper, before forming a production company called Hush, in 1970, with Hugh Murphy and working with groups like Pentangle and String Driven Thing.

The Kinks writer and frontman Ray Davies wrote the song, *Denmark Street*. The Orchids, another Page discovery, despite production from Shel Talmy, didn't have the same success. Page did find another chart-topping group though, in the Troggs, the debut single *Lost Girl* being recorded at Regent Sound. By this time Page had formed Page One with Dick James. In 1966 the President label was launched in the UK, having hits with such artists as The Symbols, Felice Taylor and the Equals who went to No.1 with *Baby Come Back*. Equals guitarist Eddy Grant was the group's songwriter, providing the Equals with their hits and becoming a major and influential solo artist and songwriter. Kassner also set up the Jay Boy label, having hits with artists such as George McRae and KC and the Sunshine Band. From the 80s onwards the company enjoyed success with keyboards virtuoso Rick Wakeman. When Ed Kassner died in 1996, David Kassner became MD. His wife Veronique and their son, Alex are also part of the family business looking after 70,000 copyrights.

No. 25 is now Macari's Musical Instruments, started in Tin Pan Alley in 1958. Founded by Larry and Joe Macari, the business has returned to its spiritual home with Joe's son, Anthony, and Larry's son, Steve at the helm. This is where Jimi Hendrix came to buy his trademark wah-wah pedal. They are the only authorised Gibson dealer in the area and Macari's is also the home of Sola Sound who have marketed the famous tone bender pedal since 1965. Their other shop is around the corner in Charing Cross Road. Above Macari's Angel Music sell vintage electric guitars, having moved there in 1999 from The Angel Islington. The company strap-line is, *'honest guitar traders since 1994.'*

No. 26

This Grade II listed property is the oldest in the street, having been originally constructed as a stable in 1635, the tenth year of the reign of Charles I. In 1888 there was a silver caster working from here, predating the Stratocasters sold next door by Macari's seventy years later. The back of No. 26 later became a forge for the St. Giles area and continued to be used until World War I. The building then became a carpenter's shop until shortly after World War II, when it was converted into store rooms. It then became Julie's Café and was much frequented by the songwriters and publishers of Denmark Street.

During the Early 1990's, the building housed The Forge Folk & Blues Club, founded by Andy Preston. It was originally a social club and music venue for the staff at the guitar centre who used the original forge area at the back as an amplifier workshop - dust-sheets would be thrown over the amplifiers in the evening before the entertainment began. In 1994, the club was expanded and renamed the 12 Bar Club. 12 bar club closed in January 2015.

The smithy was carefully and temporarily moved while Crossrail work was undertaken.

No. 27

No. 27 was built in the late 17th century, re-fronted a century later and was Grade II listed in 1974. By 1938 it was being run as a dairy.

At the rear of No. 27, running through to Little Denmark Street, was a weighing machinery business run by Valentine Anscheutz and John Schlaff between the 1760s and 1780s. It later served as the iron foundry, smithy and forge for George Medhurst's weighing machine business, based at 465 Oxford Street. Medhurst trained as a clockmaker, but the duty placed on clocks severely affected his income and he turned to engineering. By 1800 he had established himself at 1 Denmark Street as a maker of scales and weighing machines and an iron founder. His machines were for heavy goods, in carts, crates or cases as well as for weighing jockeys. In 1800 Denmark Street's engineer patented his Aoelian engine, designed to propel a carriage by compressed air contained in a tank underneath the vehicle. He also worked on a gas engine, the propulsion coming from small quantities of gunpowder being detonated at regular intervals. He also patented a compound crank for converting rotary into rectilinear motion and took over the patent for a washing and wringing machine. In 1810 he invented 'A New Method of Conveying Letters and Goods with Great Certainty and Rapidity by Air.' It comprised an iron tube six feet high and five feet wide fitted with rails and able to take carriages by using compressed air. So the street was almost a Tin Pan Alley in the early 1800s Two years later this was being applied to passengers and goods with the ability of conveying them up to sixty miles an hour. He had no opportunity to experiment with his 'atmospheric propulsion' but his conception was crystal clear. He also argued that through his idea, passengers would be able to travel across London in a tunnel at the cost of a farthing a mile. In 1817 there was a patent for an 'equal balance weighing machine' from 'George Medhurst of Denmark Street, St Giles-in-the-Fields, Middlesex.' Without question he was a founding father of a prototype of the car. In 1820 his steam carriage carried one man on the New Road (now Marylebone Road) between Paddington and Islington and the following year a more substantial version ran up and down Paddington Hill at a heady 5 mph. By 1827 he was offering to sell a carriage that would carry four persons at 7 mph. and was advertising his patent canal lock to prevent loss of water. His last invention appeared to be a water-powered railway. George Medhurst died in 1827, the business being sold fifty-four years later by his grandson, Thomas, to George Herbert. It has now been transformed into a contemporary seven-bedroomed house, retaining a little of the old warehouse wall with its double height gallery.

The front of No. 27 was a beer house for almost 100 years, but never named in the census, nor taking a traditional pub name. From at least 1848 it was run by the King family, Edward, Ellen and later their daughter Sarah, until 1861. Their oldest son Edward worked as an errand boy and a porter. From 1869 until the turn of the century John Thomas Rowland ran the place, with his daughter and son-in-law, Kathleen and Edwin Hayes taking over in 1901. Their daughter Florence worked as a gold and silver burnisher and their son Edwin as a brass and tinworker. By 1911 Frederick Langdon and his wife Rosetta had become the beer-house keepers and by 1914, they had been replaced by Richard John Hunter, who still served the ale until the early 1920s. By 1938 the alcohol had gone and milk had arrived, as No.27 became a dairy. Upstairs, Jean and Julian, the Aberbach brothers, would successfully milk the film industry at the same time.

With Jean Aberbach initially staying on at Nos. 10 and 11, Campbell Connelly, to keep the money coming in, his younger brother Julian, began to build up their own company from 1933. In 1934 the brothers had an amazing stroke of luck. In conversation with the head of the French Performing Rights Society, SACEM, they discovered that there was a little-known copyright rule that benefitted film dialogue writers that had never been exercised. The Aberbachs quickly formed a new company, the Societe Entertainment Musicale Internationale (SEMI), and immediately contacted dialogue writers in France offering to collect the monies rightfully owed to them by SACEM. The writers had no idea they were even entitled to any monies and were delighted at the prospect. Taking into consideration that thousands of films had been produced in France since 1927, the Stakes were enormous. Julian immediately quit his job at Campbell Connelly and they frantically researched every film they could and signed up the writers before anyone had the same idea and set up in opposition. It was a chaotic year for SACEM, who weren't happy, but the Aberbachs had found a legal loophole and made a

killing before SACEM changed the ruling in 1935. They invested the profits (many millions in today's money) in Austrian real estate. They also acquired the rights to *Tovarich*, a new work by Parisian playwright Jacques Deval, which proved to be an enormous success. Before agreeing to see the play, Adolf Hitler had Deval checked for any hint of antisemitism. He found none and twice bought a ticket for the play. How delightful that his money went unknowingly into the pocket of the Aberbach Brothers, who had financed the work. Their financial killing through dialogue copyright had reduced SACEM money for   all the other French publishers, so they weren't the most popular kids on the boulevard. They decided to sell SEMI to their American client Ralph Peer.

In the late 1930s Jean began working in the US for a French music publisher, while Julian was eventually drafted and ended up in the States with the Free French troops in Maryland. During this period, he had developed a keen interest in country music and to that end set up a publishing company, Hill & Range, with two partners in Los Angeles. He signed Spade Cooley, set up another publishing company with Bob Wills and made many contacts in Nashville, organising the publishing contracts for such artists as Red Foley, Hank Snow, Ernest Tubb, Eddy Arnold and later Johnny Cash. At one point some three-quarters of the music produced in Nashville was represented by Hill and Range. Rival publisher Max Dreyfus attempted to buy the company, but Julian refused, and Jean who had been working for Dreyfus, joined his brother at Hill and Range. In 1955 Hank Snow suggested they take a listen to a new singer, Elvis Presley. The Aberbachs were impressed and helped Julian's friend Colonel Tom Parker to become his manager as well as negotiating his move from Sun Records to RCA. The publishing deal was a 50/50 split between Elvis, and Hill and Range. The Aberbach's cousin, Freddy Bienstock was given the job as head of Elvis Presley Music, finding writers and songs for the singer's films and albums. The rules were simple, if you were a writer and you wanted Elvis to sing your song, you had to be signed to Hill and Range.

The brothers also contracted Johnny Halliday in France to cover Elvis' songs and they worked closely with Edith Piaf and Mort Schuman, who provided many songs for Jacques Brel. By the early 1970s Hill and Range had become the biggest independent publisher in the world. After Julian was taken ill, Jean sold 75% of Hill and Range to Warner Chappell. Julian retired from the industry and

pursued his interest in paintings and sculpture. He received the National Order of the Legion of Honour in 2003 in recognition of his unique contribution to French culture. He tragically lost both his sons in 1983.

Julian Aberbach

Jean passed away in 1992. Julian died in New York in 2004 aged 95.

After their cousin Freddy Bienstock came into the company as a song plugger, Bienstock later became Chairman/CEO of Carlin Music. Former singer and BBC Broadcaster Franklin Boyd became head of Aberbach Publishing for ten years after previously working for Chappell. Born William Price, he won the All-Britain Crooning Championship at the age of fifteen before signing with the Harry Leader Band. After WWII he joined the Teddy Foster Orchestra, dropped the name Willy Price at the behest of Foster and became Franklin Boyd, but it was with the Eric Winstone Orchestra that he had a few hits including *Weaver of Dreams* and *Only Fools*. He then signed a solo deal with Columbia, releasing several covers and making regular appearances on the BBC Light programme. In 1953 he moved to the publishing side of the business, working for Victoria

Music, before joining the Aberbachs two years later. He was soon at the centre of a controversy though, with the release of Melody Marshall's *I Don't Ever Want to be a Princess.* Boyd had to issue an apology to Princess Margaret. 'The song was published to convey the sympathies and feelings of the vast majority of the American public towards your Royal Highness.'

Boyd was Cliff Richard's first professional manager and was with him until late 1959 before returning to music publishing and becoming Musical Director for the film *Just For Fun.* Boyd set up his own company representing Burt Bacharach and Hal David as well as representing the Robert Stigwood Organisation in Canada, having emigrated to Toronto in 1973. Franklin Boyd died in Sorrento, Italy in 2007.

No. 27 is now Hank's guitar shop.

No. 28

Pictorial publicity were running their business from here in the mid-1950s and recently the Jubilee Hair Salon was at No.28, before moving to Covent Garden.

134 Charing Cross Road

Songwriter, composer, pianist and bandleader, Sydney Edmund Tolchard Evans was born in Kilburn in 1901. He began playing the piano at the age of six and went on to study orchestration and conducting with a view to becoming a classical musician. Instead he joined the staff of Lawrence Wright Publishing in Denmark Street in 1919, leaving in 1924 to work as a pianist for silent films and dance bands. When Tolchard Evans 1926 song *Barcelona* became an international hit, he formed the Cecil Lennox song publishing company at 134 Charing Cross Road, between Denmark Street and Denmark Place, with lyricists, Stanley Damerell and Robert

Hargreaves, Damerell and Hargreaves using the writing pseudonym, Erell Reaves, a condensation of their names. One of Tolchard Evans early songs, *The Road to Loch Lomond*, written with HB Tilsley, was published by the company in 1926 and in 1929 Lennox published *Fairy on the Clock* by Evans, Erell Reaves and Sherman Myers. The trio of Evans, Damerell and Hargreaves wrote *Lady of Spain* in 1931, with Al Bowlly recording it the same year, with the song becoming one of the biggest international hits of the 1930s. Tolchard Evans also had a big hit the following year with *Let's all Sing Like the Birdies Sing,* with Damarell, Hargreaves and Harry Tilsley. At one time, four of Tolchard's melodies were being used as signature tunes for major London dance bands. In 1951 his career, and that of his co-writers, was further boosted when Perry Como's version of *If* sold over a million copies in 1951 and Eddie Fisher's cover of *Lady of Spain,* became a best-seller the following year. *Lady of Spain* was covered by many other artists including Bing Crosby. Tolchard Evans' song *Ev'rywhere* won an Ivor Novello Award in 1956 for 'The Year's Most Popular Song' and the following year he picked up a second Ivor Novello for *My September Love*, which was 'The Best-selling and Most performed Song of the Year' and had been a huge hit for David Whitfield who also had success with Evans' *I'll Find You*. Evans' own recording of *The Singing Piano* was used as a signature tune at Butlins Holiday Camps. In 1973 he won a second Ivor Novello for outstanding services to British music. Tolchard Evans died in 1978 having had chart hits from 1938 to 1970. The Cecil Lennox building at 134 has escaped the demolition squad and instead of *Lady of Spain* and *My September Love*, you now get beer, spirits, cold drinks, confectionary and snacks downstairs and rent rooms upstairs.

138-140 Charing Cross Road

Music Publishers Francis, Day & Hunter were on the corner of Denmark Place at 138-140 Charing Cross Road, where Hart, Son, Peard and Co. had been in 1914.

In the 1870s, brothers William and James Francis were working for piano manufacturers and music publishers, Chappell & Co, and from 1873 were members of one of the leading music hall ensembles, The Mohawk Minstrels. Harry Hunter, born in 1840, who was the lead and lyricist with rival band the Manhattan Minstrels jumped ship to become one of the Mohawks. The Francis brothers began to set out the words of their songs so that the audiences could join in, which gave them the idea of setting up their own publishing company. Bringing in David Day, born 1850, who'd worked with publishers Hopwood and Crew, they set up their own publishing house.

They soon became established as one of the leading publishers of music hall songs and popular music in the late 19th century, setting up in London in 1877 as W. & J. Francis and Day. The founders were William Francis, James Francis, David Day and Harry Hunter. The company later became Francis Brothers and Day and by 1880, David Day was made a full partner and they settled on Francis Day & Hunter. The company moved to the corner of Charing Cross Road and Denmark Place in 1897, making them the earliest modern publisher in what would become Tin Pan Alley, save for the fact that they were technically in the Charing Cross Road at 138-140. The building had a basement, ground floor and three upper storeys. A few yards along the road was a candid peel factory, now the Phoenix Theatre.

David Day formed the Music Copyright Association in 1900 to protect publishers against sheet music piracy, while his son Frederick Day was pivotal in pushing through the 1911 Copyright Act, protecting the rights of authors and composers. In the words of Ray Davies, 'Thank you for the Days.' In 1908 the company bought a third share in New York publishers, T.B. Harms, selling their share on in 1920. After WWI the company became one of the most important publishers of educational, classical and popular music in the country. Under the leadership of David and later Frederick the company expanded to become not only one of the most successful British publishers, but one of the largest publishers in the world, looking after the works of great writers like Cole Porter, George Gershwin, Richard Rodgers, Vincent Youmans and Jerome Kern. At one time they published almost 90% of all Broadway scores.

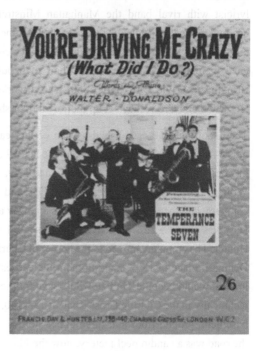

Walter Donaldson's 1930 song published by Francis, Day & Hunter, You're Driving Me Crazy, a hit over thirty years later for the Temperance Seven.

They opened offices in New York, (1905) Paris (1920) and Berlin (1928) and in 1945 bought publishers Feldman & Co. In 1972 the Francis, Day & Hunter identity was lost when the it became a subsidiary of EMI, but the David Day Memorial Scholarship which was set up at the Royal School of Speech and Drama in memory of the company's co-founder, still thrives. It is worth £3,500 and is awarded to a second- or third-year student studying on BA (Hons) Acting (Musical Theatre). David Day was also a founder of the Pivot Club, launched in the early 1900s with the aim of raising money to support talented students without financial means. Early member included Sir Laurence Olivier and Dame Peggy Ashcroft, and although the club disbanded at the outbreak of WWII, it was resurrected in 2011. David Day might not have been as well-known as many who have trodden the Tin Pan Alley Path, but there are many fellow travellers who owe him a great deal.

The Francis, Day and Hunter building in the 1950s.

Producer Johnny Franz joined Francis, Day & Hunter as an office boy in 1937 at the age of fifteen and spent most of the 1940s up and down

Denmark Street, learning the business. A gifted pianist with perfect pitch, he would often accompany such vocalists as Harry Secombe and Anne Shelton as well as play in local night clubs during the 40s and 50s. Franz was assisted during his time there by the highly-respected Paddy Fleming and between them they made many friends at the BBC. In 1952 the company published its own autobiography, *The Story of Francis, Day and Hunter,* in which they reveal that before the days of copyright protection, they weren't averse to sending 'heavies' out to deal with the problem of sheet music piracy.

In 1954 he joined Philips as Head of their A & R, going on to produce Shirley Bassey, The Beverley sisters, Frankie Vaughan, Susan Maugham, Marty Wilde, Ronnie Carroll, Winifred Atwell, The Springfields, The Four Pennies, Dusty Springfield, The Walker Brothers and Scott Walker. He also worked with America artists including Mel Torme, Johnnie Ray, Doris Day and Rosemary Clooney. His productions utilised orchestral arrangements by Wally Stott, Ivor Raymonde and Peter Knight. In 1966 he married his secretary Moira Creamer and moved to CBS in 1973, going on to manage the recording career of Peters and Lee. He produced ten UK No's between 1954 and 1973. Franz died in 1977. He was just 54-years-old.

Many of the hits written by Tin Pan Alley stalwarts Barry Mason & Les Reed were published through Francis, Day and Hunter's Donna Music imprint. By 1959, struggling Lancashire songwriter Barry Mason who was living in Notting Hill, encouraged his neighbour, Covent Garden Porter Tommy Bruce, who looked like a rock & roll star, to sing. The result was a top three hit, *Ain't Misbehavin'* and Barry's judgement didn't do any harm to his blossoming songwriting career.

In 1964 Barry and Geoff Stephens wrote the Beatle-esque *You Came Along* for Accrington group, the Warriors, featuring future Yes vocalist Jon Anderson. Jon's brother went on to become a member of Los Bravos and drummer Ian Wallace went on to play with King Crimson and Bob Dylan.

Les Reed studied at the London College of Music and joined the John Barry Seven in 1959 as their pianist. He played on many of their hits such as the *James Bond Theme* and *Hit and Miss*. He also played piano on such hits as Adam faith's *What Do You Want,* Lance Fortune's *Be Mine* and Eden Kane's *Forget Me Not.* By the mid-1960s he had a successful songwriting partnership going with Geoff Stephens, the pair writing *Tell Me When* for the Applejacks, *Here It Comes Again* for the Fortunes, *Leave a Little Love* for Lulu and *There's a Kind of Hush* for Herman's Hermits, later a hit for the Carpenters. In 1964 Les had collaborated with Gordon Mills to write *It's Not Unusual* for Tom Jones.

His partnership with Barry Mason also hit the jackpot. One of their first songs together was *I'll Try Not To Cry* for Kathy Kirby as part of A Song For Europe 1965, the BBC's contest to choose the UK entry for that year's Eurovision Song Contest in Naples.

Redd and Mason's numerous songwriting credits include *Everybody Knows* for the Dave Clark Five, the million-selling *The Last Waltz, A Man Without Love* and *Winter World of Love* and *Les Bycyclettes de Belsize* for Engelbert Humperdinck and *Here it Comes Again* for the Fortunes. They also penned *I Pretend* and *One Two Three O'Leary* for Des O'Connor, topping the chart with *The Last Waltz* and *I Pretend* in 1967, 1968 respectively. They also wrote what would become one of the world's most popular karaoke songs. *Delilah,* a massive and enduring hit for Tom Jones. Mason and Reed also wrote *Who's Doctor Who,* a novelty song recorded by Doctor who star Frazer Hines in 1967, but it failed to chart. One of their songs, *Girl of Mine* was featured on Elvis Presley's album, *Raised on Rock/For Ol' Times Sake*. Les Reed collaborated with Geoff Stephens on *This is Our Dance* featured on the album *Love Letters from Elvis,* while Stephens had a second song on the same album, called *Heart of Rome* on which he'd collaborated with UK writers Alan Blaikley and Ken Howard. Les and Johnny Worth, for whom he'd played on hit records in the early 60s, co-wrote the title track of Shirley Bassey's album *Does Anybody Miss Me?* Co-writing with Bing Crosby, Reed had a US hit in 1975 with Bing's own version of *That's What Life's All About.*

Les Reed also collaborated with Jackie Rae to write *I've Got My Eyes on You* and wrote and recorded *Man of Action*, the theme song for Radio North Sea International in 1970.

In 1970 Barry Mason collaborated with Tony Macauley to give Edison Lighthouse a No.1 with *Love Grows (Where My Rosemary Goes)*. Barry also co-wrote several hits with Roger Greenaway, including *There Goes My First Love* and *Can I Take You Home Little Girl* for the Drifters. In the 1970s Les Reed won awards for his collaborations with Geoff Stephens and Roger Greenaway. Les Reed has written several film scores including *Girl on a Motorcycle* and *One More Time*. David Essex, Charles Aznavour, Perry Como, Elvis Presley, Barbra Streisand, the Dave Clark Five, Tony Christie, Rod Stewart and Petula Clark.

Les and Barry also co-wrote *Marching on Together (aka "Leeds! Leeds! Leeds!"),* the anthem of Leeds United AFC, first released at the time of the 1972 FA Cup Final. Today, Leeds fans still use the acronym MOT (Marching on Together) when they text. Barry Mason was also the major songwriter for the English singer Declan

Galbriath for his first album, Declan (2002), including the hit *Tell Me Why* (No. 29 in UK) and *Till the Day We Meet Again.*

138—140, the building where musical and copyright history was made, was demolished in 2016 to make way for the re-development of the area.

1-6 Denmark Place

In 1916, Jack Robbins left his home in Worcester, Massachusetts to join his uncle, music pioneer Maurice Richmond, in New York. Robbins became a very successful song plugger, one of his earlier successes being with the song *Smiles* which sold 2 million copies. This led to uncle and nephew creating Richmond-Robbins Music which evolved into the Robbins-Engel catalogue and by 1924 Robbins Music Corporation. Jack led the way in brighter flashier packaging and marketing for sheet music and pioneered educational music. They encouraged the use of popular songs in school music training and school music programmes. Robbins also championed jazz before it became in vogue, spearheading the sheet music output in that genre. He and his right-hand man Jack Bergman also realised the importance and significance of the named big bands and the theme tunes with which they were identified. They started bands, kept them going, brought them to the attention of the record labels and kept the Robbins office open day and night for band arrangers, big band rehearsals and musical gatherings. As a result, big bands like Jimmy Dorsey, Glenn Miller, Benny Goodman, Count Basie and Stan Kenton featured in the Robbins catalogue. The uncannily perceptive Jack Robbins also foresaw the importance of the the big motion picture music score, with their major soundtracks and best-selling title songs. He was well ahead of the game in tying up film deals with the motion picture industry in Hollywood, bringing in top copyright lawyer, Julian T. Abeles and acquiring an interest in several major catalogues.

In 1934, M-G-M acquired a controlling interest in the Robbins Music Corporation, along with Chicago's Miller Music Publishing Co. and Leo Fiest Inc, subsequently merging the three as Robbins, Fiest, Miller Music, widely known as 'The Big Three'. Webb Rockefeller Miller had started his company in 1906 and Leo Fiest, who died in 1930, had started in music publishing way back in 1897, his slogan was, 'You can't go wrong with a Fiest song.' He was probably right; *I'll See You in My Dreams*, *What Do You Want To Make Those Eyes At Me For*, *Five Foot Two Eyes of Blue* and *In A Little Spanish Town* all ended up in Fiest's catalogue. Robbins brought in Abe Olman who anticipated the post-war communications explosion and the team were also ahead of the game in seeing the future tie-in between music and television and the power of the radio disc-jockey. During his time at the company between 1946 and 1956, Olman helped to keep the company at the cutting edge of the musical revolution and with the help of Abeles created the London office in Denmark Place. Maurice Scopp headed up the organisation from 1957 to 1965 with Arnold Maxin then taking over the reins and more hits were added to the catalogue. These included *The Shadow of Your Smile*, *You Don't Have to Say You Love Me* and *Somewhere My Love*.

By the late 1940s Jack Robbins relinquished control of the company that he'd founded but had created an incredible catalogue of songs including *Blue Moon, Deep Purple, Temptation, Moonlight Serenade, Goodnight Sweetheart, Don't Blame Me, When I Grow too Old to Dream, Maybe* and *You Are My Lucky Star.* Early in 1947, despite treacherous weather and the coal crisis prohibiting sheet music from being printed, Robbins were buoyed up as their US office announced one of their biggest ever orders. In 1960 Robbins published the

Eurovision runner-up, *Looking High, High, High* performed by Bryan Johnson and written by John Watson.

Tony Roberts, the son of Tin Pan Alley songwriter, Paddy Roberts, was at Robbins Music from 1965, having previously worked in the promotion department of Keith Prowse Music. Roberts started as Robbins' professional manager, later becoming their general manager. He moved on to become MD of Warner Bros Music, chief executive of Bell Records, a board member of Columbie Pictures and Screen Gems Music, CEO of Arista and director and general manager of Chappells.

In March 1973 Terry Slater, former professional manager at Beechwood Music, was appointed General Manager at Robbins, signing a worldwide deal with Sydney Thompson, giving Robbins the rights to music from the Invicta catalogue. Robbins were now part of Affiliated Music Publishers Ltd with Slater heading up Robbins, Ronnie Beck heading up Feldman's, also from 1-6 Denmark Place, Peter Philips in charge at KPM Music Group at 21, Denmark Street and Kay O'Dwyer the boss at Francis, Day & Hunter just around the corner in the Charing Cross Road. Classics like *Something's Gotta Give, High Noon, Three Coins in a Fountain and Friendly Persuasion,* were all published here as were the themes for such classics as *The Onedin Line, Clockwork Orange, Death in Venice* and *Tom Brown's Schooldays.*

Robbins acquired a qualified lawyer turned creative, Hal Shaper, who came to the UK from South Africa, ostensibly to pursue a career in that line, but passionate to be a songwriter, having been inspired by the film *Words and Music,* the story of Rodgers and Hart. Initially working with David Toff Music, the publisher advised him to forget songwriting and stick to the business side. Shaper plugged songs for Toff from the summer of 1955 to the summer of 1958 and discovered the hit artist Russ Hamilton. Toff was adamant that Shaper should stay firmly on the publishing side of the business and not dabble in songwriting, which is why he jumped ship to Robbins Music, who encouraged him to write. Hal's earliest songwriting success was on the 1959 Ivor Novello award-winning song *There Goes My Love.* Other early successes for Hal Shaper included *My Friend the Sea,* a top ten hit for Petula Clark in 1961 and writing the English lyric for Matt Monro's *Softly As I Leave You* in 1961. This was also covered by Frank Sinatra and when Sinatra died in 1998, his family announced the death on his website accompanied by the lyrics to *Softly as I Leave You.* It has been covered by many artists including Michael Buble, Doris Day, Shirley Bassey, Cliff Richard and Bobby Darin. The budding writer went on to have songs recorded by Elvis Presley, Barbra Streisand, Julie Andrews, Val Doonican, Jack Jones, Andy Williams, Engelbert Humperdinck, Paul Anka, Dusty Springfield, Elton John and dozens more. He wrote one of Bing Crosby's last-ever recordings, *At My Time of Life.* Shaper had sixty of his songs performed in films, his collaborators including John Williams, Michel Legrand, Ron Grainer and Ron Goodwin. Away from films his collaborators have included Herbert Kretzmer, Tony Hatch, Stanley Myers and Les Reed. In 1964 he formed Sparta Music, signing two of the Moody Blues and two British acts that did well in the States, Chad and Jeremy and Ian Whitcomb. 1967 saw him publish the major hits *Groovin'* and *It Must Be Him.* David Bowie signed to Sparta, left, returned and left again, leaving the company with some valuable copyrights. Mike Berry (not the singer) worked for Sparta for some while, bringing in acts like the UK Subs. Shaper Also acquired the administration rights to the valuable US Barton catalogue. The company published all *kinds* of music, including reggae classics, *The Israelites, The Tide is High* and *Suzanne Beware of the Devil.* Shaper's company has success through the seventies and into the eighties with the Associates. Sparta Florida as the group became also supplied music for such TV series as *The Avengers, The Sweeney* and *Dr. Who*.

6 Denmark Place

Although it was claimed in his biographies that he was born in Surrey, Robert Mellin was actually born in Ukraine in 1902, his parents, Joseph and Anna Melnikoff bringing him briefly as a baby en route to Chicago. Robert began his career as song plugger for Remick Music in Chicago, going on to become the manager. In 1938 he became an American citizen, changed his name to Mellin and became an executive of BMI in New York soon after it was formed. In 1947 he launched his own company, Robert Mellin Inc. in Europe and America, founding the company in the UK in 1952. His first success as a songwriter was in 1952 when Eddie Fisher released *I'm Yours*. The Ames Brother recorded *You, You, You* and Nat King Cole, *My One Sin*. Frank Sinatra recorded *My One and Only Love* and *Rain (Falling From the Sky)*. Louis Armstrong, Chet Baker, Ella Fitzgerald and later Sting all recorded *My One and Only Love*. Mellin's most successful lyrics were those he set to Acker Bilk's *Stranger on the Shore*. Acker Bilk took the original instrumental version to No.2 in the UK, the record staying on the chart for 55 weeks, and No.1 in the States. Both Andy Williams and the Drifters had hits with the vocal version and Ruby and the Romantics also covered it. In 1968 Mellin's publishing group acquired exclusive rights to all film scores coming out of Czechoslovakia and Romania as well as many from Italy. Robert Mellin wrote the music for such films as the *Dirty Game, Sun of a Gunfighter* and *The Last of the Mohicans*, as well as the music for the TV series, *The Adventures of Robinson Crusoe*. In the mid-1950s Len Edwards was the office manager and Pat Williams and the young office lad, Tony Hatch. A good pianist and reader of music, he proved useful in that he could play new songs to artists. Tony went on to become one of the country's top songwriters. When Mellin's company was sold, in 1968, the asking price was $1.6 million. He died in Rome in 1994.

Sixteen-year-old Tony Hatch began work at Robert Mellin after attending the London Choir School. 'I got a very nice job making the tea, doing the filing, running the errands and whenever any artists came in I would sit down and play the piano for them….sheet music was very big, so if you played piano, you were one step ahead and that's how I managed to get my job.'

One morning, Decca's Dick Rowe arrived at the office and Tony had the opportunity to play him some of his own songs. This not only resulted in singer Gerry Dorsey (prior to becoming Engelbert Humperdinck) recording Hatch's *Crazy Bells,* but also to the offer of a job, working as Dick Rowe's assistant at a new company that had been formed by the Rank organisation, the Top Rank label. After two years learning his craft in Denmark Place, Tony Hatch was on the way to establishing himself as a top producer and one of the great British songwriters.

Middlesex-born Hatch attended the London Choir School before landing the job with Robert Mellin., his role being to play the company's songs on the piano to singers and artists. After a couple of years Dick Rowe poached him for Top Rank Records and after his National Service, with the Band of the Coldstream Guards, he began to write songs. His first success was Garry Mills' *Look for a Star,* which was featured in the film *Circus of Horrors,* with four versions of the song charting in the US. In 1961 Top Rank was sold to EMI and Hatch moved to Pye Records to work with Alan A. Freeman. Hatch wrote for several artists, sometimes under the pseudonym of Mark Anthony and sometimes Fred Nightingale. In 1963 he wrote Bobby Rydell's big hit, *Forget Him,* as well as peening songs for Connie Francis, Pat Boone and Keely Smith. In 1964 he wrote the

Searchers *Sugar and Spice.* After Petula Clark recorded *Valentino,* she and Tony Hatch collaborated on many songs. In 1964, on a trip to New York, he wrote her hit *Downtown, I Know a Place, You'd Better Come Home* and *Round Every Corner* followed, with Hatch and Clark writing *You're the One,* which also became a major hit for the Vogues in the US. Both Petula and Chris Montez had success with Hatch's *Call Me.* Their run of success continued with *My Love, Call Me, I Couldn't Live Without Your Love, The Other Man's Grass is Always Greener* and *Don't Sleep in the Subway,* all written with his then wife, Jackie Trent. In 1964 Hatch had been hired to write the theme for the TV soap, *Crossroads* (also recorded by Paul McCartney and Wings) and also penned a song for the *Inspector Rose* series, with Jackie Trent, called *Where Are You Now?* Which went to No.1. Hatch went on to compose many TV themes, including *Sportsnight, The Doctors, The Champions, Hadleigh, Mr and Mrs.,* and *Whodunit.* Tony and Jackie also wrote *Joanna,* a hit for Scott Walker and *We'll Be with You* for Stoke City FC. During the 1970s they diversified into musical theatre with *The Card* and *Rock Nativity.* Hatch also wrote the original theme for the TV series *Emmerdale Farm* and became a regular panellist on the TV talent show *New Faces.* Tony Hatch also wrote the score for the film *Sweeney 2* before moving to Dublin where he and Jackie hosted the TV series' *Words and Music* and *It's a Musical World.* After moving to Australia in 1982, the couple wrote the theme to the TV Series, *Neighbours.* They separated in 1995, divorced in 2002 and he's now married to Maggie. In 2013 Tony Hatch was inducted into the Songwriter's Hall of Fame.

18 Denmark Place

The fire that claimed the most lives since World War II raged through two nightclubs in Denmark Street on the evening of 16th August 1980. At the time it was home to several illegal gambling dens and the odd unlicensed nightclub. On the top two floors of 18 Denmark Place which backed on to Denmark Street, were *The Spanish Rooms,* also known as *El Hueco (the Hole)* a late night bar frequented by the Irish and Jamaican communities and *Rodo's* also known as *El Dandy,* a salsa club popular with South Americans. Both were scheduled to be shut down on the 18th. They were two days too late. Some hundred and fifty people were packed into the three-storey building that night, one of whom, John 'The Gypsy' Thompson, convinced he'd been overcharged, got into an argument with the barman and was subsequently thrown out for fighting. He returned with a two-gallon can of petrol, poured it through the letterbox and set fire to it. Dozens and dozens of the revellers were locked into what was a building with a heavily wooded interior with no means of escape. Thirty-seven people were killed from eight different nationalities. One fire officer said, 'People seemed to have died on the spot without even having time to move an inch. Some were slumped at tables. Seven were at the bar and appeared to have fallen as they stood, with drinks still in their hands. Some people had ripped shutters from the windows and broken the glass with their bare hands, then jumped to the ground with their clothes on fire, smashing bones. Survivors spoke of the screaming, the skin peeling off faces, of trying to get out by the back door but finding it locked.' Many tried to escape by breaking the windows of the adjacent building in No. 22 Denmark Street with guitars from the shop. Diana Coward, named after the Paul Anka hit *Diana,* was just eighteen when she perished in the conflagration. Another of those who died, Alejandro Vargas Bernett, was an architectural graduate from Bogota, who it's said helped others to escape while hero Alex Reid went back inside to try and save a pregnant woman. It took a full two months to identify all those that had died. In May 1981 Thompson, a small-time crook with delusions that he was a big-time gangster, was sentenced to life, dying of lung cancer on 16th August 2008, the 28th anniversary of the fire.

The aftermath of the fire at 18 Denmark Place.

20 Denmark Place

Picture restorer, Edward Robert Davis (1881-1929) traded at 20 Denmark Place from 1905-1909. His bill head referred to him as, 'E. Davis, Lining and Stretching Frame Maker', and described him as a 'Specialist in panel work. Old panels rejoined and cradled. Transferring a speciality.' Sometimes referred to as 'Edwin' as well as 'Edward', from 1920 he teamed up with John Reeve as Reeve and Davis at 77, Cleveland Street.

22 & 23 Denmark Place

In 1909, a short-lived record company named Musogram was based at No. 22. The Musogram 'Long Playing Record' was the brainchild of piccolo player and electrician Percy Packman and first appeared in December 1909, having been established in May 1907. Several people working with the company having previously been with Neophone and later becoming Marathon, both of which he was involved with at different times. They were vertical-cut with a fine U-shaped groove giving an extended playing time. These were followed in 1910 by Musogram's 'Living Record', featuring a coarser groove. Among their early releases were various marches performed by the Royal Military Band, including *Stars & Stripes.* The company's final release, just six months after their debut was in May 1910. Packman's system was then used by the Marathon label, formed in 1911, and manufactured at the Edison Bell factory for the National Gramophone Company. The company failed in 1915. Packman was listed on the 1911 census as a 'Talking Machine Record Recorder.' In April 1910 his was interviewed at Demark Place in *Talking Machine News.* 'We now have the famous Musogram Records made by that skilful expert Mr. P.J. Packman. Indeed it was to see this gentleman that we paid our visit and we found him upstairs in the recording room, busily making arrangements for the arrival of one of the artists who was to make a few records. In fact all three of the productions are excellent and reflect the greatest credit not only upon the singer but upon Mr. Packman, who we may here mention was the very first to introduce the close-cut phono disc which enables a record to be made which will play for over six minutes, long enough to embrace the entire song without cutting.' The principle of Packman's cutter was later adopted by the rest of the sound recording industry. Recording pioneer Percy Packham was born in Rainham. Kent in 1875, married a St Giles girl, Edith Shenton in 1906 and died at Hammersmith in 1941. His two sons, born around the time Packman was based in Denmark Place, both lived until their 86th year.

No.23 Denmark Place appears to have been built, or rebuilt, circa 1908, with Robert Charles Jones, a 'model maker' also working from there from 1911.

132 Charing Cross Road
(On the corner of Denmark Street)

This address would become the office of Dick James. Born Leon Vapnick in London's East End, Dick James began singing at the age of fifteen, before WWII, turning professional at seventeen and first broadcasting in 1940. He continued to sing during his time in the army and after the war performed with many top dance bands including Geraldo, Billy Ternant, Cyril Stapleton, Henry Hall, Geraldo and Stanley Black, sometimes using the name Lee Sheridan. He was also one of the original Stargazers, founded by Cliff Adams and Ronnie Milne in 1949, alongside Marie Benson and Fred Datchler, before leaving to resume his solo career.

By 1953 though he was planning a change: 'I was thirty-two and couldn't see much future for a fat, bald-headed singer. It was a choice between becoming an agent or becoming a publisher....and as songs can't answer you back I decided to become a publisher.' In the summer of 1953 he joined Sydney Bron's publishing company at 122 Charing Cross Road. It was fortuitous that he still kept up with his singing to some extent, as he was approached by his close friend George Martin in 1955, who asked him to record the theme to a new TV series, *The Adventures of Robin Hood,* being made at Nettlefold Studios Walton-on-Thames and starring Richard Greene. He was paid £100 for the recording, which went on to sell over half a million copies, although he admitted: 'It made me one of the world's most famous unknown singers.' He also provided the vocals on another series filmed at Nettlefold Studios, *The Buccaneers*, starring Robert Shaw and produced by Hannah Weinstein. He also had hit singles with In the *Garden of Eden* and *The Ballad of Davy Crockett,* which was a double A side with *Robin Hood.*

It took Dick James eighteen months before he picked up his first hit song for Bron, when Perry Como's *Idle Gossip* became a hit, but James soon began to gather momentum, in his eight years there chalking up twenty-eight hits, including five No.1s. It convinced him that, although money was tight, he could make it on his own. In 1961 he set up at Suite Two Shaldon Mansions, 132 Charing Cross Road on the corner of Denmark Street. With goodwill from former writers he'd worked with: 'Tolchard Evans, who had a number of hits with us at Bron Music, came into the office and threw about twenty manuscripts on to the desk. He told me to take what I wanted and to pay him the royalties whenever I could. That was a really magnificent gesture in helping me get started.' With songs from Tolchard Evans, who worked out of the same building, and some assistance from George Martin he managed to bump along with just two staff and three copyrights. But things were to change dramatically.

A young songwriter called Mitch Murray turned up with a song called *How Do You Do It* and as George Martin was producing a new group called the Beatles he got them to record it. Neither George nor Dick James thought their version was up to much and although George was hoping it might be the Beatles second single, the group themselves weren't convinced and wanted their own song *Please, Please Me* as the next release. Brian Epstein told George that he was looking for a good publisher who might get his boys a good TV slot. George recommended Dick, Epstein went to see him and in one phone call to Philip Jones at *Thank Your Lucky Stars* landed not only the Beatles' first major TV slot, but one of the most valuable publishing deals of all-time: *Please, Please Me* and *Ask Me Why*. The Beatles were regular visitors during 1963 before Dick James moved round the corner to larger offices at New Oxford Street.

George Martin, Dick James and Brian Epstein

Dick James and Brian Epstein formed Northern Songs to publish the material from all four Beatles. On January 12th 1963 the Beatles performed on the show and were on their way to global stardom. The bonus was securing the publishing on other Epstein groups, like Billy J. Kramer and Gerry and the Pacemakers, whose *How Do You Do It?* went to No.1. Dick James published a remarkable seven No.1s in the following seven months. 'From the moment I picked up the phone to organise the Beatles first television show, it became the order of the day that I fixed all the radio and TV appearances, all the business side was taken care of by Brian and the recording side of things was handled by George Martin. That was the way things worked.'

It was a fortuitous day when Mitch Murray walked into Dick James office, as he went on to win two Ivor Novello Awards including the Jimmy Kennedy Award and wrote or co-wrote five UK and three US chart-topping songs. His song *How Do You Do It?* was picked up by George Martin for the Beatles, and although they recorded it, their version wasn't officially released until 1995. The song became a No.1

for Gerry and the Pacemakers, as did the follow-up, *I Like It*, another Mitch Murray song. He wrote two big hits for Freddie and the Dreamers, *You Were Made for Me* and *I'm Telling You Now*. The songs were published by Dick James with neighbours Campbell Connelly as sole selling agents. Mitch Murray began collaborating with Peter Callander after meeting in 1966, Callander having started as a song plugger for Bron Music before becoming a manager at Shapiro Bernstein Music.

Mitch and Peter Callander penned many more hits, such as *Even the Bad Times Are Good*, for the Tremeloes, *Ragamuffin Man* for Manfred Mann, *The Ballad of Bonnie and Clyde* for Georgie Fame, *Hitchin' a Ride* for Vanity Fare and with Geoff Stephens, *Goodbye Sam, Hello Samantha*, for Cliff Richard. Murray and Callander not only wrote *Avenues and Alleyways, I Did What I did for Maria* and *Las Vegas* for Tony Christie, they also produced them.

Mitch released a humorous single as Mr. Murray, *Down Came the Rain* and wrote the much-requested children's favourite, *My Brother* recorded by Terry Scott. Murray and Callander formed the Bus Stop label through which they launched Paper Lace, for whom they wrote *Billy Don't Be A Hero* and *The Night Chicago Died*. Covered in the US by Bo Donaldson and the Heywoods, both songs became US No.1s. Mitch Murray and Peter Callander formed the Society of Distinguished Songwriters in 1971. Mitch Murray is also an accomplished speech writer. He was married to singer Grazina Frame and their daughters, singers and actresses Mazz and Gina, are in Woman the Band and both successful in their own right. Aside from the Murray/Callander partnership, Peter also wrote for Cilla Black, PJ Proby, Dusty Springfield and Sandie Shaw as well writing the million-selling *Daddy Don't You Walk so Fast* with Geoff Stephens. Much-missed by the songwriting fraternity, Peter Callander passed away in February 2014.

In 1969 James sold Northern Songs, although the Beatles were upset at not being given an opportunity to buy their own songs back. Dick James also got involved with record production, forming a partnership with Larry Page of Page One Records late in 1965 and having hits with The Troggs. Larry Page and Dick James would part company in the summer of 1969.

Dick James' son Stephen had joined the company in 1963, learning the trade and doing every job in the office before setting up the This Record Co. four years later, in 1967. Dick and Stephen also set up their own recording studio, which is where the young Reg Dwight, the former tea boy at Mills Music, began coming to record his early demos. Steve Brown, the former EMI plugger who'd joined Dick James, suggested that the young singer should write more commercial songs, resulting in an advertisement being placed and the appearance of the guy who would become Elton's long-term collaborator, Bernie Taupin. He changed his name to Elton John, taken from Bluesology band-mates Elton Dean and Long John Baldry. This Record Co. had a deal with Philips, through whom they released Elton's first single *Lady Samantha,* which sold 7,000 copies. Late in 1968 Stephen james set up a new deal with Louis Benjamin at Pye Records, resulting in the formation of the DJM label in 1969. The label's first success was by Mr Bloe, called *Groovin' with Mr. Bloe,* which was Zack Lawrence and a bunch of session musicians. A decision that may seem blindingly obvious with hindsight, but wasn't at the time, was agreeing to spend $10,000 promoting Elton John in the States. It worked, echoing the way George Martin and Brian Epstein had made the Beatles happen, and that was, '...the principle of complete co-ordination of all elements in one organisation...production, publishing, promotion, management. It's essential that all these factions work together rather than operate in a fragmented way.'

Ten years after he started with a handful of copyrights, little money and a company employing two people, he had forty companies, forty staff (in London alone) and over 7,000 copyrights. After just seven years in existence, Northern Songs, with fewer than 200 copyrights sold for £10 million. Dick died in 1986 and Dick James Music was acquired by Polygram which in turn was bought out by Universal.

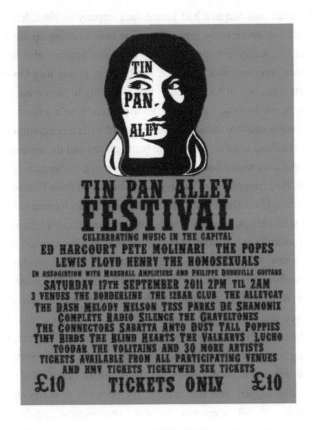

Tin Pan Alley heritage was still being celebrated by new artists in 2011

In 2016 the TV series for undiscovered songwriters, *Tin Pan Alley*, was broadcast over eight weeks on Sky in the UK. The series included songwriters Lamont Dozier, Gary Kemp, Graham Gouldman and Cathy Dennis and Tin Pan Alley songwriters, Don Black, Barry Mason, Guy Fletcher and Mike Batt. The Tin Pan Alley/PRS for Music Trophy was won by Nikki Murray for his song *Complicated Head.*

Whatever happens to Denmark Street in the future, it certainly has a hell of a past.

Key to characters on the front cover

1. Donovan

2. Queen Matilda

3. Eddy Grant

4. Frankie Fraser

5. Henry Flitcroft

6. Ray davies

7. Billy Cotton

8. Lord Wharton

9. Casanova

10. Jimmy Kennedy

11. Syed Sajjad Zaheer

12. Harry Wellmon

13. Andrew Marvell

14. Mary Shelley

15. Dick James

16. Vera Lynn

17. Don Black

18. Dennis Nilsen

19. Ringo Starr

20. John Lennon

21. George Harrison

22. Paul McCartney

23. Earl of Southampton

24. 24. Bill Wyman

25. Keith Richards

26. Mick Jagger

27. Charlie Watts

28. Brian Jones

29. Elton John

30. Buddy Holly

31. Prince George of Denmark

32. Tony Iommi

33. Reggie Kray

34. Jack Sheppard

35. Ronnie Kray

36. Rahere

37. John Lydon

38. Charlie Chaplin

39. David Bowie

40. Mary Anne Talbot

41. Tom Thumb

BV - #0001 - 310519 - C22 - 197/132/17 - PB - 9781912964208